Praise for

The Politically Incorrect Guide™ to
ISLAM (AND THE CRUSADES)

"With a provocative and irreverent style, Robert Spencer assails, with much erudition, the taboos imposed by the Politically Correct League. A daring tonic that teaches fundamental truths."

> —**Bat Ye'or**, author, *Eurabia and The Decline of Eastern Christianity Under Islam*

"The jihad that the Western world faces today is identical in its motivations and goals to that which Europe managed to stave off almost a thousand years ago, thanks in large part to the Crusades of which the West is now ashamed. In this book, Robert Spencer tells the truth that few in the U.S. or Europe wish to face. Today's jihad, as Spencer illustrates here, is proceeding on two fronts: one of violence and terror, and another of cultural shaming and the rewriting of history. Here is a devastating riposte to that revisionism—and a clarion call for the defense of the West, before it is too late."

> —**Ibn Warraq**, author, *Why I Am Not A Muslim*, and editor of *Leaving Islam* and *What the Koran Really Says*

"The value of Spencer's book is twofold. He reminds us of the consequences of our failure to come to grips with the message and implications of Islam. And he warns against the spirit of masochistic self-loathing that permeates the Western elite class. In a sane world, Spencer's recommendations—notably that the upholders of sharia should be treated as political radicals and subjected to appropriate supervision—would not be deemed "politically incorrect" but eminently sensible."

> —**Serge Trifkovic**, author, *Sword of the Prophet*

"With the 2005 *Kingdom of Heaven* movie trying to visualize the actual scenes that occurred between European Crusaders and Arab Muslim armies in the Middle Ages, the whole issue of the clash of civilizations came back to haunt politicians. Traditional historians used to relate facts. Politicized historians, such as Amine Maalouf, insisted that Western Crusaders were evil, and their enemies were righteous. Robert Spencer, an expert on historical jihad, responds with a "politically incorrect" but academically sound and challenging work. Spencer displays an enormous amount of well-researched material. He throws the ball back into the camp of Arabist historians."

—**Dr. Walid Phares**, author, *Lebanese Christian Nationalism: The Rise and Fall of an Ethnic Resistance*

"Sweeping away the politically correct myths about a tolerant, peaceful Islam brutalized by demonic Christian Crusaders, Robert Spencer in this powerful, important book lets the facts of history speak for themselves. The truth he recovers is simple: an aggressive, violent Islamic creed for fourteen centuries has waged war against the infidel West, a scourge of conquest and persecution that roused the Crusaders to restore the Near East to the Christian and Hellenic culture devastated by the armies of Islam. Spencer's rousing, straight-talking book is a much-needed antidote to the poisonous propaganda that compromises our current battle against jihadist murder."

—**Bruce S. Thornton**, author, *Greek Ways: How the Greeks Created Western Civilization*

The Politically Incorrect Guide™ to

ISLAM

(AND THE CRUSADES)

The Politically Incorrect Guide™ to

ISLAM
(AND THE CRUSADES)

ROBERT SPENCER

Since 1947
REGNERY
PUBLISHING, INC.
An Eagle Publishing Company • Washington, DC

Library of Congress Cataloging-in-Publication Data

Spencer, Robert, 1962–
    The politically incorrect guide to Islam and the Crusades/ Robert Spencer.
    p. cm.
    Includes bibliographical references and index.
    ISBN 0-89526-013-1
    1. Islam—Controversial literature. 2. Jihad. 3. Crusades. I. Title.
    BT1170.S655 2005
    297—dc22

                             2005017128

Published in the United States by
Regnery Publishing, Inc.
One Massachusetts Avenue, NW
Washington, DC 20001
www.regnery.com

Distributed to the trade by
National Book Network
Lanham, MD 20706

Manufactured in the United States of America

10 9 8 7 6 5 4 3 2 1

Books are available in quantity for promotional or premium use. Write to Director of Special Sales, Regnery Publishing, Inc., One Massachusetts Avenue NW, Washington, DC 20001, for information on discounts and terms or call (202) 216-0600.

DEUS VULT!

CONTENTS

Introduction   xiii

Part I: ISLAM   1

Chapter 1:   **Muhammad: Prophet of War**   3

    Muhammad the raider

    The Battle of Badr

    Assassination and deceit

    Revenge and pretexts

    In victory and defeat, more Islam

    PC Myth: We can negotiate with these people

Chapter 2:   **The Qur'an: Book of War**   19

    The Qur'an counsels war

    PC Myth: The Qur'an teaches tolerance and peace

    PC Myth: The Qur'an teaches believers to take up arms
        only in self-defense

    The Qur'an's tolerant verses: "canceled"

    PC Myth: The Qur'an and the Bible are equally violent

Chapter 3:   **Islam: Religion of War**   33

    PC Myth: Islam's war teachings are only a tiny element of
        the religion

    Three choices

    It's not just Muhammad's opinion. It's the law.

    PC Myth: Islam is a religion of peace that has been
        hijacked by a tiny minority of extremists

    But what about moderate Muslims?

Chapter 4:   **Islam: Religion of Intolerance**   47

    PC Myth: Islam is a tolerant faith

    The dhimma

PC Myth: Historically the dhimma wasn't so bad

Taxpayer woes

Pushing too hard

PC Myth: Jews had it better in Muslim lands than in Christian Europe

PC Myth: Dhimmitude is a thing of the past

PC Myth: Islam values pre-Islamic cultures in Muslim countries

Chapter 5: **Islam Oppresses Women**   **65**

PC Myth: Islam respects and honors women

The great Islamic cover-up

Child marriage

Wife-beating

An offer they can't refuse

Don't go out alone

Temporary husbands

Prophetic license

Temporary wives

Rape: Four witnesses needed

Female circumcision

Long-term prospects? Dim

Chapter 6: **Islamic Law: Lie, Steal, and Kill**   **79**

Lying: It's wrong—except when it isn't

Theft: It all depends on who you're stealing from

Murder: It all depends on whom you're killing

Universal moral values? Can't find them.

PC Myth: Islam forbids the killing of the innocent

Chapter 7: **How Allah Killed Science**   **87**

What about art and music?

PC Myth: Islam was once the foundation of a great cultural and scientific flowering

What happened to the Golden Age?

Contents

Allah kills science

But all is not lost: Some things for which we can
thank Islam

Chapter 8: **The Lure of Islamic Paradise**   **99**

What's behind Door Number One

The joy of sex

How to gain entry into Paradise

The Assassins and the lure of Paradise

Chapter 9: **Islam—Spread by the Sword? You Bet.**   **107**

PC Myth: Early Muslims had no bellicose designs on
neighboring lands

PC Myth: The native Christians of the Middle East and
North Africa welcomed the Muslims as liberators

PC Myth: Early jihad warriors were merely defending
Muslim lands from their non-Muslim neighbors

Not only West, but East

What did the Muslims want?

PC Myth: Christianity and Islam spread in pretty much
the same way

Part II: THE CRUSADES   **119**

Chapter 10: **Why the Crusades Were Called**   **121**

PC Myth: The Crusades were an unprovoked attack by
Europe against the Islamic world

PC Myth: The Crusades were an early example of the
West's predatory imperialism

PC Myth: The Crusades were fought by Westerners greedy
for gain

PC Myth: The Crusades were fought to convert Muslims
to Christianity by force

Chapter 11: **The Crusades: Myth and Reality**   **133**

PC Myth: The Crusaders established European colonies in
the Middle East

PC Myth: The capture of Jerusalem was unique in medieval history and caused Muslim mistrust of the West

PC Myth: The Muslim leader Saladin was more merciful and magnanimous than the Crusaders

PC Myth: Crusades were called against Jews in addition to Muslims

PC Myth: The Crusades were bloodier than the Islamic jihads

Did the pope apologize for the Crusades?

Chapter 12: **What the Crusades Accomplished—And What They Didn't**   147

Making deals with the Mongols

Making deals with the Muslims

The jihad in Eastern Europe

Help from an unlikely quarter

Chapter 13: **What If the Crusades Had Never Happened?**   159

PC Myth: The Crusades accomplished nothing

Case study: The Zoroastrians

Case study: The Assyrians

Chapter 14: **Islam and Christianity: Equivalent Traditions?**   171

The whitewash of *Kingdom of Heaven*

PC Myth: The problem the world faces today is religious fundamentalism

But surely you're not saying that Islam is the problem?

That makes sense. Why is it so hard for people to accept?

Recovering pride in Western civilization

Why the truth must be told

Part III: TODAY'S JIHAD   **181**

Chapter 15: **The Jihad Continues**   **183**

What are they fighting for?

That was when our heartaches began

Only one thing will fix this problem

Caliphate dreams in Britain—and the United States

Khomeini in Dearborn and Dallas

A tiny minority of extremists?

Restoration of Muslim unity

Chapter 16: **"Islamophobia" and Today's Ideological Jihad**   **195**

At the UN: A new word for a new tool of political manipulation

The Universal Declaration of Human Rights: Islamic responses

What is Islamophobia, anyway?

"Islamophobia" as a weapon of jihad

Reform or denial?

News flash: Islam as Muslims live it is false Islam!

Misrepresenting Islam

Dhimmitude from media and officials

Chapter 17: **Criticizing Islam May Be Hazardous to Your Health**   **209**

The chilling of free speech in America: FOX's *24* and CAIR

Dealing with the devil

Death knell for the West?

A predetermined outcome

To criticize is not to incite

The murder of Theo van Gogh

Van Gogh was not the first

The costs of maintaining the PC myths

Living in fear of being a Christian—in Falls Church, Virginia

If you leave Islam, you must die

What happens when the law looks the other way

Chapter 18: **The Crusade We Must Fight Today**   **221**

The Islamization of Europe

What is to be done?

Defeating the jihad internationally

Defeating the jihad domestically

Acknowledgments   233

Notes   235

Index   257

Introduction

ISLAM AND THE CRUSADES

The Crusades may be causing more devastation today than they ever did in the three centuries when most of them were fought. Not in terms of lives lost and property destroyed—today's is a more subtle destruction. The Crusades have become a cardinal sin not only of the Catholic Church but also of the Western world in general. They are Exhibit A for the case that the current strife between the Muslim world and Western, post-Christian civilization is ultimately the responsibility of the West, which has provoked, exploited, and brutalized Muslims ever since the first Frankish warriors entered Jerusalem and—well, let Bill Clinton tell it:

> Indeed, in the first Crusade, when the Christian soldiers took Jerusalem, they first burned a synagogue with three hundred Jews in it, and proceeded to kill every woman and child who was Muslim on the Temple mound. The contemporaneous descriptions of the event describe soldiers walking on the Temple mound, a holy place to Christians, with blood running up to their knees. *I can tell you that that story is still being told today in the Middle East and we are still paying for it.*[1] (Emphasis added)

In this analysis Clinton curiously echoed Osama bin Laden himself, some of whose own communiqués spoke of his organization not as "al Qaeda" but of a "World Islamic Front for Jihad Against Jews and Crusaders," and called in a fatwa for "jihad against Jews and Crusaders."[2]

Such usage is quite widespread. Shortly before the beginning of the Iraqi war that toppled Saddam Hussein, on November 8, 2002, Sheikh Bakr Abed Al-Razzaq Al-Samaraai preached in Baghdad's Mother of All Battles mosque about "this difficult hour in which the Islamic nation [is] experiencing, an hour in which it faces the challenge of [forces] of disbelief of infidels, Jews, crusaders, Americans and Britons."[3]

Similarly, when Islamic jihadists bombed the U.S. consulate in Jeddah, Saudi Arabia, in December 2004, they explained that the attack was part of a larger plan to strike back at "Crusaders:" "This operation comes as part of several operations that are organized and planned by al Qaeda as part of the battle against the crusaders and the Jews, as well as part of the plan to force the unbelievers to leave the Arabian Peninsula." They said that jihad warriors "managed to enter one of the crusaders' big castles in the Arabian Peninsula and managed to enter the American consulate in Jeddah, in which they control and run the country."[4]

"One of the crusaders' big castles in the Arabian Peninsula?" Why would Islamic jihad terrorists have such a fixation with thousand-year-old castles? Could Clinton be right that they see the Crusades as the time that their troubles with the West began, and present-day conflicts in Iraq and Afghanistan as a revival of the Crusader ethos?

In a sense, yes. The more one understands the Crusades—why they were fought, and from what forces within Christianity and Islam they sprang—the more one will understand the present conflict. The Crusades, in ways that Bill Clinton and those who bombed the consulate in Jiddah only dimly fathom, hold the keys to understanding the present world situation in numerous ways.

This book explains why, with its first half devoted to Islam and second half to the Crusades. It will, in the process, clear away some of the fog of misinformation that surrounds Islam and the Crusades today. That fog is thicker than ever. One of the people most responsible for it, Western apologist for Islam Karen Armstrong, even blames Westerners' misperceptions of Islam on the Crusades:

> Ever since the Crusades, the people of Western Christendom developed a stereotypical and distorted vision of Islam, which they regarded as the enemy of decent civilization. . . . It was, for example, during the Crusades, when it was Christians who had instigated a series of brutal holy wars against the Muslim world, that Islam was described by the learned scholar-monks of Europe as an inherently violent and intolerant faith, which had only been able to establish itself by the sword. The myth of the supposed fanatical intolerance of Islam has become one of the received ideas of the West.[5]

Armstrong is right in a sense (no human being, it seems, can be wrong *all* the time): when it comes to talk of Islam, you can't believe everything you hear—especially after the September 11 attacks. Misinformation and half-truths about what Islam teaches and what Muslims in the United States believe have filled the airwaves and have even influenced public policy.

Much of this misapprehension comes in analyses of the "root causes" of the jihad terrorism that took so many lives on September 11 and has continued to threaten the peace and stability of non-Muslims around the world. It has become fashionable among certain media people and academics to place much, if not all, of the blame for what happened on September 11, 2001, not on Islam and Muslims, but on the United States and other Western countries. A pattern of mistreatment of the Islamic world by the West, say learned professors and self-important commentators, is continuing. It began centuries ago, they say—at the time of the Crusades.

But in fact, the seeds of today's conflict were planted much earlier than the First Crusade. In order to understand the Crusades properly, and the peculiar resonance they have in today's global conflict with Islamic jihad terrorists, we must begin with a survey of the prophet of Arabia and the religion he founded. For the Crusades, as we shall see, were fundamentally a reaction to events that were set in motion over 450 years before the battles began.

I intend this book to be neither a general introduction to the Islamic religion, nor a comprehensive historical survey of the Crusades. Rather, it is an examination of certain highly tendentious assertions about both Islam and the Crusades that have entered the popular discourse. This book is an attempt to move the public discourse about both subjects a bit closer to the truth.

Part I

ISLAM

Chapter 1

MUHAMMAD: PROPHET OF WAR

Why does the life of Muhammad, the Prophet of Islam, matter today? Fourteen centuries have passed since he was born. Millions of Muslims have lived and died since then, and many leaders have risen to lead the faithful, including descendents of the Prophet himself. Surely Islam, like other religions, has changed over 1,400 years.

Here's why the life of Muhammad matters: Contrary to what many secularists would have us believe, religions are *not* entirely determined (or distorted) by the faithful over time. The lives and words of the founders remain central, no matter how long ago they lived. The idea that believers shape religion is derived, instead, from the fashionable 1960s philosophy of deconstructionism, which teaches that written words have no meaning other than that given to them by the reader. Equally important, it follows that if the reader alone finds meaning, there can be no truth (and certainly no religious truth); one person's meaning is equal to another's. Ultimately, according to deconstructionism, we all create our own set of "truths," none better or worse than any other.

Yet for the religious man or woman on the streets of Chicago, Rome, Jerusalem, Damascus, Calcutta, and Bangkok, the words of Jesus, Moses, Muhammad, Krishna, and Buddha mean something far greater than any individual's reading of them. And even to the less-than-devout reader,

Guess what?

● Muhammad did not teach "peace and tolerance."

● Muhammad led armies and ordered assassinations of his enemies.

● Islamic tradition allows for negotiated settlements only in service of the ultimate goal of Islamic conquest.

the words of these great religious teachers are clearly not equal in their meaning.

That's why I have placed a "Muhammad vs. Jesus" sidebar in every chapter to emphasize the fallacy of those who claim that Islam and Christianity—and all other religious traditions, for that matter—are basically equal in their ability to inspire good or evil. It is also meant to emphasize that the West, built on Christianity, is worth defending, even if we live in a so-called post-Christian era. Furthermore, through the words of Muhammad and Jesus, we can draw a distinction between the core principles that guide the faithful Muslim and Christian. These principles are important. The followers of Muhammad read his words and imitate his actions, which leads to an expression of faith quite different from Christians. One does not have to look too far to see that life in an Islamic country is different from life in the United States or Britain. The difference begins with Muhammad. In these days when so many invoke Muhammad's words and deeds to justify actions of violence and bloodshed, it is important to become familiar with this pivotal figure.

For many in the West, Muhammad remains more mysterious than other major religious figures. Most people know, for example, that Moses received the Ten Commandments on Mount Sinai, that Jesus died on a cross at Calvary and was raised from the dead, and maybe even that Buddha sat under a tree and received enlightenment. But less is known about Muhammad, and even that much is disputed. Hence, what follows will be taken solely from Islamic texts.

First basic fact: Muhammad ibn Abdallah ibn Abd al-Muttalib (570–632), the prophet of Islam, was a man of war. He taught his followers to fight for his new religion. He said that their god, Allah, had commanded them to take up arms. And Muhammad, no armchair general, fought in numerous battles. These facts are crucial to anyone who really wants to understand what caused the Crusades centuries ago or, in our own time, what has led to the rise of the global jihad movement.

In the course of these battles, Muhammad articulated numerous principles that have been followed by Muslims to this day. Therefore, it is important to record some features of Muhammad's battles, which can provide insight into today's newspaper headlines—insights that continue, sadly, to elude many analysts and experts.

Muhammad the raider

Muhammad already had experience as a warrior before he assumed the role of prophet. He had participated in two local wars between his Quraysh tribe and their neighboring rivals Banu Hawazin. But his unique role as prophet-warrior would come later. After receiving revelations from Allah through the angel Gabriel in 610, he began by just preaching to his tribe the worship of One God and his own position as a prophet. But he was not well received by his Quraysh brethren in Mecca, who reacted disdainfully to his prophetic call and refused to give up their gods. Muhammad's frustration and rage became evident. When even his uncle, Abu Lahab, rejected his message, Muhammad cursed him and his wife in violent language that has been preserved in the Qur'an, the holy book of Islam: "May the hands of Abu Lahab perish! May he himself perish! Nothing shall his wealth and gains avail him. He shall be burnt in a flaming fire, and his wife, laden with faggots, shall have a rope of fibre around her neck!" (Qur'an 111:1–5).

Ultimately, Muhammad would turn from violent words to violent deeds. In 622, he finally fled his native Mecca for a nearby town, Medina, where a band of tribal warriors had accepted him as a prophet and pledged loyalty to him. In Medina, these new Muslims began raiding the caravans of the Quraysh, with Muhammad personally leading many of these raids. These raids kept the nascent Muslim movement solvent and helped form Islamic theology—as in one notorious incident when a band of Muslims raided a Quraysh caravan at Nakhla, a settlement not far from

Mecca. The raiders attacked the caravan during the sacred month of Rajab, when fighting was forbidden. When they returned to the Muslim camp laden with booty, Muhammad refused to share in the loot or to have anything to do with them, saying only, "I did not order you to fight in the sacred month."[1]

But then a new revelation came from Allah, explaining that the Quraysh's opposition to Muhammad was a worse transgression than the violation of the sacred month. In other words, the raid was justified. "They question thee, O Muhammad, with regard to warfare in the sacred month. Say: warfare therein is a great transgression, but to turn men from the way of Allah, and to disbelieve in Him and in the Inviolable Place of Worship, and to expel His people thence, is a greater sin with Allah; for persecution is worse than killing" (Qur'an 2:214). Whatever sin the Nakhla raiders had committed was overshadowed by the Quraysh's rejection of Muhammad.

Just Like Today: Killing non-combatants

When Osama bin Laden killed innocent non-combatants in the World Trade Center on September 11, 2001, and later his co-religionists captured and beheaded civilian hostages in Iraq, American Muslim spokesmen blandly asserted that this targeting of innocent people was forbidden by Islam. This was debatable, since some Islamic legal authorities allow the killing of non-combatants if they are seen as aiding the enemies of Islam in war.[2] However, even if the principle were correct, it would give way to another that arose out of the Nakhla raid: "Persecution is worse than killing." And therefore, to fight against the persecution of Muslims, by any means necessary, is the highest good.

This was a momentous revelation, for it led to an Islamic principle that has had repercussions throughout the ages. Good became identified with anything that redounded to the benefit of Muslims, regardless of whether it violated moral or other laws. The moral absolutes enshrined in the Ten Commandments, and other teachings of the great religions that preceded Islam, were swept aside in favor of an overarching principle of expediency.

The Battle of Badr

Soon after Nakhla came the first major battle the Muslims fought. Muhammad heard that a large Quraysh caravan, laden with money and goods, was coming from Syria. "This is the Quraysh caravan containing their property," he told his followers. "Go out to attack it, perhaps God will give it as a prey."[3] He set out toward Mecca to lead the raid. But this time the Quraysh were ready for him, coming out to meet Muhammad's three hundred men with a force nearly a thousand strong. Muhammad seems not to have expected these numbers and cried out to Allah in anxiety, "O God, if this band perish today Thou wilt be worshipped no more."[4]

Despite their superior numbers, the Quraysh were routed. Some Muslim traditions say that Muhammad himself participated in the fighting, others that he exhorted his followers from the sidelines. In any event, it was an occasion for him to see years of frustration, resentment, and hatred toward his own people, who had rejected him, avenged. One of his followers later recalled a curse Muhammad had pronounced on the leaders of the Quraysh: "The Prophet said, 'O Allah! Destroy the chiefs of Quraish, O Allah! Destroy Abu Jahl bin Hisham, 'Utba bin Rabi'a, Shaiba bin Rabi'a, 'Uqba bin Abi Mu'ait, 'Umaiya bin Khalaf (or Ubai bin Kalaf).'"[5]

All these men were captured or killed during the battle of Badr. One Quraysh leader named in this curse, 'Uqba, pleaded for his life, "But who will look after my children, O Muhammad?"

"Hell," responded the Prophet of Islam, and ordered 'Uqba killed.[6]

Another Quraysh chieftain, Abu Jahl (which means "Father of Ignorance," a name given him by Muslim chroniclers; his real name was 'Amr ibn Hisham) was beheaded. The Muslim who severed the head proudly carried his trophy to Muhammad: "I cut off his head and brought it to the apostle, saying, 'This is the head of the enemy of God, Abu Jahl.'"

Muhammad was delighted. "By God than Whom there is no other, is it?" he exclaimed, and gave thanks to Allah for the death of his enemy.[7]

The bodies of all those named in the curse were thrown into a pit. As an eyewitness recalled, "Later on I saw all of them killed during the battle of Badr and their bodies were thrown into a well except the body of Umaiya or Ubai, because he was a fat man, and when he was pulled, the parts of his body got separated before he was thrown into the well."[8] Then Muhammad taunted them as "people of the pit" and posed a theological question: "Have you found what God promised you is true? I have found that what my Lord promised me is true." When asked why he was speaking to dead bodies, he replied: "You cannot hear what I say better than they, but they cannot answer me."[9]

The victory at Badr was the legendary turning point for the Muslims. Muhammad even claimed that armies of angels joined with the Muslims to smite the Quraysh—and that similar help would come in the future to Muslims who remained faithful to Allah: "Allah had helped you at Badr, when ye were a contemptible little force; then fear Allah; thus may ye show your gratitude. Remember thou saidst to the Faithful: 'Is it not enough for you that Allah should help you with three thousand angels specially sent down? Yea, if ye remain firm, and act aright, even if the enemy should rush here on you in hot haste, your Lord would help you with five thousand angels making a terrific onslaught" (Qur'an 3:123–

125). Another revelation from Allah emphasized that it was piety, not military might, that brought victory at Badr: "There has already been for you a Sign in the two armies that met in combat: one was fighting in the cause of Allah, the other resisting Allah; these saw with their own eyes twice their number. But Allah doth support with His aid whom He pleaseth. In this is a warning for such as have eyes to see" (Qur'an 3:13). Another Qur'anic passage asserts that the Muslims were merely passive instruments at Badr: "It is not ye who slew them; it was Allah" (Qur'an 8:17). And Allah would grant such victories to pious Muslims even though they faced odds even more overwhelming than those they had overcome at Badr: "O Prophet! Rouse the Believers to the fight. If there are twenty amongst you, patient and persevering, they will vanquish two hundred: if a hundred, they will vanquish a thousand of the unbelievers: for these are a people without understanding" (Qur'an 8:65).

Allah rewarded those he had granted victory at Badr: There was great booty—so much, in fact, that it became a bone of contention. So divisive did this become that Allah himself spoke about it in a chapter (sura) of the Qur'an devoted entirely to reflections on the battle of Badr: the eighth chapter, titled Al-Anfal, "The Spoils of War" or "Booty." Allah warns the Muslims not to consider booty won at Badr to belong to anyone but Muhammad: "They ask thee concerning things taken as spoils of war. Say: '(Such) spoils are at the disposal of Allah and the Messenger: so fear Allah, and keep straight the relations between yourselves. Obey Allah and His Messenger, if ye do believe'" (Qur'an 8:1). Ultimately, Muhammad distributed the booty among the Muslims equally, keeping a fifth for himself: "And know that whatever ye take as spoils of war, lo! a fifth thereof is for Allah, and for the messenger and for the kinsman (who hath need) and orphans and the needy and the wayfarer, if ye believe in Allah and that which We revealed unto Our slave on the Day of Discrimination, the day when the two armies met" (Qur'an 8:41). Allah emphasized that it was a reward for obedience to him: "Now enjoy what ye have won, as lawful and good, and keep your duty to Allah. Lo! Allah is Forgiving, Merciful" (Qur'an 8:69).[10]

From being a tiny, despised community, the Muslims were now a force with which the pagans of Arabia had to reckon—and they began to strike terror in the hearts of their enemies. Muhammad's claim to be the last prophet of the One, True God appeared validated by a victory against enormous odds. With this victory, certain attitudes and assumptions were being planted in the minds of Muslims, which remain with many of them to this day. These include:

- ❀ Allah will grant victory to his people against foes that are superior in numbers or firepower, so long as they remain faithful to his commands.
- ❀ Victories entitle the Muslims to appropriate the possessions of the vanquished as booty.
- ❀ Bloody vengeance against one's enemies belongs not solely to the Lord, but also to those who submit to him on earth. That is the meaning of the word Islam: submission.
- ❀ Prisoners taken in battle against the Muslims may be put to death at the discretion of Muslim leaders.
- ❀ Those who reject Islam are "the vilest of creatures" (Qur'an 98:6) and thus deserve no mercy.
- ❀ Anyone who insults or even opposes Muhammad or his people deserves a humiliating death—by beheading if possible. (This is in accordance with Allah's command to "smite the necks" of the "unbelievers" (Qur'an 47:4)).

Above all, the battle of Badr was the first practical example of what came to be known as the Islamic doctrine of jihad—a doctrine that holds the key to the understanding of both the Crusades and the conflicts of today.

Assassination and deceit

Flushed with victory, Muhammad stepped up his raiding operations. He also hardened in his attitudes toward the Jewish tribes of the region, who kept their faith and rejected Muhammad as a prophet of God. With this rejection, Muhammad's prophetic calls to Jews began to get violent, emphasizing earthly punishment. Striding into the center of the marketplace of the Banu Qaynuqa, a Jewish tribe with whom he had a truce, he announced to the crowds, "O Jews, beware lest God bring upon you the vengeance that He brought upon Quraysh and become Muslims. You know that I am a prophet who has been sent—you will find that in your scriptures and God's covenant with you."[11] The Jews of the Banu Qaynuqa were not persuaded, frustrating the Prophet even more. He laid siege on them until they offered him unconditional surrender.

Even then Muhammad's anger was not assuaged. He found a new focus for it in a Jewish poet, K'ab bin Al-Ashraf, who, according to Muhammad's first biographer, Ibn Ishaq, "composed amatory verses of an insulting nature about the Muslim women."[12] Muhammad asked his followers, "Who is willing to kill Ka'b bin Al-Ashraf who has hurt Allah and His Apostle?"[13]

Ibn Warraq on Islam:

"The theory and practice of jihad was not concocted in the Pentagon.... It was taken from the Koran, the Hadith and Islamic tradition. Western liberals, especially humanists, find it hard to believe this.... It is extraordinary the amount of people who have written about the 11th of September without once mentioning Islam. We must take seriously what the Islamists say to understand their motivation, [that] it is the divinely ordained duty of all Muslims to fight in the literal sense until man-made law has been replaced by God's law, the Sharia, and Islamic law has conquered the entire world.... For every text the liberal Muslims produce, the mullahs will use dozens of counter-examples [that are] exegetically, philosophically, historically far more legitimate."

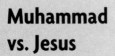

Muhammad vs. Jesus

"Love your enemies and pray for those who persecute you."

Jesus (Matthew 5:44)

"Against them make ready your strength to the utmost of your power, including steeds of war, to strike terror into the hearts of the enemies, of Allah and your enemies, and others besides, whom ye may not know, but whom Allah doth know."

Qur'an 8:60

He found a volunteer in a young Muslim named Muhammad bin Maslama: "O Allah's Apostle! Would you like that I kill him?" After the Prophet answered, "Yes," Muhammad bin Maslama asked him for permission to lie in order to deceive K'ab bin Al-Ashraf into walking into an ambush.[14] The Prophet granted him this permission, and Muhammad bin Maslama duly deceived and murdered K'ab.[15]

After the murder of K'ab, Muhammad issued a blanket command: "Kill any Jew that falls into your power." This was not a military order: The first victim was a Jewish merchant, Ibn Sunayna, who had "social and business relations" with the Muslims. The murderer, Muhayissa, was rebuked for the deed by his brother Huwayissa, who was not yet a Muslim. Muhayissa was unrepentant. He told his brother, "Had the one who ordered me to kill him ordered me to kill you I would have cut your head off."

Huwayissa was impressed: "By God, a religion which can bring you to this is marvelous!" He became a Muslim.[16] The world is still witnessing such marvels to this day.

Revenge and pretexts

After their humiliation at Badr, the Quraysh were anxious for revenge. They assembled three thousand troops against one thousand Muslims at Uhud. Muhammad wore two coats of mail and, brandishing a sword, led the Muslims into battle. But this time they were routed. The Prophet himself had his face bloodied and a tooth knocked out; rumors even flew around the battlefield that he had been killed. When he was able to find water to wash the blood off his face, Muhammad vowed revenge: "The wrath of God is fierce against him who bloodied the face of His prophet."[17] When Abu Sufyan, the Quraysh leader, taunted the Muslims, Muhammad was adamant, and emphasized the traditional sharp Islamic distinction between believers and unbelievers. He told his lieutenant

Just Like Today: Pretexts

Another pattern was set at Uhud that played out across the centuries: Muslims would see any aggression as a pretext for revenge, regardless of whether they provoked it. With a canny understanding of how to sway public opinion, jihadists and their PC allies on the American Left today use current events as pretexts to justify what they are doing: Time and again they portray themselves as merely reacting to grievous provocations from the enemies of Islam. By this they gain recruits and sway popular opinion.

Conventional wisdom among a surprisingly broad political spectrum today holds that the global jihad movement is a response to some provocation or other: the invasion of Iraq, the establishment of Israel, the toppling of Iran's Mossadegh—or a more generalized offense such as "American neo-colonialism" or "the lust for oil." Those who are particularly forgetful of history blame it on newly minted epiphenomena such as the Abu Ghraib prison scandals, which cast a shadow over America's presence in Iraq in 2004. But the jihadists were fighting long before Abu Ghraib, Iraq, Israel, or American independence. Indeed, they have been fighting and imitating their warrior Prophet ever since the seventh century, casting their actions as responses to the enormities of their enemies ever since Muhammad discovered his uncle's mutilated body.

'Umar to respond: "God is most high and most glorious. We are not equal. Our dead are in paradise; your dead in hell."[18]

Muhammad vowed revenge again when he found the body of his uncle Hamza. Hamza had been killed at Uhud and his body horribly mutilated by a woman, Hind bint 'Utba, who cut off Hamza's nose and ears and ate a part of his liver. She did this in revenge for the killing of her father, brother, uncle, and eldest son at Badr. The Prophet was not in the least moved by the fact that she had done these terrible deeds in revenge: "If God gives me victory over Quraysh in the future," he exclaimed, "I will mutilate thirty of their men." Touched by his grief and anger, his followers made a similar vow: "By God, if God gives us victory over them in the future we will mutilate them as no Arab has ever mutilated anyone."[19]

In victory and defeat, more Islam

Defeat at Uhud, meanwhile, did nothing to shake Muslims' faith or dull its fervor. Allah told them they would have gained another victory if they had not disobeyed him: "Allah verily made good His promise unto you when ye routed them by His leave, until (the moment) when your courage failed you, and ye disagreed about the order and ye disobeyed, after He had shown you that for which ye long" (Qur'an 3:152).

Here again a pattern was set: When things go wrong for the Muslims, it is punishment for not being faithful to Islam. In 1948, Sayyid Qutb, the great theorist of the Muslim Brotherhood, which holds the distinction of being the first modern Islamic terrorist group, declared of the Islamic world: "We only have to look in order to see that our social situation is as bad as it can be." Yet "we continually cast aside all our own spiritual heritage, all our intellectual endowment, and all the solutions which might well be revealed by a glance at these things; we cast aside our own fundamental principles and doctrines, and we bring in those of democracy, or socialism, or communism."[20] In other words, Islam alone guarantees success, and to abandon it brings failure.

The theological connection between victory and obedience and defeat and disobedience was reinforced after the Muslim victory at the Battle of the Trench in 627. Muhammad again received a revelation that attributed the victory to Allah's supernatural intervention: "O ye who believe! Remember Allah's favor unto you when there came against you hosts, and We sent against them a great wind and hosts ye could not see" (Qur'an 33:9).

PC Myth: We can negotiate with these people

Yet another key Islamic principle was formulated by events surrounding the Treaty of Hudaybiyya. In 628, Muhammad had a vision in which he performed a pilgrimage to Mecca—a pagan custom that he wanted to make part of Islam, but had so far been unable to do because of Quraysh control of the city. He directed Muslims to prepare to make the pilgrimage to Mecca, and advanced on the city with 1,500 men. The Quraysh met him outside the city, and the two sides concluded a ten-year truce (*hudna*), the treaty of Hudaybiyya.

The Muslims agreed to return home without making the pilgrimage, and the Quraysh would allow them to make the pilgrimage the following year. Muhammad shocked his men by agreeing further to provisions that

Just Like Today: Tsunami calls for more Islam

After a tsunami devastated the South Pacific on December 26, 2004, Australia and the United States alone pledged more than one billion dollars in aid. Oil-soaked Arab countries—Saudi Arabia, Qatar, UAE, Kuwait, Algeria, Bahrain, and Libya—made a combined pledge of less than one-tenth this amount. One reason for this: Islamic teachers attributed the tsunami to the sins committed by infidels and Muslims in heavily Islamic Indonesia. As one Saudi cleric said, "It happened at Christmas when fornicators and corrupt people from all over the world come to commit fornication and sexual perversion."[21]

seemed highly disadvantageous to the Muslims: Those fleeing the Quraysh and seeking refuge with the Muslims would be returned to the Quraysh, while those fleeing the Muslims and seeking refuge with the Quraysh would not be returned to the Muslims. The Quraysh negotiator, Suhayl bin 'Amr, even compelled Muhammad not to identify himself as "Muhammad, the apostle of God." Said Suhayl, "If I witnessed that you were God's apostle I would not have fought you. Write your own name and the name of your father." To the dismay of his companions, Muhammad did so.

Then, contrary to all appearances, he insisted that the Muslims had been victorious, producing a new revelation from Allah: "Verily We have granted thee a manifest victory" (Qur'an 48:1). He promised that his followers would reap much booty: "Allah was well pleased with the believers when they swore allegiance unto thee beneath the tree, and He knew what was in their hearts, and He sent down peace of reassurance on them, and hath rewarded them with a near victory; and much booty that they will capture. Allah is ever Mighty, Wise. Allah promiseth you much booty that ye will capture, and hath given you this in advance, and hath withheld men's hands from you, that it may be a token for the believers, and that He may guide you on a right path" (Qur'an 48:18–20).

If any of his followers were still skeptical, their fears would soon be assuaged. A woman of the Quraysh, Umm Kulthum, joined the Muslims in Medina; her two brothers came to Muhammad, asking that she be returned, "in accordance with the agreement between him and the Quraysh at Hudaybiya."[22] Muhammad refused because Allah forbade it. He gave Muhammad a new revelation: "O ye who believe! When there come to you believing women refugees, examine and test them:

A Book You're Not Supposed to Read

A. Guillaume, *The Life of Muhammad: A Translation of Ibn Ishaq's Sirat Rasul Allah*, Oxford University Press, 1955. An English translation of the earliest biography of Muhammad—written by a pious Muslim. Virtually every page presents a devastating refutation of the whitewashed, peaceful Muhammad of PC myth.

Allah knows best as to their faith: if ye ascertain that they are believers, then send them not back to the unbelievers" (Qur'an 60:10).

In refusing to send Umm Kulthum back to the Quraysh, Muhammad broke the treaty. Although Muslim apologists have claimed throughout history that the Quraysh broke it first, this incident came before any treaty violations by the Quraysh. Furthermore, breaking the treaty reinforced the principle that nothing was good except what was advantageous to Islam, and nothing evil except what hindered it. Once the treaty was formally discarded, Islamic jurists enunciated the principle that, in general, truces were to be concluded for no longer than ten years and only entered into for the purpose of allowing weakened Muslim forces to gain strength.

Subsequent events would illustrate the dark implications of this principle.

Chapter 2

THE QUR'AN: BOOK OF WAR

With Muhammad's prophetic career so thoroughly marked by blood and warfare, it should be no surprise that the sacred book bequeathed by the Prophet of Islam to the world, the Qur'an, would be similarly violent and intransigent. And it's true: The Qur'an is unique among the sacred writings of the world in counseling its adherents to make war against unbelievers.

The Qur'an counsels war

There are over a hundred verses in the Qur'an that exhort believers to wage jihad against unbelievers. "O Prophet! Strive hard against the unbelievers and the hypocrites, and be firm against them. Their abode is Hell, an evil refuge indeed" (Qur'an 9:73). "Strive hard" in Arabic is *jahidi*, a verbal form of the noun *jihad*. This striving was to be on the battlefield: "When you meet the unbelievers in the battlefield, strike off their heads and, when you have laid them low, bind your captives firmly" (Qur'an 47:4). This is emphasized repeatedly: "O ye who believe! Fight the unbelievers who gird you about, and let them find firmness in you: and know that Allah is with those who fear Him" (Qur'an 9:123).

This warfare was to be directed against both those who rejected Islam and those who professed to be Muslims but did not hold to the fullness

- The Qur'an commands Muslims to make war on Jews and Christians.

- Oft-quoted tolerant, peaceful Qur'anic verses have actually been *canceled*, according to Islamic theology.

- There is nothing in the Bible that rivals the Qur'an's exhortations to violence.

of the faith: "Prophet, make war on the unbelievers and the hypocrites and deal rigorously with them. Hell shall be their home: an evil fate" (Qur'an 9:73). This warfare was only part of the larger spiritual conflict between Allah and Satan: "Those who believe fight in the cause of Allah, and those who reject faith fight in the cause of evil: so fight ye against the friends of Satan" (Qur'an 4:76).

"Then, when the sacred months have passed, slay the idolaters wherever ye find them, and take them captive, and besiege them, and prepare for them each ambush. But if they repent and establish worship and pay the poor-due, then leave their way free. Lo! Allah is Forgiving, Merciful" (Qur'an 9:5). The "poor-due" in this verse is *zakat*, which is one of the Five Pillars of Islam, and regulates religious tithes. Thus the verse is saying that if the "idolaters" become Muslims, leave them alone.

Jews and Christians were to be fought, along with "idolaters": "Fight those who believe not in Allah nor the Last Day, nor hold that forbidden which hath been forbidden by Allah and His Messenger, nor acknowledge the religion of Truth, (even if they are) of the People of the Book, until they pay the Jizya with willing submission, and feel themselves subdued" (Qur'an 9:29). The jizya was a tax inflicted upon nonbelievers.

Jihad is the highest duty of Muslims: "Do ye make the giving of drink to pilgrims, or the maintenance of the Sacred Mosque, equal to the pious service of those who believe in Allah and the Last Day, and strive with might and main in the cause of Allah [*jihad fi sabil Allah*]? They are not comparable in the sight of Allah: and Allah guides not those who do wrong. Those who believe, and suffer exile and strive with might and main, in Allah's cause [*jihad fi sabil Allah*], with their goods and their persons, have the highest rank in the sight of Allah: they are the people who will achieve salvation" (Qur'an 9:19–20). In Islamic theology, *jihad fi sabil Allah* refers specifically to taking up arms for Islam.

Paradise is guaranteed to those who "slay and are slain" for Allah: "Allah hath purchased of the believers their persons and their goods; for theirs (in return) is the garden (of Paradise): they fight in His cause, and slay and are slain: a promise binding on Him in truth" (Qur'an 9:111).

One may attempt to spiritualize such verses, but there is no doubt from the historical record that Muhammad meant them literally.

PC Myth: The Qur'an teaches tolerance and peace

But wait a minute: Doesn't the Qur'an *really* teach tolerance and peace? Sure, there are a few bad verses here and there, but there are also a lot of verses that affirm the brotherhood of man and the equality and dignity of all people, right?

No. The closest the Qur'an comes actually to counseling tolerance or peaceful coexistence is to counsel believers to leave the unbelievers alone in their errors: "Say: O disbelievers! I worship not that which ye worship; nor worship ye that which I worship. And I shall not worship that which ye worship. Nor will ye worship that which I worship. Unto you your religion, and unto me my religion" (Qur'an 109:1–6). Of course, they are to be left alone so that Allah can deal with them: "And have patience with what they say, and leave them with noble dignity. And leave Me alone to deal with those in possession of the good things of life, who yet deny the Truth; and bear with them for a little while" (Qur'an 73:10–11).

Above all, no Muslim should force anyone to accept Islam: "Let there be no compulsion in religion: Truth stands out clear from Error: whoever rejects evil and believes in Allah hath grasped the most trustworthy hand-hold, that never breaks" (Qur'an 2:256).

But is this really tolerance the way that modern Westerners understand it? It might be a reasonable facsimile if that were all the Qur'an has to say about the subject. But it isn't.

PC Myth: The Qur'an teaches believers to take up arms only in self-defense

At this point, Islamic apologists might grant that the Qur'an doesn't leave relations between believers and unbelievers at the live-and-let-live stage. They may admit that it counsels believers to defend themselves, and will argue that it is somewhat akin to the Catholic Church's just-war theory.

There is support for this view in the Qur'an: "Fight in the way of Allah against those who fight against you, but begin not hostilities. Lo! Allah loveth not aggressors." So Muslims are, in this verse at least, not to start conflicts with unbelievers. Once hostilities have begun, however, Muslims should wage them furiously: "And slay them wherever ye find them, and drive them out of the places whence they drove you out, for persecution is worse than slaughter. And fight not with them at the Inviolable Place of Worship until they first attack you there, but if they attack you there then slay them. Such is the reward of disbelievers. But if they desist, then lo! Allah is Forgiving, Merciful."

And what is to be the conclusion of this war? "And fight them until persecution is no more, and religion is for Allah" (Qur'an 2:190–193). This would seem to indicate that the war must continue until the world is Islam—the "religion is for Allah"—or under the hegemony of Islamic law.

Consequently, there is a problem with the interpretation that jihad warfare can only be defensive. The South African mufti Ebrahim Desai repeated a common teaching in Islam when he answered a question at "Islam Q & A Online." The questioner asked, "I have a question about offensive jihad. Does it mean that we are to attack even those non-Muslims which don't [sic] do anything against Islam just because we have to propagate Islam?" Desai responded:

> You should understand that we as Muslims firmly believe that
> the person who doesn't believe in Allah as he is required to, is
> a disbeliever who would be doomed to Hell eternally. Thus

one of the primary responsibilities of the Muslim ruler is to spread Islam throughout the world, thus saving people from eternal damnation. Thus what is meant by the passage in Tafsir Uthmani [a commentary on the Qur'an] is that if a country doesn't allow the propagation of Islam to its inhabitants in a suitable manner or creates hindrances to this, then the Muslim ruler would be justifying in waging Jihad against this country, so that the message of Islam can reach its inhabitants, thus saving them from the Fire of Jahannum [Hell]. If the Kuffaar [unbelievers] allow us to spread Islam peacefully, then we would not wage Jihad against them.[1]

Just Like Today: Jihadists cite Muhammad's battles to prove jihad is not just defensive

In an article titled "The True Meaning of Jihad," posted in 2003 at the website Khilafah.com, which is affiliated with the jihadist group Hizb ut-Tahrir, one Sidik Aucbur cites the example of Muhammad against those who would argue that jihad is purely defensive:

Moreover some will say that Jihad was only defensive; this is incorrect. A quick study of the Life of the Prophet (SalAllahu Alaihi Wasallam) shows us something different:

⚘ The Battle of Mut'ah was instigated by the Muslims against the Romans; the Muslims were 3,000 faced against a Roman army of 200,000.

⚘ The Battle of Hunayn was inevitable shortly after the Muslims had conquered Makkah.

⚘ The Battle of Tabuk was also instigated to finally destroy the Romans.

We see from the ijmaa (Consensus) of Sahaba [the companions of Muhammad], that they too instigated Jihad, through As-Sham, Iraq, Iran, Egypt and North Africa. Moreover, the status of Martyr in Islam is of the highest, so how can it be that Jihad is reduced to anything lower that that.[2]

In other words, if a country is perceived to be hindering the spread of Islam, Muslims are obliged to wage war against it. This would, of course, be a defensive conflict, since the hindrances came first. Here then is another illustration of how elastic and essentially meaningless the concept of fighting only in self-defense has become. What constitutes a sufficient provocation? Must the defending side wait until the enemy strikes the first military blow? These questions have no clear or definitive answers in Islamic law, making it possible for anyone to portray virtually any struggle as defensive without violating the strict canons of that law. But this also renders meaningless the oft-repeated claims that jihad warfare can only be defensive.

The Qur'an's tolerant verses: "canceled"

What's more, the Qur'an's last word on jihad is not defensive, but offensive. The suras of the Qur'an are not arranged chronologically, but according to length. However, Islamic theology divides the Qur'an into "Meccan" and "Medinan" suras. The Meccan ones come from the first segment of Muhammad's career as a prophet, when he simply called the Meccans to Islam. Later, after he had fled to Medina, his positions hardened. The Medinan suras are less poetic and generally much longer than those from Mecca; they're also filled with matters of law and ritual—and exhortations to jihad warfare against unbelievers. The relatively tolerant verses quoted above and others like them generally date from the Meccan period, while those with a more violent and intolerant edge are mostly from Medina.

Why does this distinction matter? Because of the Islamic doctrine of abrogation (*naskh*). This is the idea that Allah can change or cancel what he tells Muslims: "None of Our revelations do We abrogate or cause to be forgotten, but We substitute something better or similar: knowest thou not that Allah Hath power over all things?" (Qur'an 2:106). According to this idea, the violent verses of the ninth sura, including the Verse of the Sword (9:5), abrogate the peaceful verses, because they were revealed later in Muhammad's prophetic career: In fact, most Muslim authorities agree that the ninth sura was the very last section of the Qur'an to be revealed.

In line with this, some Islamic theologians have asserted that the Verse of the Sword abrogates no fewer than 124 more peaceful and tolerant verses of the Qur'an.[3] *Tafsir al-Jalalayn*, a commentary on the Qur'an by the respected imams Jalal al-Din Muhammad ibn Ahmad al-Mahalli (1389–1459) and Jalal al-Din 'Abd al-Rahman ibn Abi Bakr al-Suyuti (1445–1505), asserts that the ninth sura "was sent down when security was removed by the sword."[4] Another mainstream and respected Qur'an commentator, Isma'il bin 'Amr bin Kathir al Dimashqi (1301–1372), known popularly as Ibn Kathir, declares that sura 9:5 "abrogated every agreement of peace between the Prophet and any idolater, every treaty, and every term.... No idolater had any more treaty or promise of safety ever since Surah Bara'ah [the ninth sura] was revealed."[5] Ibn Juzayy (d. 1340), yet another Qur'an commentator whose works are still read in the Islamic world, agrees: The Verse of the Sword's purpose is "abrogating every peace treaty in the Qur'an."[6]

Ibn Kathir makes this clear in his commentary on another "tolerance verse": "And he [Muhammad] saith: O my Lord! Lo! these are a folk who believe not. Then bear with them, O Muhammad, and say: Peace. But they will come to know" (Qur'an 43:88–89). Ibn Kathir explains: "*Say Salam* (peace!) means, 'do not

Alexis de Tocqueville on Islam:

"I studied the Quran a great deal. I came away from that study with the conviction that by and large there have been few religions in the world as deadly to men as that of Muhammad. So far as I can see, it is the principal cause of the decadence so visible today in the Muslim world and, though less absurd than the polytheism of old, its social and political tendencies are in my opinion more to be feared, and I therefore regard it as a form of decadence rather than a form of progress in relation to paganism itself."

respond to them in the same evil manner in which they address you; but try to soften their hearts and forgive them in word and deed.'" However, that is not the end of the passage. Ibn Kathir then takes up the last part: "But they will come to know. This is a warning from Allah for them. His punishment, which cannot be warded off, struck them, and His religion and His word was supreme. Subsequently Jihad and striving were prescribed until the people entered the religion of Allah in crowds, and Islam spread throughout the east and the west."[7]

That work is not yet complete.

All this means that warfare against unbelievers until they either become Muslim or pay the jizya—the special tax on non-Muslims in Islamic law—"with willing submission" (Qur'an 9:29) is the Qur'an's last word on jihad. Mainstream Islamic tradition has interpreted this as Allah's enduring marching orders to the human race: The Islamic *umma* (community) must exist in a state of perpetual war with the non-Muslim world, punctuated only by temporary truces.

Some Islamic theologians today are attempting to construct alternative visions of Islam based on a different understanding of abrogation; however, such efforts have met with little interest and support among Muslims worldwide—not least because they fly in the face of interpretations that have been mainstream for centuries.

PC Myth: The Qur'an and the Bible are equally violent

All right, so the Qur'an teaches war. But so does the Bible, right? Islamic apologists and their non-Muslim allies frequently try to make a case for moral equivalence between Islam and Christianity: "Muslims have been violent? So have Christians. Muslims are waging jihad? Well, what about the Crusades? The Qur'an teaches warfare? Well, I could cherry-pick violent verses out of the Bible." You can find that sort of thing in *all* religious traditions we're told. None of them is more or less likely to incite its followers to violence we're assured.

Just Like Today: The peaceful verses *still* abrogated

The doctrine of abrogation is not the province of long-dead muftis whose works no longer carry any weight in the Islamic world. The Saudi Sheikh Muhammad Saalih al-Munajid (b. 1962), whose lectures and Islamic rulings (*fatawa*) circulate widely throughout the Islamic world, demonstrates this in a discussion of whether Muslims should force others to accept Islam. In considering Qur'an 2:256 ("There is no compulsion in religion,") the sheikh quotes Qur'an 9:29, 8:39, "And fight them until there is no more Fitnah (disbelief and polytheism, i.e. worshipping others besides Allaah), and the religion (worship) will all be for Allaah Alone [in the whole of the world]", and the Verse of the Sword. Of the latter, Sheikh Muhammad says simply: "This verse is known as Ayat al-Sayf (the Verse of the Sword). These and similar verses abrogate those saying that there is no compulsion to become Muslim."[8]

But is all this really true? Some Islamic apologists and non-Muslim purveyors of moral equivalence claim to find even in the New Testament passages that exhort believers to violence. They most often point to two passages:

- "I tell you that to everyone who has, more shall be given, but from the one who does not have, even what he does have shall be taken away. But these enemies of mine, who did not want me to reign over them, bring them here and slay them in my presence" (Luke 19:26–27). Of course, the fallacy here is that these are the words of a king in a parable, not Jesus' instructions to His followers, but such subtleties are often ignored in the modern communications age.

- "Do not think that I have come to bring peace on earth. I did not come to bring peace, but a sword. I am sent to set a man against his father, a daughter against her mother, and a daughter-in-law against her mother-in-law" (Matthew 10:34–35). If this passage were really calling for any literal violence, it would seem to be intra-familial jihad. But to invoke it as the equivalent of the Qur'an's jihad passages, which number over a hundred, is absurd: Even the Crusaders at their most venal and grasping didn't invoke passages like these. Also, given the completely peaceful message of Jesus, it is clear that he meant "a sword" in an allegorical and metaphorical way. To interpret this text literally is to misunderstand Jesus, who, unlike Muhammad, did not take part in battles. It fails to recognize the poetry of the Bible, which is everywhere.

Perhaps aware of how absurd such New Testament arguments are, Islamic apologists more often tend to focus on several Old Testament passages.

- ✿ "When the LORD your God brings you into the land where you are entering to possess it, and clears away many nations before you, the Hittites and the Girgashites and the Amorites and the Canaanites and the Perizzites and the Hivites and the Jebusites, seven nations greater and stronger than you. And when the LORD your God delivers them before you and you defeat them, then you shall utterly destroy them. You shall make no covenant with them and show no favor to them" (Deuteronomy 7:1–2).
- ✿ "When you approach a city to fight against it, you shall offer it terms of peace. If it agrees to make peace with you and opens to you, then all the people who are found in it shall become your forced labor and shall serve you. However, if it does not make peace with you, but makes war against you,

then you shall besiege it. When the LORD your God gives it into your hand, you shall strike all the men in it with the edge of the sword. Only the women and the children and the animals and all that is in the city, all its spoil, you shall take as booty for yourself; and you shall use the spoil of your enemies which the LORD your God has given you. Only in the cities of these peoples that the LORD your God is giving you as an inheritance, you shall not leave alive anything that breathes" (Deuteronomy 20:10–17).

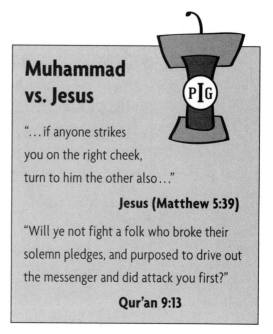

Muhammad vs. Jesus

"…if anyone strikes you on the right cheek, turn to him the other also…"

Jesus (Matthew 5:39)

"Will ye not fight a folk who broke their solemn pledges, and purposed to drive out the messenger and did attack you first?"

Qur'an 9:13

❀ "Now therefore, kill every male among the little ones, and kill every woman who has known man intimately. But all the girls who have not known man intimately, spare for yourselves" (Numbers 31:17–18).

Strong stuff, right? Just as bad as "slay the unbelievers wherever you find them" (Qur'an 9:5) and "Therefore, when ye meet the unbelievers in fight, smite at their necks; at length, when ye have thoroughly subdued them, bind a bond firmly on them" (Qur'an 47:4) and all the rest, right?

Wrong. Unless you happen to be a Hittite, Girgashite, Amorite, Canaanite, Perizzite, Hivite, or Jebusite, these Biblical passages simply do not apply to you. The Qur'an exhorts believers to fight unbelievers without specifying anywhere in the text that only certain unbelievers are to be fought, or only for a certain period of time, or some other distinction. Taking the texts at face value, the command to make war against unbelievers is open-ended and universal. The Old Testament, in contrast, records God's commands to the Israelites to make war against particular people

Just Like Today:
Using the Qur'an to justify terrorism

In a sermon broadcast on official Palestinian Authority television in 2000, Dr. Ahmad Abu Halabiya, a member of the Palestinian Authority's Fatwa Council, declared: "Allah the almighty has called upon us not to ally with the Jews or the Christians, not to like them, not to become their partners, not to support them, and not to sign agreements with them. And he who does that is one of them, as Allah said: 'O you who believe, do not take the Jews and the Christians as allies, for they are allies of one another. Who from among you takes them as allies will indeed be one of them.'... Have no mercy on the Jews, no matter where they are, in any country. Fight them, wherever you are. Wherever you meet them, kill them."

In this Abu Halabiya was quoting Qur'an 5:51 ("O ye who believe! Take not the Jews and the Christians for your friends and protectors: they are but friends and protectors to each other. And he amongst you that turns to them (for friendship) is of them") and 9:5 ("slay the idolaters wherever ye find them"). He applied these words to the contemporary political situation: "Wherever you are, kill those Jews and those Americans who are like them—and those who stand by them—they are all in one trench, against the Arabs and the Muslims—because they established Israel here, in the beating heart of the Arab world, in Palestine. They created it to be the outpost of their civilization—and the vanguard of their army, and to be the sword of the West and the crusaders, hanging over the necks of the monotheists, the Muslims in these lands."[9]

only. This is jarring to modern sensibilities, to be sure, but it does not amount to the same thing. That's one reason why Jews and Christians haven't formed terror groups around the world that quote these Scriptures to justify killing civilian non-combatants.

By contrast, Osama bin Laden, who is only the most visible exponent of a terror network that extends from Indonesia to Nigeria and into Western Europe and the Americas, quotes the Qur'an copiously in his communiqués. In his 1996 "Declaration of War against the Americans Occupying the Land of the Two Holy Places," he quotes suras 3:145; 47:4–6; 2:154; 9:14; 47:19; 8:72; and of course the notorious "Verse of the Sword," sura 9:5.[10] In 2003, on the first day of the Muslim holy celebration Eid al-Adha, the Feast of Sacrifice, he began a sermon: "Praise be to Allah who revealed the verse of the Sword to his servant and messenger [the Prophet Muhammad], in order to establish truth and abolish falsehood."[11]

Of course, the devil can quote Scripture for his own purpose, but Osama's use of these and other passages in his messages is consistent (as we shall see) with traditional Islamic understanding of the Qur'an. When modern-day Jews and Christians read their Bibles, they simply don't interpret the passages cited as exhorting them to violent actions against unbelievers. This is due to the influence of centuries of interpretative traditions that have moved away from literalism regarding these passages. But in Islam, there is no comparable interpretative tradition. The jihad passages in the Qur'an are anything but a dead letter. In Saudi Arabia,

A Book You're Not Supposed to Read

Don't believe what I am saying about the Qur'an? Read it for yourself. The clearest and most accurate English translation is that of N. J. Dawood, *The Koran* (Penguin), but Muslims tend to dislike it because Dawood was not a Muslim. The two most accurate English translations by Muslims are those by Abdullah Yusuf Ali and Mohammed Marmaduke Pickthall, both of which are available in multiple editions under various titles. Both are marred by a pseudo-King James Bible English, which makes them irritating to read.

Pakistan, and elsewhere, a key recruiting ground for jihad terrorist groups is the Islamic school: The students learn that they must wage jihad warfare, and then these groups give them the opportunity.

Chapter 3

ISLAM: RELIGION OF WAR

The Qur'an is clear enough about the warfare that Muslims must wage against unbelievers, but it lacks overall clarity. In its entirety, the Qur'an is a monologue: Allah is the only speaker (with a few notable exceptions), and with no particular concern for narrative continuity, he speaks with Muhammad about various events in the Prophet's life and about the earlier Muslim prophets (most notably, Abraham, Moses, and Jesus). That makes reading the Qur'an somewhat like walking in on a private conversation between two unknown people: It's confusing, disorienting, and ultimately incomprehensible.

That's where the Hadith, the traditions of Muhammad, enter. The Hadith are volumes upon volumes of stories of Muhammad in which he (and sometimes his followers) explains how and in what situations various verses of the Qur'an came to him, pronounces on disputed questions, and leads by example. In a very small number of ahadith (the plural of hadith), Muhammad quotes words of Allah that do not appear in the Qur'an; these are known as the *hadith qudsi*, or holy hadith, and Muslims consider them to be just as much the revealed Word of Allah as the Qur'an itself. Other ahadith that Muslims consider authentic are second in authority only to the Qur'an itself—and often the Qur'anic text is simply incomprehensible without them.

The focus of many ahadith, not surprisingly, is war.

Guess what?

- Muhammad taught his followers that there was nothing better (or holier) than jihad warfare.

- Muhammad told his men to offer non-Muslims only three choices: conversion, subjugation, or death.

- These teachings are not marginal doctrines or historical relics—they are still taught in mainstream Islam.

PC Myth: Islam's war teachings are only a tiny element of the religion

Okay, even if the Qur'an does contain some verses about war, that doesn't mean Muslims agree with them, right? After all, there are a lot of Christians who don't take every aspect of Christian doctrine seriously, aren't there?

Of course; however, there is no mistaking the centrality of violent jihad in Islam. In fact, the Prophet of Islam repeatedly emphasized that there was nothing better his followers could do than engage in jihad warfare. When a Muslim asked him to name the "best deed" one could do, besides the act of becoming a Muslim, the Prophet responded, "To participate in Jihad (holy fighting) in Allah's Cause."[1] He explained that "to guard Muslims from infidels in Allah's Cause for one day is better than the world and whatever is on its surface."[2] For "a journey undertaken for jihad in the evening or morning merits a reward better than the world and all that is in it."[3]

Muhammad also warned that Muslims who did not engage in jihad would be punished: "Muhammad was firm about the necessity of jihad not only for himself personally, but for every Muslim. He warned believers that 'he who does not join the warlike expedition (jihad), or equip, or looks well after a warrior's family when he is away, will be smitten by Allah with a sudden calamity.'"[4]

Those who fought in jihads would enjoy a level of Paradise higher than that enjoyed by others:

> It has been narrated on the authority of Abu Sa'id Khudri that the Messenger of Allah (may peace be upon him) said (to him): Abu Sa'id, whoever cheerfully accepts Allah as his Lord, Islam as his religion and Muhammad as his Apostle is necessarily entitled to enter Paradise. He (Abu Sa'id) wondered at it and said: Messenger of Allah, repeat it for me. He (the Messenger

of Allah) did that and said: There is another act which elevates the position of a man in Paradise to a grade one hundred (higher), and the elevation between one grade and the other is equal to the height of the heaven from the earth. He (Abu Sa'id) said: What is that act? He replied: Jihad in the way of Allah! Jihad in the way of Allah![5]

On another occasion "a man came to Allah's Apostle and said, 'Instruct me as to such a deed as equals Jihad (in reward).' He replied, 'I do not find such a deed.'"[6]

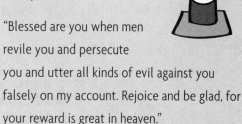

Muhammad vs. Jesus

"Blessed are you when men revile you and persecute you and utter all kinds of evil against you falsely on my account. Rejoice and be glad, for your reward is great in heaven."

Jesus (Matthew 5:11)

"And slay them wherever ye find them, and drive them out of the places whence they drove you out, for persecution is worse than slaughter."

Qur'an 2:191

Three choices

In one key hadith, Muhammad delineates three choices that Muslims are to offer to non-Muslims:

> It has been reported from Sulaiman b. Buraid through his father that when the Messenger of Allah (may peace be upon him) appointed anyone as leader of an army or detachment he would especially exhort him to fear Allah and to be good to the Muslims who were with him. He would say: Fight in the name of Allah and in the way of Allah. Fight against those who disbelieve in Allah. Make a holy war.... When you meet your enemies who are polytheists, invite them to three courses of action. If they respond to any one of these, you also accept it and withhold yourself from doing them any harm. Invite them to accept Islam; if they respond to you, accept it from them and

desist from fighting against them. . . . If they refuse to accept Islam, demand from them the Jizya. If they agree to pay, accept it from them and hold off your hands. If they refuse to pay the tax, seek Allah's help and fight them.[7]

Just Like Today: Osama invites America to Islam

following the example of the Prophet, Osama bin Laden called Americans to Islam in his November 2002 "letter to the American people":

What are we calling you to, and what do we want from you?

(1) The first thing that we are calling you to is Islam. . . .

It is the religion of Jihad in the way of Allah so that Allah's Word and religion reign Supreme.[8]

"Allah's Word and religion" may only "reign Supreme" in this view when the fullness of Islamic law is imposed and enforced in society. Jihadist theorists and groups have declared their intention to unify the Islamic nations of the world under a single ruler: the caliph. Historically, the caliph was the successor of the Prophet as the spiritual and political leader of the Muslims, or at least the Sunnis. The caliphate was abolished in 1924; many contemporary jihadists date the woes of the Islamic world from this event. They want to restore the caliphate, unite the Islamic world behind it, and reimpose Islamic law (the Sharia) on Islamic countries. Apart from Saudi Arabia and Iran, Sharia is today only partially enforced, if at all. Modern Islamic warriors seek to carry Sharia to non-Muslim states by force, under the banner of jihad.

The choices for unbelievers are:

1. Accept Islam.

2. Pay the jizya, the poll-tax on non-Muslims, which (as we
   shall see) is the cornerstone of an entire system of humiliating regulations that institutionalize inferior status for non-
   Muslims in Islamic law.

3. War with Muslims.

Always remember, "peaceful coexistence as equals in a pluralistic society" isn't one of the choices.

In another hadith repeated several times in the collection of traditions
that Muslims consider most reliable, Muhammad says that he has been
"commanded to fight against people" until they become Muslim, and that
those who resist risk forfeiting their lives and property: "The Prophet
spoke clearly about his own responsibility to wage war for the religion he
had founded: 'I have been ordered (by Allah) to fight against the people
until they testify that none has the right to be worshipped but Allah and
that Muhammad is the Messenger of Allah, and perform *As-Salat*
(prayers) and give *Zakat*, so if they perform all that, then they save their
lives and properties from me except for Islamic laws, and their reckon-
ing (accounts) will be with (done by) Allah.'"[9]

It's not just Muhammad's opinion. It's the law.

Okay, so Muhammad was commanded to fight against people until they
became Muslims or submitted to Islamic law. And the Qur'an teaches warfare. But that doesn't mean Muslims have taught all this, right? Didn't we
see in chapter two that certain portions of the Bible aren't taken literally
by most Jews and Christians? Isn't it the same with Islam? Aren't you just
cherry-picking embarrassing verses in an attempt to make Islam look bad?

In a word: no. The unpleasant fact is that violent jihad warfare against unbelievers is not a heretical doctrine held by a tiny minority of extremists, but a constant element of mainstream Islamic theology. Islam is preoccupied with legal questions; indeed, Islamic law contains instructions for the minutest details of individual behavior, as well as regulations on the structuring of government and relations between states. It also contains unmistakable affirmations of the centrality of jihad warfare against unbelievers. This is true of all four principal schools of Sunni Muslim jurisprudence, the Maliki, Hanafi, Hanbali, and Shafi'i, to which the great majority of Muslims worldwide belong. These schools formulated laws centuries ago regarding the importance of jihad and the ways in which it was to be practiced; however, that doesn't mean that these laws are ancient history and have been superseded by more recent rulings. It is a commonly accepted principle in the Islamic world that the "gates of ijtihad," or free inquiry into the Qur'an and Islamic tradition in order to discover Allah's rulings, have been closed for centuries. In other words, Islamic teaching on principal matters has long been settled and is not to be called into question. (To be sure, there are reform-minded Muslims today who have called for a reopening of the "gates of ijtihad" so that Islam can be reinterpreted, but so far these calls have gone unheeded by the most important and influential authorities in the Islamic world.)

Therefore, barring a general reopening of the "gates of ijtihad," which seems extremely unlikely, these rulings will remain normative for mainstream Muslims. All four principal Sunni schools agree on the importance of jihad. Ibn Abi Zayd al-Qayrawani (d. 996), a Maliki jurist, declared:

> Jihad is a precept of Divine institution. Its performance by certain individuals may dispense others from it. We Malikis maintain that it is preferable not to begin hostilities with the enemy before having invited the latter to embrace the religion

of Allah except where the enemy attacks first. They have the alternative of either converting to Islam or paying the poll tax (*jizya*), short of which war will be declared against them."[10]

Likewise, Ibn Taymiyya (d. 1328), a Hanbali jurist who is a favorite of Osama bin Laden and other modern-day jihadists, proclaimed:

Since lawful warfare is essentially jihad and since its aim is that the religion is God's entirely and God's word is upper-most, therefore according to all Muslims, those who stand in the way of this aim must be fought. As for those who cannot offer resistance or cannot fight, such as women, children, monks, old people, the blind, handicapped and their likes, they shall not be killed unless they actually fight with words (e.g. by propaganda) and acts (e.g. by spying or otherwise assisting in the warfare)."[11]

The Hanafi school sounds the same notes:

It is not lawful to make war upon any people who have never before been called to the faith, without previously requiring them to embrace it, because the Prophet so instructed his com-manders, directing them to call the infidels to the faith, and also because the people will hence perceive that they are attacked for the sake of religion, and not for the sake of taking their property, or making slaves of their children, and on this consideration it is possible that they may be induced to agree to the call, in order to save themselves from the troubles of war... If the infidels, upon receiving the call, neither consent to it nor agree to pay capitation tax, it is then incumbent on the Muslims to call upon God for assistance, and to make war upon them, because God is the assistant of those who serve Him, and the destroyer of His enemies, the infidels, and it is necessary to implore His aid upon every occasion; the Prophet, moreover, commands us so to do."[12]

Shafi'i scholar Abu'l Hasan al-Mawardi (d. 1058), who echoes Muhammad's instructions to invite the unbelievers to accept Islam or fight them if they refuse, also agrees:

> The mushrikun [infidels] of Dar al-Harb (the arena of battle) are of two types: First, those whom the call of Islam has reached, but they have refused it and have taken up arms. The amir of the army has the option of fighting them...in accordance with what he judges to be in the best interest of the Muslims and most harmful to the mushrikun...Second, those whom the invitation to Islam has not reached, although such persons are few nowadays since Allah has made manifest the call of his Messenger...it is forbidden to...begin an attack before explaining the invitation to Islam to them, informing them of the miracles of the Prophet and making plain the proofs so as to encourage acceptance on their part; if they still refuse to accept after this, war is waged against them and they are treated as those whom the call has reached.[13]

Proof that none of this is merely of historical interest is another Shafi'i manual of Islamic law that was certified in 1991 by the highest authority in Sunni Islam, Cairo's Al-Azhar University. The manual, 'Umdat al-Salik (available in English as Reliance of the Traveller), was declared to conform "to the practice and faith of the orthodox Sunni community."[14] After defining the "greater jihad" as "spiritual warfare against the lower self," it devotes eleven pages to the "lesser jihad." It defines this jihad as "war against non-Muslims," noting that the word itself "is etymologically derived from the word *mujahada*, signifying warfare to establish the religion."[15]

'Umdat al-Salik spells out the nature of this warfare in quite specific terms: "The caliph makes war upon Jews, Christians, and Zoroastrians . . . until they become Muslim or pay the non-Muslim poll tax." There follows a comment by a Jordanian jurist that corresponds to Muhammad's instructions to call the unbelievers to Islam before fighting them: The caliph wages this war only "provided that he has first invited [Jews, Christians, and Zoroastrians] to enter Islam in faith and practice, and if they will not, then invited them to enter the social order of Islam by paying the non-Muslim poll tax (jizya) . . . while remaining in their ancestral religions."[16] Also, if there is no caliph, Muslims must still wage jihad.[17]

These laws have been well known for centuries to those who suffered because of them. Gregory Palamas (1296–1359), a Greek monk and theologian (today revered as a saint by the Orthodox Church) who was imprisoned for a time by the Turks, remarked trenchantly about Muslims: "These infamous people, hated by God and infamous, boast of having got the better of the Romans [i.e., Byzantines] by their love of God . . . They live by the bow, the sword, and debauchery, finding pleasure in taking slaves, devoting themselves to murder, pillage, spoil . . . and not only do they commit these crimes, but even—what an aberration—they believe that God approves of them."[18]

PC Myth: Islam is a religion of peace that has been hijacked by a tiny minority of extremists

This, of course, is the mother of all PC myths about Islam. Yet its persistence and resilience in the face of mountains of evidence to the contrary, both from Islamic theology and today's newspapers, is not simply due to naïve multiculturalism and cynical duplicity. Even the Muslim Brotherhood theorist Sayyid Qutb, one of the twentieth century's foremost advocates of violent jihad, taught (without a trace of irony) that Islam is a religion of peace. However, he had a very specific kind of peace in mind: "When Islam strives for peace, its objective is not that superficial peace which requires that only that part of the earth where the followers of Islam are residing remain secure. The peace which Islam desires is that the religion (i.e. the law of the society) be purified for God, that the obedience of all people be for God alone, and that some people should not be lords over others. After the period of the Prophet—peace be on him— only the final stages of the movement of Jihaad are to be followed; the initial or middle stages are not applicable."[20]

In other words, Islam is a religion of the peace that will come when everyone is Muslim or at least subject to the Islamic state. And to establish that peace, Muslims must wage war.

Just Like Today: Chechen jihadists cite Islamic law on jihad

Islamic legal treatises enjoining jihad do not gather dust on the shelf. Jihadists use them to convince recruits that they need to fulfill their responsibility as Muslims by waging war against unbelievers. One example of this came in late 2003 from the Shariah Council of the State Defense Council (Majlis al-Shura) of the Chechen Republic of Ichkeria. In its underground publication *Jihad Today*, the Sharia Council published an article titled "Jihad and Its Solution Today." In it three of the four main schools of Sunni jurisprudence were cited to argue for jihad against the Russians in Chechnya:

First, what is Jihad?

Hanbali School defined it as spending power and energy in the war in the way of Allah by personal participation, property, word, etc.

Maliki School considers it a war (a battle) of a Muslim with a Kafir (an infidel) who has no treaty, to exalt the Word of Allah, or who trespassed on the territories of Muslims.

Hanbalis say that this is a war against Kafirs (the infidels), unlike an armed fight with the Muslims bordering on being rebels, or brigands or robbers for an example. (Mugni-Muhtaj, vol. 6, page 4).[20]

But what about moderate Muslims?

As I have demonstrated in the first three chapters, Islam is unique among the religions of the world in having a developed doctrine, theology, and legal system that mandates warfare against unbelievers. However, many will claim that even by marshalling this evidence, I am trying to make people think that every Muslim is a terrorist, and that your Arab or Pakistani convenience store clerk is secretly plotting the violent downfall of the United States. Some will even say that I am trying to incite violence against that convenience store clerk and other innocents.

This is, of course, arrant nonsense, but it does indicate that some clarification is needed. In the first place, the fact that warfare against unbelievers is not a twisting of Islam, but is repeatedly affirmed in the Qur'an, the Hadith, the example of Muhammad, and the rulings of every school of Islamic jurisprudence, does not make every Muslim a terrorist.

There are several principal reasons for this. One is that because the Qur'an is in difficult, classical Arabic, and must be read and recited during Muslim prayers in that language only, a surprisingly large number of those who identify themselves as Muslims have scant acquaintance with what it actually says. Although the media establishment continues to interchange the words "Muslim" and "Arab," most Muslims worldwide today are not Arabs. Even modern Arabic, much less classical Qur'anic Arabic, is foreign to them. They often memorize the Qur'an by rote without any clear idea of what it actually says. A Pakistani Muslim once proudly told me that he had memorized large sections of the Qur'an, and planned to buy a translation one day so that he could find out exactly what it was saying. Such instances are common to a degree that may surprise most non-Muslims.

Up until recent times, other cultural factors have also prevented Muslims, particularly in Eastern Europe and Central Asia, from acting on or even knowing much about Islam's actual teachings on how to deal with

A Book You're Not Supposed to Read

An Introduction to Islamic Law by Joseph Schacht; Oxford: Clarendon Press, 1982. This is a weighty book, as eye-opening as it is scholarly: Schacht is a serious scholar who is refreshingly free of the bias that dominates studies of Islam in universities today. A sampling: "The basis of the Islamic attitude towards unbelievers is the law of war; they must be either converted or subjugated or killed."

unbelievers. That is changing, however: In those areas and elsewhere around the world, Muslim hardliners, though not always financed by Saudi Arabia, have made deep inroads into peaceful Muslim communities by preaching violent Islam as the "pure Islam" and calling Muslims back to the full observance of their religion.[21]

This recruitment focuses on the Qur'an and other key Islamic texts. Take, for example, the case of Sahim Alwan, an American citizen and leader of the Yemeni community in Lackawanna, New York, and onetime president of the mosque there. He has the distinction of being the first American to attend an al Qaeda training camp. Why did he go? He was convinced to do so by Kamal Derwish, an al Qaeda recruiter. Alwan explained that Derwish taught him that the Qur'an "says you have to learn how to prepare. Like, you gotta be prepared just in case you do have to go to war. If there is war, then you would have to be called for jihad. And that was the aspect of the camp itself, for going to learn how to use weapons, and stuff like that."[22]

Of course, there are some Muslims who are working to bring about change within Islam, but it is difficult to discern their motives. The prominent American Muslim spokesman Siraj Wahaj, for instance, is often presented as a moderate. In 1991, he even became the first Muslim to give an invocation to the U.S. Congress. And why not? Not long after the September 11 attacks, he said just what jittery Americans wanted to hear from Muslims: "I now feel responsible to preach, actually to go on a jihad against extremism."[23]

Whether his true thoughts are more extreme remains unclear; after all, he has also warned that the United States will fall unless it "accepts the

Islamic agenda."[24] He has lamented that "if only Muslims were clever politically, they could take over the United States and replace its constitutional government with a caliphate."[25] In the early 1990s, he sponsored talks by Sheikh Omar Abdel Rahman in mosques in New York City and New Jersey. Rahman was later convicted for conspiring to blow up the World Trade Center in 1993, and Wahaj was designated a "potential unindicted co-conspirator."[26]

The fact that someone who would like to see the Constitution replaced has led a prayer for those sworn to uphold it is just a symptom of a larger, ongoing problem: The government and media are eager to find moderate Muslims—and as their desperation has increased, their standards have declined. Unfortunately, it is not so easy to find Muslim leaders who have genuinely renounced violent jihad and any intention, now or in the future, to impose Sharia on non-Muslim countries.

Nonetheless, there are enormous numbers of Muslims in the United States and around the world who want nothing to do with today's global jihad. While their theological foundation is weak, many are heroically laboring to create a viable moderate Islam that will allow Muslims to coexist peacefully with their non-Muslim neighbors. They are to be commended, but make no mistake: This moderate Islam does not exist to any significant extent in the world today. Where Muslims do coexist peacefully with non-Muslims, as in Central Asia and elsewhere, it is not because the teachings of jihad have been reformed or rejected; they have simply been ignored, and history teaches us that they can be remembered at any time.

Chapter 4

ISLAM: RELIGION OF INTOLERANCE

Muslim spokesmen in the United States have worked hard to present a vision of Islam as benign, open, and accepting—worlds away from the fanatical intransigence of Osama bin Laden and his ilk. PC watchdogs, both Muslim and non-Muslim, have virtually ruled out any dissent from the idea that Islam is peaceful, benign, and tolerant to a degree that will present no problem whatsoever for Western societies. They depict Islam as akin to Judaism and Christianity and, like them, liable to be "hijacked" (through no fault of its own) by "extremists." Most Americans today accept this as axiomatic—and many would consider rejecting it an act of "racism," despite the fact that Islam is not a race and most Muslims in the world today are not members of the ethnic group with which they are most often identified, the Arabs.

But there's just one problem with the common view: It isn't true. We've already seen how thoroughly Islam is a religion of war; it is also, profoundly, a religion of intolerance.

PC Myth: Islam is a tolerant faith

Jews and Christians, goes the PC line, lived in harmony with Muslims during the era of the great Islamic empires of the past. When jihad terrorists

Guess what?

- Islamic law mandates second-class status for Jews, Christians, and other non-Muslims in Islamic societies.

- These laws have never been abrogated or revised by any Islamic authority.

- The idea that Jews fared better in Islamic lands than in Christian Europe is false.

bombed Madrid on March 11, 2004, commentators unctuously reminded the world that when Muslims ruled Spain, it was a beacon of tolerance where Muslims, Jews, and Christians lived together in peace and harmony. When jihadists bombed synagogues in Istanbul on November 15, 2003, the commentators intoned that the bombings were particularly heartbreaking in a city that for so long had known tranquility among Muslims, Jews, and Christians.

This unquestionable dogma of Islamic tolerance has important political implications. It discourages anti-terrorism investigators in Europe and America from monitoring activity in mosques. It helps perpetuate the mistaken notion that Islamic terrorism comes from political grievances and socioeconomic imbalances. European governments with rapidly growing Muslim populations use it to reassure themselves that in old Al-Andalus, Islamic hegemony wasn't all that bad. European and American politicians and religious leaders woo the growing Islamic communities in their nations, trying to win their political support and assuming that they will assimilate easily and become peaceful, active participants in the political process. Why not? Islam is tolerant and teaches pluralism. What could be a better foundation for participation in Western democracy?

The idea of a tolerant Islam has even been taken up at the United Nations. The Turkish daily *Zaman* reported in March 2005 that at a UN seminar, "Confronting Islamophobia: Education for Tolerance and Understanding," "the tolerance that Ottomans showed to people of different religions was held up as an example to be adopted even today" and was lauded as a "social model in which different religions and nations lived under the same roof for hundreds of years."[1]

It doesn't seem to have come up at the UN that when the different religions lived under the same roof, one was the master and the others lived as despised inferiors.

The dhimma

The Qur'an calls Jews and Christians "People of the Book;" Islamic law calls them *dhimmis*, which means "protected" or "guilty" people—the Arabic word means both. They are "protected" because, as People of the Book, they have received genuine revelations ("the Book") from Allah and thus differ in status from out-and-out pagans and idolaters like Hindus and Buddhists. (Historically, the latter two groups have been treated even worse by Islamic conquerors, although as a practical matter their Muslim masters ultimately awarded them dhimmi status.) Jews and Christians are "guilty" because they have not only rejected Muhammad as a prophet, but have also distorted the legitimate revelations they received from Allah. Because of that guilt, Islamic law dictates that Jews and Christians may live in Islamic states, but not as equals with Muslims. One Muslim jurist explained that the caliph must "make jihad against those who resist Islam after having been called to it until they submit or accept to live as a protected dhimmi-community—so that Allah's rights, may He be exalted, 'be made uppermost above all [other] religion' (Qur'an 9:33)."[2] While Jews, Christians, and other non-Muslims are allowed to practice their religions, they must do so under severely restrictive conditions that remind them of their second-class status at every turn.

This lower status was first articulated by Umar ibn al-Khattab, who was caliph from 634 to 644. According to the Qur'anic commentary of Ibn Kathir, the Christians making this pact with Umar pledged:

> We made a condition on ourselves that we will neither erect in our areas a monastery, church, or a sanctuary for a monk, nor restore any place of worship that needs restoration nor use any of them for the purpose of enmity against Muslims.[3]

This, of course, allowed Islamic authorities to seize churches whenever they wanted. Since testimony of Christians was discounted and disallowed in many cases, it was often enough for a Muslim simply to charge that a church was being used to foment "enmity against Muslims" and then seize it.

The Christians' agreement with the caliph Umar continues: "We will not prevent any Muslim from resting in our churches whether they come by day or night.... Those Muslims who come as guests will enjoy boarding and food for three days."[4] The agreement also mandates a number of humiliating regulations to make sure that the dhimmis "feel themselves subdued" in accordance with Qur'an 9:29. The Christians promised:

> We will not... prevent any of our fellows from embracing Islam, if they choose to do so. We will respect Muslims, move from the places we sit in if they choose to sit in them. We will not imitate their clothing, caps, turbans, sandals, hairstyles, speech, nicknames and title names, or ride on saddles, hang swords on the shoulders, collect weapons of any kind or carry these weapons.... We will not encrypt our stamps in Arabic, or sell liquor. We will have the front of our hair cut, wear our customary clothes wherever we are, wear belts around our waist, refrain from erecting crosses on the outside of our churches and demonstrating them and our books in public in Muslim fairways and markets. We will not sound the bells in our churches, except discreetly, or raise our voices while reciting our holy books inside our churches in the presence of Muslims.

After these and other rules are fully laid out, the agreement concludes: "These are the conditions that we set against ourselves and followers of our religion in return for safety and protection. If we break any of these promises that we set for your benefit against ourselves, then our *Dhimmah* (promise of protection) is broken and you are allowed to do with us what you are allowed of people of defiance and rebellion."[5]

All this is still part of the Sharia today. "The subject peoples," according to a contemporary manual of Islamic law, must "pay the non-Muslim poll tax (jizya)" and "are distinguished from Muslims in dress, wearing a wide cloth belt (zunnar); are not greeted with 'as-Salamu 'alaykum' [the traditional Muslim greeting "Peace be with you"]; must keep to the side of the street; may not build higher than or as high as the Muslims' buildings, though if they acquire a tall house, it is not razed; are forbidden to openly display wine or pork...recite the Torah or Evangel aloud, or make public display of their funerals or feast days; and are forbidden to build new churches."[6] If they violate these terms, the law further stipulates that they can be killed or sold into slavery at the discretion of the Muslim leader.

Dhimmis were also strictly forbidden, on pain of death, to proselytize among Muslims—a prohibition accompanied by a similar death sentence for Muslims who left Islam. Both of these, along with the other provisions of dhimmitude, remain part of Islamic law today.

These laws largely governed the relations between Muslims and non-Muslims in Islamic states for centuries, until Western pressure brought to bear on the weakened Ottoman Empire in the mid-nineteenth century led to the emancipation of the dhimmis. Here and there they were relaxed or ignored for various periods, but they always remained on the books, ready to be enforced again by any ruler with the will to do so.

And from the charter of the Islamic Resistance Movement, better known as Hamas, comes a keen awareness of how to manipulate the myth of Islamic tolerance: "Under the shadow of Islam, it is possible for the members of the three religions: Islam, Christianity and Judaism to coexist in safety and security. Safety and security can only prevail under the shadow of Islam, and recent and ancient history is the best witness to that effect.... Islam accords his rights to everyone who has rights and averts aggression against the rights of others."[7] Hamas doesn't exactly

Just Like Today: Muslim leaders call for restoration of the dhimma

Sure, Jews and Christians lived as dhimmis in the old Islamic empires, but that's a relic of the past, right? No Muslims want to reinstitute dhimmi status for them today, do they?

Of course they do. Sheikh Omar Bakri Muhammad, a controversial pro-Osama Muslim leader in Great Britain, wrote in October 2002 that even though there was no caliph in the Islamic world today, that didn't mean Muslims could simply kill unbelievers. He affirmed that they must still be offered the choice to live subject to the Muslims: "We cannot simply say that because we have no Khilafah [caliphate] we can just go ahead and kill any non-Muslim, rather, we must still fulfill their Dhimmah."[8]

Likewise, Sheikh Yussef Salameh, the Palestinian Authority's undersecretary for religious endowment, in May 1999 "praised the idea that Christians should become dhimmis under Muslim rule, and such suggestions have become more common since the second intifada began in October 2000."[9]

In a recent Friday sermon at a mosque in Mecca, Sheikh Marzouq Salem Al-Ghamdi spelled out the Sharia's injunctions for dhimmis:

> If the infidels live among the Muslims, in accordance with the conditions set out by the Prophet—there is nothing wrong with it provided they pay *Jizya* to the Islamic treasury. Other conditions are...that they do not renovate a church or a monastery, do not rebuild ones that were destroyed, that they feed for three days any Muslim who passes by their homes...that they rise when a Muslim wishes to sit, that they do not imitate Muslims in dress and speech, nor ride horses, nor own swords, nor arm themselves with any kind of weapon; that they do not sell wine, do not show the cross, do not ring church bells, do not raise their voices during prayer, that they shave their hair in front so as to make them easily identifiable, do not incite anyone against the Muslims, and do not strike a Muslim...If they violate these conditions, they have no protection.[10]

spell out the deprivation of rights entailed by living "under the shadow of Islam," however.

Sheikh Abdullah Azzam (1941–1989), one of the founders of al Qaeda, also assumes that the Islamic state he fought to restore would collect the jizya from dhimmis. In his book *Defence of the Muslim Lands* he discusses various categories of jihad. In accordance with traditional Islamic theology, he explains that offensive jihad is an obligation of the Islamic community, and adds, "And the Ulama [Muslim scholars] have mentioned that this type of jihad is for maintaining the payment of Jizya."[11]

PC Myth: Historically the dhimma wasn't so bad

But in practice, it couldn't really have been like that, could it? Islamic apologist Stephen Schwartz, a convert to Islam, argues that in reality, dhimmitude wasn't all that bad and maintains that its horrors have been exaggerated: "The dhimma is now held out by a demagogic element in the West as a terrifying symbol of Islamic domination."[12] And it is certainly true that no law is ever universally enforced with uniform zeal and thoroughness. In the ninth century, Theodosius, the patriarch of Jerusalem, wrote that the Muslims "are just and do us no wrong nor show us any violence."[13] But the legal status of the Christians and Jews was still precarious at best. Historian A. S. Tritton notes:

> At one moment the dhimmi appears as a persecuted worm who is entirely negligible, and the next complaint is made of his pernicious influence on the Muslims around him. Laws were made, observed for a time, and then forgotten till something brought them to the remembrance of the authorities.... One feels that if events had been governed by logic, Islam would have swallowed up the subject religions; but they survive, vigorous though battered.[14]

Battered, indeed. The humiliations took various forms, but they were almost always present. Historian Philip Hitti notes one notorious example from the ninth century: "The Caliph al-Mutawakkil in 850 and 854 decreed that Christians and Jews should affix wooden images of devils to their houses, level their graves even with the ground, wear outer garments of honey color, i.e. yellow, put two honey-colored patches on the clothes of their slaves, . . . and ride only on mules and asses with wooden saddles marked by two pomegranate-like balls on the cantle."[15]

Later, Christians in the Ottoman Empire, according to historian Steven Runciman, "were never allowed to forget that they were a subject people."[16] This extended to the appropriation of their holy places by the conquering people: When the Turks took Constantinople in 1453, according to Hoca Sa'eddin, tutor of the sixteenth-century Sultans Murad III and Mehmed III, "churches which were within the city were emptied of their vile idols and cleansed from the filthy and idolatrous impurities and by the defacement of their images and the erection of Islamic prayer niches and pulpits . . . many monasteries and chapels became the envy of the gardens of Paradise."[17]

In the fourteenth century, the pioneering sociologist Ibn Khaldun explained the options for Christians: "It is [for them to choose between] conversion to Islam, payment of the poll tax, or death."[18]

Taxpayer woes

Paying the special tax on non-Muslims, the jizya, wasn't as easy as filling out a 1040. The Syrian orthodox patriarch of Antioch, chronicler Michael the Syrian (1126–1199), recorded how crushing this burden was for the Christians in the time of the Caliph Marwan II (744–750):

> Marwan's main concern was to amass gold and his yoke bore
> heavily on the people of the country. His troops inflicted many

evils on the men: blows, pillages, outrages on women in their husbands' presence.[19]

Marwan was not alone. One of his successors, al-Mansur (754–775), according to Michael, "raised every kind of tax on all the people in every place. He doubled every type of tribute on Christians."[20]

Payment of the jizya often took place in a peculiar and demeaning ceremony in which the Muslim tax official hit the dhimmi on the head or back of the neck. Tritton explained, "The dhimmi has to be made to feel that he is an inferior person when he pays, he is not to be treated with honour."[21] This ensured that the dhimmi felt "subdued," as commanded by Qur'an 9:29. The twelfth-century Qur'anic commentator Zamakhshari even directed that the jizya should be collected "with belittlement and humiliation."[22] The thirteenth-century Shafi'i jurist an-Nawawi directed that "the infidel who wishes to pay his poll tax must be treated with disdain by the collector: the collector remains seated and the infidel remains standing in front of him, his head bowed and his back bent. The infidel personally must place the money on the scales, while the collector holds him by the beard, and strikes him on both cheeks."[23]

According to historian Bat Ye'or, this blow as part of the payment process "survived unchanged till the dawn of the twentieth century, being ritually performed in Arab-Muslim countries, such as Yemen and Morocco, where the Koranic tax continued to be extorted from the Jews."[24]

Non-Muslims often converted to Islam to avoid this tax: This is how the vast Christian populations of North Africa and the Middle East ultimately became tiny, demoralized minorities. According to the seventeenth-century European traveler Jean-Baptiste Tavernier, in Cyprus in 1651 "over four hundred Christians had become Muhammadans because they could not pay their *kharaj* [a land tax that was also levied on non-Muslims, sometimes synonymous with the jizya], which is the tribute that the Grand Seigneur levies on Christians in his states." The following year in Baghdad, when Christians "had to pay their debts or their kharaj, they were forced to sell their children to the Turks to cover it."[25]

In other instances, however, conversion to Islam was forbidden for dhimmis—it would destroy the tax base.[26]

Pushing too hard

Eventually, all this oppression provoked a reaction. Historian Apostolos E. Vacalopoulos describes an instructive set of circumstances surrounding Greece's early nineteenth century struggle for independence:

> The Revolution of 1821 is no more than the last great phase of the resistance of the Greeks to Ottoman domination; it was a relentless, undeclared war, which had begun already in the first years of servitude. The brutality of an autocratic regime, which was characterized by economic spoliation, intellectual decay and cultural retrogression, was sure to provoke opposition. Restrictions of all kinds, unlawful taxation, forced labor, persecutions, violence, imprisonment, death, abductions of girls and boys and their confinement to Turkish harems, and various deeds of wantonness and lust, along with numerous less offensive excesses—all these were a constant challenge to the instinct of survival and they defied every sense of human decency. The Greeks bitterly resented all insults and humiliations, and their anguish and frustration pushed them into the arms of rebellion. There was no exaggeration in the statement made by one of the beys of Arta, when he sought to explain the ferocity of the struggle. He said: 'We have wronged the rayas [dhimmis] (i.e. our Christian subjects) and destroyed both their wealth and honor; they became desperate and took up arms. This is just the begin-

ning and will finally lead to the destruction of our empire.' The sufferings of the Greeks under Ottoman rule were therefore the basic cause of the insurrection; a psychological incentive was provided by the very nature of the circumstances.[27]

Today the jihadist terrorists complain that the West has destroyed their wealth and honor; however, as they continue to commit acts of violence against innocent people—as they did on September 11 and in many other attacks—this complaint will ring increasingly hollow. It is even possible that these continued acts of violence will eventually give rise to a stronger and more forthright resistance to Islamization than we have seen.

PC Myth: Jews had it better in Muslim lands than in Christian Europe

PC spokesmen assert every day that even if the dhimma really did subject Jews and Christians to ongoing and institutionalized discrimination and harassment, it certainly wasn't as bad as the way Jews were treated in Christian Europe. Historian Paul Johnson explains: "In theory,...the status of the Jewish *dhimmi* under Moslem rule was worse than under the Christians, since their right to practise their religion, and even their right to live, might be arbitrarily removed at any time. In practice, however, the Arab warriors who conquered half the civilized world so rapidly in the seventh and eighth centuries had no wish to exterminate literate and industrious Jewish communities who provided them with reliable tax incomes and served them in innumerable ways."[28]

Certainly in terms of legal restrictions, the Muslim laws were much harsher for Jews than those of Christendom. In 1272, Pope Gregory X repeated what Pope Gregory I first affirmed in 598: Jews "ought not to suffer any disadvantage in those [privileges] which have been granted them." Gregory X also repeated earlier papal decrees forbidding forced conversions (as does Islamic law) and commanding that "no Christian shall presume to seize, imprison, wound, torture, mutilate, kill, or inflict violence on them; furthermore, no one shall presume, except by judicial action of the authorities of the country, to change the good customs in the land where they live for the purpose of taking their money or goods from them or from others."

So far this is similar to the Islamic "protection" of the subject peoples. But then Gregory adds, "In addition, no one shall disturb them in any

Muhammad vs. Jesus

"And he sent messengers ahead of him, who went and entered a village of the Samaritans, to make ready for him; but the people would not receive him, because his face was set toward Jerusalem. And when his disciples James and John saw it, they said, 'Lord, do you want us to bid fire come down from heaven and consume them?' But he turned and rebuked them."

Luke 9:52–55

"Narrated Ibn Abbas: When the Verse: 'And warn your tribe (O Muhammad) of near-kindred (and your chosen group from among them)' [Qur'an 26:214] was revealed, Allah's Messenger went out, and when he had ascended As-Safa mountain, he shouted, 'Ya Sabahah!'[29] The people said, 'Who is that?' Then they gathered around him, whereupon he said, 'Do you see? If I inform you that cavalrymen are proceeding up the side of this mountain, will you believe me?' They said, 'We have never heard you telling a lie.' Then he said, 'I am a plain warner to you of a coming severe punishment.' Abu Lahab said, 'May you perish! You gathered us only for this reason?' Then Abu Lahab went away. So the *Surat Al-Masad*: 'Perish the two hands of Abu Lahab!' was revealed."[30] *Surat Al-Masad* is the Qur'an's 111th sura: "May the hands of Abu Lahab perish! May he himself perish! Nothing shall his wealth and gains avail him. He shall be burnt in a flaming fire, and his wife, laden with faggots, shall have a rope of fibre around her neck!"

Qur'an 111:1–5

way during the celebration of their festivals, whether by day or by night, with clubs or stones or anything else." This is clearly distinct from the Sharia prohibitions of dhimmis celebrating their religious festivals in public. Also, in view of the fact that a Jew's testimony was not admissible against a Christian, the pope also forbids Christians to testify against Jews—while the Sharia forbids a dhimmi from testifying against a Muslim, but has no problem with a Muslim testifying against a dhimmi.[31]

This is not to say that there weren't abuses. Protections of the Jews, such as those enunciated by Gregory X, were often honored in the breach. But it was no accident that by the dawn of the modern age, the great majority of Jews lived in the West, not within the confines of Islam. The reasons for this may be because in Christian lands there was the idea, however imperfect, of the equality of dignity and rights for all people— an idea that contradicted the Qur'an and Islamic theology and never took root in the Islamic world.

PC Myth: Dhimmitude is a thing of the past

But surely all this is a question of history, isn't it? Islamic apologists have maintained that no one is calling for restoration of the dhimma today. We have already seen that that is not true. Also false is the widespread assumption that dhimmitude is not found in the Islamic world today. Since Sharia is not fully in place anywhere except Saudi Arabia (where non-Muslims are not allowed to practice their religions at all) and Iran, the laws of the dhimma are not fully in effect in the Islamic world. However, elements of them remain on the books in every Muslim country. Nowhere in the Islamic world today do non-Muslims enjoy full equality of rights with Muslims.

A few recent and representative incidents from Egypt:

> ❀ Apostasy—leaving the faith—is a capital offense in Islamic law. Egyptian officials arrested twenty-two Christians, many

Three Books You're Not Supposed To Read

The Dhimmi: Jews and Christian Under Islam (1985), *The Decline of Eastern Christianity Under Islam: From Jihad to Dhimmitude* (1996), and *Islam and Dhimmitude: Where Civilizations Collide* (2001), written by Bat Ye'or and published by Fairleigh Dickinson University Press. Ye'or is the pioneering scholar of the dhimma. Each book is full of primary source documents that bring the harsh realities of dhimmitude home and give the lie to Islamic apologists and whitewashers who try to explain it away.

of them former Muslims who had secretly converted to Christianity, in October 2003. They were questioned and tortured; authorities suspected that several of them were trying to bring other Muslims to Christianity.[32]

❀ In December 2003, the Brethren Church of Assiout was demolished, with official permission, so that church members could build a new structure. But before they could do so, their building license was revoked—recalling the dhimmi prohibition against building new churches or repairing old ones.[33]

❀ On November 25, 2003, Boulos Farid Rezek-Allah Awad, a Coptic Christian married to a Christian convert from Islam, was arrested while attempting to leave the country and held for twelve hours. When an Egyptian security police officer asked him about his wife, Rezek-Allah told him that she had already left Egypt. Perhaps mindful of the death penalty for apostates, the officer responded, "I'll bring her back and cut her into pieces in front of you."[34] Several months later, however, Rezek-Allah was allowed to leave Egypt and settle in Canada.[35]

From Pakistan:

❀ In November 2003, Pakistani police arrested Anwar Masih, a Christian, on a charge of blasphemy. According to the *Daily Times* of Pakistan, Masih began discussing Islam with a Muslim neighbor, Naseer. "During the discussion, the sub-inspector said, Masih got angry and blasphemed. Naseer related the discussion to two other neighbours of his mother, Attaullah and Younas Salfi. The three subsequently gathered other locals and pelted stones at Masih's house, on which police reached the scene and taking no notice of the attack on his home, arrested Masih."[36]

🏵 The following month, a church in the Pakistani village of Dajkot was attacked during a prayer service by a mob of Muslims shouting, "You infidels, stop praying and accept Islam!" According to the *Pakistan Christian Post*, the mob "entered the church and started beating the worshipers. The Muslim attackers desecrated the Holy Bible and broke every thing in the church." However, the police "refused to lodge any report," and at the local hospital, Muslim doctors ignored the injured Christians at the direction of an influential local Muslim.[37]

🏵 In May 2004, another Christian charged with blasphemy, Samuel Masih, was beaten to death with a hammer by a Muslim policeman as he lay in a hospital bed suffering from tuberculosis.[38]

And from Kuwait:

🏵 Hussein Qambar Ali, a Kuwaiti, converted from Islam to Christianity in the 1990s. Even though the Kuwaiti constitution guarantees the freedom of religion and says nothing about the traditional Islamic prohibition on conversion to another faith, he was arrested and tried for apostasy. During his trial, a prosecutor declared that the Sharia took precedence over Kuwait's secular legal code: "With grief I have to say that our criminal law does not include a penalty for apostasy. The fact is that the legislature, in our humble opinion, cannot enforce a penalty for apostasy any more or less than what our Allah and his messenger have decreed. The ones who will make the decision about his apostasy are: our Book, the Sunna, the agreement of the prophets and their legislation given by Allah."[39]

PC Myth: Islam values pre-Islamic cultures in Muslim countries

Islam doesn't just denigrate and devalue non-Muslims, but also leads Muslims to denigrate and devalue the pre-Islamic cultures of their own countries. "In 637 A.D.," notes the Nobel Prize–winning author V. S. Naipaul, "just five years after the death of the Prophet, the Arabs began to overrun Persia, and all Persia's great past, the past before Islam, was declared a time of blackness."[40]

There was nothing unusual in that. It is a scene that has been repeated throughout the history of Islam. Islamic theology so devalues non-believers that there is no room in Islamic culture for any generosity toward their achievements. Muslims call the age before any country adopted Islam the time of *jahiliyya*, or ignorance. Naipaul explains that "the time before Islam is a time of blackness: that is part of Muslim theology. History has to serve theology." An example of this is how Pakistanis denigrated the famous archaeological site at Mohenjo Daro, seeing its value only as a chance to preach Islam:

> A featured letter in *Dawn* offered its own ideas for the site. Verses from the Koran, the writer said, should be engraved and set up in Mohenjo-Daro in "appropriate places": "Say (unto them, O Mohammed):
>
> Travel in the land and see the nature of the sequel for the guilty
>
> . . .

Say (O Mohammed, to the disbelievers): Travel in the land and see the nature of the consequence for those who were before you.

Most of them were idolaters."[41]

Just Like Today: Muslims devalue ancient sites of other religions

Muslims in Turkish-occupied northern Cyprus attempted to turn the fourth-century monastery of San Makar into a hotel. In Libya, the daffy Colonel Qaddafi turned Tripoli's Catholic cathedral into a mosque. And in Afghanistan, of course, the Taliban government dynamited the famous Buddhas of Bamiyan in March 2001. Could the Christian monuments of Europe possibly suffer the same fate?

If the warriors of jihad, who are as energized today as they have been at any time during the last millennium, get their way, they certainly could. Edward Gibbon, author of *The Decline and Fall of the Roman Empire*, observed that if the eighth-century Muslim incursion into France had been successful, "perhaps the interpretation of the Koran would now be taught in the schools of Oxford and her pulpits might demonstrate to a circumcised people the sanctity and truth of the revelation of Mahomet."[42]

That day may be yet to come.

Chapter 5

ISLAM OPPRESSES WOMEN

On March 18, 2005, a Muslim woman named Amina Wadud led an Islamic prayer service in New York City. Because she is a woman, three mosques refused to host the service, so it was set for an art gallery, but the galley withdrew the invitation after receiving a bomb threat. Finally, it was held in an Episcopal church. A Muslim protester outside the event fumed, "These people do not represent Islam. If this was an Islamic state, this woman would be hanged, she would be killed, she would be diced into pieces."[1] Undoubtedly true; nevertheless, Wadud maintained that such treatment was fundamentally un-Islamic: in the Qur'an, she asserted, men and women are equal. It is only by distorting the Qur'an that Muslim men have come to regard women as only good for sex and housekeeping.[2]

PC Myth: Islam respects and honors women

It's widely accepted, almost to the point of being axiomatic, that Islamic mistreatment of women is cultural and does not stem from the Qur'an—and that Islam actually offers women a better life than they can enjoy in the West. The Los Angeles-based Muslim Women's League claims that "spiritual equality, responsibility, and accountability for both men and women is a well-developed theme in the Quran. Spiritual equality between men and women in the sight of God is not limited to purely

Guess what?

- The Qur'an and Islamic law treat women as nothing more than possessions of men.

- The Qur'an sanctions wife-beating.

- Islam also allows for child marriage, the virtual imprisonment of women in their homes, "temporary marriage" (i.e., prostitution—but only for Shi'ites!), and more.

spiritual, religious issues, but is the basis for equality in all temporal aspects of human endeavor."[3]

Another Muslim women's advocate, the Egyptian Dr. Nawal el-Saadawi, who has run afoul of the Egyptian authorities because Muslim divines consider her opinions less than Islamic, goes still further: "Our Islamic religion has given women more rights than any other religion has, and has guaranteed her honour and pride."[4]

In the same vein, the *Christian Science Monitor* in December 2004 featured several Latin American female converts to Islam.[5] One of them, Jasmine Pinet, explained that she "has found greater respect as a woman by converting to Islam." Pinet praised Muslim men for their respect for women: "They're not gonna say, 'Hey *mami*, how are you?' Usually they say, 'Hello, sister.' And they don't look at you like a sex object." The *Monitor* reports that there are forty thousand Latin American Muslims in the United States today, and that "many of the Latina converts say that their belief that women are treated better in Islam was a significant factor in converting."

For readers who might find this surprising—given the burqa, polygamy, the prohibition of female drivers in Saudi Arabia, and other elements of the Islamic record on women that are well known in the West—the *Monitor* quotes Leila Ahmed, professor of women's studies and religion at Harvard: "It astounds me, the extent to which people think Afghanistan and the Taliban represent women and Islam." Ahmed says that "we're in the early stages of a major rethinking of Islam that will open Islam for women. [Muslim scholars] are rereading the core texts of Islam—from the Koran to legal texts—in every possible way."

But did the Taliban really originate the features of Islam that discriminate against women? Will a "rereading" of the Qur'an and other core texts of Islam really help "open Islam for women"? These are some of the texts that will have to be "reread":

- ❀ Women are inferior to men, and must be ruled by them: "Men have authority over women because God has made the one superior to the other" (Qur'an 4:34)

- ❀ The Qur'an likens a woman to a field (*tilth*), to be used by a man as he wills: "Your women are a tilth for you to cultivate so go to your tilth as ye will" (2:223)

- ❀ It declares that a woman's testimony is worth half that of a man: "Get two witnesses, out of your own men, and if there are not two men, then a man and two women, such as ye choose, for witnesses, so that if one of them errs, the other can remind her" (2:282)

- ❀ It allows men to marry up to four wives, and have sex with slave girls also: "If ye fear that ye shall not be able to deal justly with the orphans, marry women of your choice, two or three or four; but if ye fear that ye shall not be able to deal justly with them, then only one, or a captive that your right hands possess, that will be more suitable, to prevent you from doing injustice" (4:3)

- ❀ It rules that a son's inheritance should be twice the size of that of a daughter: "Allah thus directs you as regards your children's inheritance: to the male, a portion equal to that of two females" (4:11)

- ❀ It tells husbands to beat their disobedient wives: "Good women are the obedient, guarding in secret that which Allah hath guarded. As for those from whom ye fear rebellion, admonish them and banish them to beds apart, and scourge them" (4:34)

Aisha, the most beloved of Muhammad's many wives, admonished women in no uncertain terms: "O womenfolk, if you knew the rights that your husbands have over you, every one of you would wipe the dust from her husband's feet with her face."[6]

Individual Muslims may respect and honor women, but Islam doesn't.

The great Islamic cover-up

The Qur'an directs that women must "lower their gaze and guard their modesty; that they should not display their beauty and ornaments except what must ordinarily appear thereof; that they should draw their veils over their bosoms and not display their beauty except to their husbands, their fathers" and a few others (Qur'an 24:31).

Muhammad was more specific when Asma, daughter of one of his leading companions (and first successor) Abu Bakr, came to see him while "wearing thin clothes." "O Asma," exclaimed the Prophet, "when a woman reaches the age of menstruation, it does not suit her that she displays her parts of body except this and this, and he pointed to her face and hands."[7]

In our own day, this covering has become the foremost symbol of the place of women in Islam.

Just Like Today: Girls die for the burqa

A graphic example of the oppression that Islamic dress regulations for women engender came in March 2002 in Mecca, when fifteen girls were killed in a fire at their school. Saudi Arabia's religious police, the *muttawa*, wouldn't let the girls out of the building. Since only women were in the school, the girls had shed their all-concealing outer garments. The *muttawa* preferred the girls' death to transgression of Islamic law—to the extent that they actually battled police and firemen who were trying to open the school's doors.[8]

Child marriage

The Qur'an takes child marriage for granted in its directives about divorce. Discussing the waiting period required in order to determine if the woman is pregnant, it says:

"If you are in doubt concerning those of your wives who have ceased menstruating, know that their waiting period shall be three months. The same shall apply to *those who have not yet menstruated*" (Qur'an 65:4, emphasis added). In other words, Allah is here envisioning a scenario in which a pre-pubescent woman is not only married, but is being divorced by her husband.

One reason why such a verse might have been "revealed" to Muhammad is that he himself had a child bride: The Prophet "married 'Aisha when she was a girl of six years of age, and he consummated that marriage when she was nine years old."[10] Child marriages were common in seventh-century Arabia—and here again the Qur'an has taken a practice that should have been abandoned long ago and given it the sanction of divine revelation.

Wife-beating

Muhammad was once told that "women have become emboldened towards their husbands," whereupon he "gave permission to beat them." When some women complained, Muhammad noted: "Many women have gone round Muhammad's family complaining against their husbands. They are not the best among you."[14] He was unhappy

Just Like Today: Child marriages in the Islamic world

This has touched millions of women and girls in societies where the Qur'an is absolute truth and Muhammad is the model for all human behavior. More than half of the teenage girls in Afghanistan and Bangladesh are married.[9] Ayatollah Khomeini told the Muslim faithful that marrying a girl before she began menstruating was "a divine blessing." He counseled fathers: "Do your best to ensure that your daughters do not see their first blood in your house."[11]

Iranian girls can get married when they are as young as nine with parental permission, or thirteen without consent.[12] With child marriage comes domestic violence: "In Egypt 29 percent of married adolescents have been beaten by their husbands; of those, 41 percent were beaten during pregnancy. A study in Jordan indicated that 26 percent of reported cases of domestic violence were committed against wives under 18."[13]

with the women who complained, not with their husbands who beat them. At another point he added: "A man will not be asked as to why he beat his wife."[15]

Another hadith recounts that on one occasion a woman came to Muhammad looking for justice. "'Aishah said that the lady (came), wearing a green veil (and complained to her ('Aishah) of her husband and showed her a green spot on her skin caused by beating). It was the habit of ladies to support each other, so when Allah's Messenger came, 'Aishah said, 'I have not seen any woman suffering as much as the believing women. Look! Her skin is greener than her clothes!'"[16]

"I have not seen any woman suffering as much as the believing women"? Aisha doesn't seem to have had any illusions that, in Nawal El-Saadawi's words, "our Islamic religion has given women more rights than any other religion has." But Muhammad is unmoved by Aisha's alarm at the woman's bruises: When her husband appears, Muhammad does not reprove him for beating his wife—in fact, he doesn't mention it at all. And why would he, since Allah had already revealed to him that a man should treat his disobedient wife this way?

Muhammad even struck Aisha herself. One night, thinking she was asleep, he went out. Aisha surreptitiously followed him. When he found out what she had done, he hit her: "He struck me on the chest which caused me pain, and then said: Did you think that Allah and His Apostle would deal unjustly with you?"[18]

Just Like Today: Wife-beating

The Pakistan Institute of Medical Sciences has determined that *over 90 percent* of Pakistani wives have been struck, beaten, or abused sexually—for offenses on the order of cooking an unsatisfactory meal. Others were punished for failing to give birth to a male child.[17]

An offer they can't refuse

Muhammad emphasized that women were possessions of their husbands: "Allah's Messenger said, 'If a husband calls his wife to his bed (i.e. to have sexual relations) and she refuses and causes him to sleep in anger, the angels will curse her till morning.'"[19] This has become enshrined in Islamic law: "The husband is only obliged to support his wife when she gives herself to him or offers to, meaning she allows him full enjoyment of her person and does not refuse him sex at any time of the night or day."[20]

Don't go out alone

Islamic law stipulates that "the husband may forbid his wife to leave the home"[21] and that "a woman may not leave the city without her husband or a member of her unmarriageable kin accompanying her, unless the journey is obligatory, like the hajj. It is unlawful for her to travel otherwise, and unlawful for her husband to allow her to."[22]

According to Amnesty International, in Saudi Arabia "women . . . who walk unaccompanied, or are in the company of a man who is neither their husband nor a close relative, are at risk of arrest on suspicion of prostitution or other 'moral' offences."[23]

Temporary husbands

Nothing is easier than divorce for a Muslim male: All he has to do is tell his wife, "I divorce you," and the divorce is consummated. The apparent harshness of this seems to be mitigated by another verse from the Qur'an: "If a wife fears cruelty or desertion on her husband's part, there is no blame on them if they arrange an amicable settlement between themselves; and such settlement is best" (Qur'an 4:128). But this call for an agreement is not a call for a meeting of equals—at least as it has been interpreted in the hadith. Aisha explains this verse: "It concerns the woman whose husband does not want to keep her with him any longer, but wants to divorce her and marry some other lady, so she says to him: 'Keep me and do not divorce me, and then marry another woman, and you may neither spend on me, nor sleep with me.'"[24]

Meanwhile, the likelihood that a man may divorce his wife in a fit of anger and then want to reconcile with her later gives rise to another odd point of Islamic law: Once a Muslim woman has been thrice divorced by the same husband, she must marry and divorce another man before going back to him: "When a free man has pronounced a threefold divorce, it is unlawful for him to remarry the divorced wife until she has married another husband in a valid marriage and the new husband has copulated with her."[25]

Muhammad insisted on this. Once a woman came to him for help. Her husband had divorced her and she had remarried. However, her second husband was impotent, and she wanted to remarry her first husband. The Prophet was unyielding, telling her that she could not remarry her first husband "unless you had a complete sexual relation with your present husband and he enjoys a complete sexual relation with you.'"[26]

This has given rise to the phenomenon of "temporary husbands." After a husband has divorced his wife in a fit of pique, these men will "marry" the hapless divorcee for one night in order to allow her to return to her husband and family.

Prophetic license

When Muhammad already had nine wives and numerous concubines, Allah gave him special permission to have as many women as he desired: "O Prophet! Lo! We have made lawful unto thee thy wives unto whom thou hast paid their dowries, and those whom thy right hand possesseth of those whom Allah hath given thee as spoils of war, and the daughters of thine uncle on the father's side and the daughters of thine aunts on the father's

side, and the daughters of thine
uncle on the mother's side and the
daughters of thine aunts on the
mother's side who emigrated with
thee, and a believing woman if she
give herself unto the Prophet and
the Prophet desire to ask her in marriage—a privilege for thee only, not
for the (rest of) believers" (Qur'an
33:50). Such convenient prophecies
are numerous in the Qur'an—Allah
even commands Muhammad to
marry the comely divorced wife of his adopted son (33:37).

Just Like Today: Put down that book

Islamic hardliners in Pakistan were so opposed to the education of women that, in one tumultuous five-day period in February 2004, they burned down eight girls' schools.[27]

Muhammad's desire has borne bitter fruit. These two Qur'anic passages are just two elements of a pervasive assumption that women are not
entitled to equality of dignity with men as human beings, but are objects
to be awarded to men and used by them. Polygamy, of course, is a foundation of this assumption, and is moving westward with Islam. In late
2004, polygamy had become so common among Muslims in Britain that
the British were considering recognizing it for tax purposes.[28]

Temporary wives

Shi'ite Islam, the dominant form of Islam in Iran, also allows for "temporary wives." This is a provision for men to gain female companionship
on a short-term basis. In a temporary marriage, or *mut'a*, the couple signs
a marriage agreement that is ordinary in every respect except that it car-
ries a time limit. One tradition of Muhammad stipulates that a temporary
marriage "should last for three nights, and if they like to continue, they
can do so, and if they want to separate, they can do so."[29] Many such
unions, however, don't last as long as three nights.

The authority for this practice rests upon a variant Shi'ite reading of a verse of the Qur'an (4:24), as well as this passage from the Hadith: "Narrated Jabir bin Abdullah and Salama bin Al-Akwa: While we were in an army, Allah's Messenger came to us and said, 'You have been allowed to do the *Mut'a* (marriage), so do it."[30] Sunni Muslims, who account for 85 percent of all Muslims, claim that Muhammad later revoked this provision—but Shi'ites disagree. In any case, temporary wives tend to congregate in Shi'ite holy cities, where they can offer companionship to lonely seminarians.

Rape: Four witnesses needed

Most threatening of all to women may be the Muslim understanding of rape as it plays out in conjunction with Islamic restrictions on the validity of a woman's testimony. In court, a woman's testimony is worth half as much as that of a man. (Qur'an 2:282).

Islamic legal theorists have restricted the validity of a woman's testimony even further by limiting it to, in the words of one Muslim legal manual, "cases involving property, or transactions dealing with property, such as sales."[31] Otherwise only men can testify. And in cases of sexual misbehavior, four male witnesses are required. These witnesses must be able to do more than simply testify that an instance of fornication, adultery, or rape happened; they must have seen the act itself. This peculiar and destructive stipulation had its genesis in an incident in Muhammad's life, when his wife Aisha, was accused of infidelity. The accusation particularly distressed Muhammad, since Aisha was his favorite wife. But in this case, as in many others, Allah came to the aid of his Prophet: He revealed Aisha's innocence and instituted the stipulation of four witnesses for sexual sins: "Why did they not produce four witnesses? Since they produce not witnesses, they verily are liars in the sight of Allah" (Qur'an 24:13).[32]

Muhammad vs. Jesus

"Then the scribes and the Pharisees brought a woman who had been caught in adultery and made her stand in the middle. They said to Him, 'Teacher, this woman was caught in the very act of committing adultery. Now in the law, Moses commanded us to stone such women. So what do you say?' They said this to test Him, so that they could have some charge to bring against Him. Jesus bent down and began to write on the ground with His finger. But when they continued asking Him, He straightened up and said to them, 'Let the one among you who is without sin be the first to throw a stone at her.' Again He bent down and wrote on the ground. And in response, they went away one by one, beginning with the elders. So He was left alone with the woman before Him. Then Jesus straightened up and said to her, 'Woman, where are they? Has no one condemned you?' She replied, 'No one, sir.' Then Jesus said, 'Neither do I condemn you. Go, and from now on do not sin any more.'"

John 7:53–8:11

"There came to him (the Holy Prophet) a woman from Ghamid and said: Allah's Messenger, I have committed adultery, so purify me. He (the Holy Prophet) turned her away. On the following day she said: Allah's Messenger, Why do you turn me away?...By Allah, I have become pregnant. He said: Well, if you insist upon it, then go away until you give birth to the child. When she was delivered she came with the child wrapped in a rag and said: Here is the child whom I have given birth to. He said: Go away and suckle him until you wean him. When she had weaned him, she came to him...She said: Allah's Apostle, here is he as I have weaned him and he eats food. He (the Holy Prophet) entrusted the child to one of the Muslims and then pronounced punishment. And she was put in a ditch up to her chest and he commanded people and they stoned her. Khalid bin Walid came forward with a stone which he flung at her head and there spurted blood on the face of Khalid and so he abused her. Allah's Apostle heard his (Khalid's) curse that he had hurled upon her. Thereupon he (the Holy Prophet) said: Khalid, be gentle. By Him in Whose Hand is my life, she has made such a repentance that even if a wrongful tax-collector were to repent, he would have been forgiven. Then giving command regarding her, he prayed over her and she was buried."[33]

A Book You're Not Supposed to Read

Voices Behind the Veil: The World of Islam Through the Eyes of Women, edited by Ergun Mehmet Caner; Grand Rapids, MI: Kregel Publications, 2004.

Consequently, it is almost impossible to prove rape in lands that follow the dictates of the Sharia. Men can commit rape with impunity: As long as they deny the charge and there are no witnesses, they will get off scot-free, because the victim's testimony is inadmissible. Even worse, if a woman accuses a man of rape, she may end up incriminating herself. If the required male witnesses can't be found, the victim's charge of rape becomes an admission of adultery. That accounts for the grim fact that as many as 75 percent of the imprisoned women in Pakistan are, in fact, behind bars for the crime of being a victim of rape.[34] Several high-profile cases in Nigeria recently have also revolved around rape accusations being turned around by Islamic authorities into charges of fornication, resulting in death sentences that were modified only after international pressure.[35]

Female circumcision

Female circumcision is yet another source of misery for women in some Islamic countries. This is not a specifically Islamic custom, for it's found among a number of cultural and religious groups in Africa and South Asia. Among Muslims, it's prevalent mainly in Egypt and the surrounding lands. Yet despite the fact that there is scant (at best) attestation in the Qur'an or Hadith for this horrific practice, the Muslims who do practice it invest it with religious significance. An Islamic legal manual states that circumcision is required "for both men and women."[36]

To Sheikh Muhammad Sayyed Tantawi, the grand sheikh of al-Azhar, female circumcision is "a laudable practice that [does] honor to women."[37] As the grand imam of al-Azhar, Tantawi is, in the words of a BBC report, "the highest spiritual authority for nearly a billion Sunni Muslims."[38]

Perhaps in the eyes of Sheikh Tantawi, the pain that female circumcision causes its victims is worth the result; most authorities agree that female circumcision is designed to diminish a woman's sexual response, so that she will be less likely to commit adultery.

Long-term prospects? Dim

As long as men read and believe the Qur'an, women will be despised, second-class citizens, subject to the heartbreak and dehumanization of polygamy, the threat of an easy and capricious divorce, and worse—including beatings, false accusations, and the loss of virtually all of the most basic human freedoms. These are not phenomena of a group, party, or anything so ephemeral. They are the consequences of regarding the Qur'an as the absolute, eternally valid, and perfect word of Allah. As long as men continue to take the Qur'an at face value, women will be at risk.

Chapter 6

ISLAMIC LAW:
LIE, STEAL, AND KILL

Not only does Islam command warfare against unbelievers and their subjugation under Islamic rule; it also—as we have already seen in part—sanctions lying, stealing, and killing in order to advance Islam. In fact, Islam doesn't have a moral code analogous to the Ten Commandments; the idea that Islam shares the general moral outlook of Judaism and Christianity is another PC myth. In Islam, virtually anything is acceptable if it fosters the growth of Islam.

Lying: It's wrong—except when it isn't

Muhammad minced no words about the necessity of telling the truth: "It is obligatory for you to tell the truth, for truth leads to virtue and virtue leads to Paradise, and the man who continues to speak the truth and endeavours to tell the truth is eventually recorded as truthful with Allah, and beware of telling of a lie for telling of a lie leads to obscenity and obscenity leads to Hell-Fire, and the person who keeps telling lies and endeavours to tell a lie is recorded as a liar with Allah."[1]

However, as with so many other Islamic principles, this is largely a matter between believers. When it comes to unbelievers—particularly those who are at war with Muslims—Muhammad enunciated a quite different principle: "War is deceit."

Specifically, he taught that lying was permissible in battle.[2] Thus were born two enduring Islamic principles: the permissibility of political assassination for the honor of the Prophet and his religion and an allowance for the practice of deception in wartime. The doctrines of religious deception (*taqiyya* and *kitman*) are most often identified with Shi'ite Islam and are ostensibly rejected by Sunnis (over 85 percent of Muslims worldwide) because they were sanctioned by the Prophet. However, they can still be found in traditions that Sunni Muslims consider most reliable.

Also, religious deception (practiced on hapless unbelievers) is taught by the Qur'an itself, telling Muslims: "Let not the believers take for friends or helpers unbelievers rather than believers. If any do that, in nothing will there be help from Allah; except by way of precaution, that ye may guard yourselves from them" (Qur'an 3:28). In other words, don't make friends with unbelievers except to "guard yourselves from them": Pretend to be their friends so that you can strengthen yourself against them. The distinguished Qur'anic commentator Ibn Kathir explains that, in this verse, "Allah prohibited His believing servants from becoming supporters of the disbelievers, or to take them as comrades with whom they develop friendships, rather than the believers." However, exempted from this rule were "those believers who in some areas or times fear for their safety from the disbelievers. In this case, such believers are allowed to show friendship to the disbelievers outwardly, but never inwardly."[3]

When Shi'ite Muslims were persecuted by Sunnis, they developed the doctrine of *taqiyya*, or concealment: They could lie about what they believed, denying aspects of their faith that were offensive to Sunnis. This practice is sanctioned by the Qur'an warning Muslims that those who forsake Islam will be consigned to Hell—except those forced to do so, but who remain true Muslims inwardly: "Any one who, after accepting faith in Allah, utters unbelief—except under compulsion, his heart remaining firm in faith—but such as open their breast to unbelief, on them is wrath from Allah, and theirs will be a dreadful penalty" (Qur'an

16:106). Closely related to this is the doctrine of *kitman*, or mental reservation, which is telling the truth, but not the whole truth, with an intention to mislead. Although these doctrines are commonly associated with Shi'ites, Sunnis have also practiced them throughout Islamic history, because of their Qur'anic foundation.[4] Ibn Kathir, who was no Shi'ite, explains that "the scholars agreed that if a person is forced into disbelief, it is permissible for him to either go along with them in the interests of self-preservation, or to refuse."[5]

Jihadists today have spoken of the usefulness of deceptive practices. Remember that the next time you see a Muslim spokesman on television professing his friendship with non-Muslim Americans and his loyalty to the United States. Of course, he may be telling the truth—but he may not be telling the whole truth or he may be just lying. And it's virtually certain that whoever is conducting the interview will not ask him about this passage of the Qur'an.

But what constitutes force in this case? Ibn Kathir seems to envision only physical force, but force can take many forms. Might Islamic spokesmen in this country feel constrained to downplay or deny aspects of their religion that unbelievers might find unpalatable?

Theft: It all depends on who you're stealing from

Islamic law is notorious for mandating harsh punishments—and perhaps most notable is amputation for theft: "As for the thief, both male and female, cut off their hands. It is the reward of their own deeds, an exemplary punishment from Allah. Allah is Mighty, Wise" (Qur'an 5:38).

But here again, the situation is different when it comes to unbelievers who are perceived as warring against Islam. We know that the Qur'an makes laws for the division of the spoils of war, mandating that a fifth go to Allah and charitable works (Qur'an 8:41). And after Muhammad signed the Treaty of Hudaybiyya with the Quraysh (see chapter one), he reassured his confused and disappointed followers with the promise of more spoils: "Allah promiseth you much booty that ye will capture, and hath given you this in advance, and hath withheld men's hands from you, that it may be a token for the believers, and that He may guide you on a right path." (Qur'an 48:18–20). The instances in which Muslims actually captured booty in raids are numerous.

Murder: It all depends on whom you're killing

Muslim apologists like to quote Qur'an 5:32: "Whosoever killeth a human being for other than manslaughter or corruption in the earth, it shall be as if he had killed all mankind, and whoso saveth the life of one, it shall be as if he had saved the life of all mankind." However, this oft-quoted verse is not actually the all-encompassing prohibition of murder that it may seem. For one thing, it is addressed to the "Children of Israel" and set in the past; it is not addressed to Muslims. It actually comes as part of a warning to Jews not to make war against Muhammad, or they will face terrible punishment. The point is that Allah warned the Children of Israel not to spread "mischief in the land," and yet they continued to do so:

> On that account We ordained for the Children of Israel that if any one slew a person—unless it be for murder or for spreading mischief in the land—it would be as if he slew the whole people: and if any one saved a life, it would be as if he saved the life of the whole people. Then although there came to them Our messengers with clear signs, yet, even after that, many of them continued to commit excesses in the land. The punishment of those who wage war against Allah and His Messenger, and strive with might and main for mischief through the land is: execution, or crucifixion, or the cutting off of hands and feet from opposite sides, or exile from the

John Quincy Adams on Islam:

"In the seventh century of the Christian era, a wandering Arab of the lineage of Hagar [i.e., Muhammad], the Egyptian, combining the powers of transcendent genius, with the preternatural energy of a fanatic, and the fraudulent spirit of an impostor, proclaimed himself as a messenger from Heaven, and spread desolation and delusion over an extensive portion of the earth. Adopting from the sublime conception of the Mosaic law, the doctrine of one omnipotent God; he connected indissolubly with it, the audacious falsehood, that he was himself his prophet and apostle. Adopting from the new Revelation of Jesus, the faith and hope of immortal life, and of future retribution, he humbled it to the dust by adapting all the rewards and sanctions of his religion to the gratification of the sexual passion. He poisoned the sources of human felicity at the fountain, by degrading the condition of the female sex, and the allowance of polygamy; and he declared undistinguishing and exterminating war, as a part of his religion, against all the rest of mankind. *THE ESSENCE OF HIS DOCTRINE WAS VIOLENCE AND LUST: TO EXALT THE BRUTAL OVER THE SPIRITUAL PART OF HUMAN NATURE....* Between these two religions, thus contrasted in their characters, a war of twelve hundred years has already raged. The war is yet flagrant... While the merciless and dissolute dogmas of the false prophet shall furnish motives to human action, there can never be peace upon earth, and good will towards men." (Emphasis in the original)

land: that is their disgrace in this world, and a heavy punishment is theirs in the Hereafter. (Qur'an 5:31–33)

In fact, in light of the Qur'an's bellicose commands to "slay the unbelievers" (9:5; 2:191), it should be clear that in this case, as in so many others, there is one standard for Muslims and another for non-Muslims. Indeed, the Qur'an stipulates that "it is not for a believer to kill a believer unless it be by mistake" (4:92), but it never makes a similar statement regarding unbelievers.

This led to a predictable double standard in Islamic law. "Killing without right," according to the Shafi'i school of Sunni Muslim jurisprudence, "is, after unbelief, one of the very worst enormities." It stipulates that "retaliation is obligatory... against anyone who kills a human being purely intentionally and without right." However, no retaliation is permitted in the case of "a Muslim killing a non-Muslim."[6]

An Iranian Sufi leader, Sheikh Sultanhussein Tabandeh, who wielded considerable influence in fashioning the jurisprudence of Khomeini's Islamic Republic, wrote *A Muslim Commentary on the Universal Declaration of Human Rights*. While arguing for capital punishment if a Muslim is killed, Tabandeh argues against it if the murderer is Muslim and the victim non-Muslim: "Since Islam regards non-Muslims as on a lower level of belief and conviction, if a Muslim kills a non-Muslim... then his punishment must not be the retaliatory death, since the faith and conviction he possesses is loftier than that of the man slain. A fine only may be exacted from him."[7]

Universal moral values? Can't find them.

In his landmark book *The Abolition of Man*, the Christian apologist C. S. Lewis (1898–1963) assembled examples of what he called the Tao, or the Natural Law: principles held by people in a wide variety of cultures and civilizations. These principles include "Duties to Parents, Elders, Ancestors"; "Duties to Children and Posterity"; "The Law of Good Faith and Veracity"; "The Law of Magnanimity"; and more. He illustrates the universality of these principles by quotations from sources as diverse as the Old Testament, the New Testament, Virgil's *Aeneid*, the Bhagavad Gita, Confucius' *Analects*, the writings of Australian aborigines, and many others. Completely missing are any quotations from the Qur'an or other Muslim sources.

This omission may be due to Lewis somehow lacking knowledge of Islam. Yet this is highly unlikely, given when Lewis lived and the role his country, the United Kingdom, played in the Middle East and Asia. Certainly, you would have thought, he could have found illustrations for some of his principles from the Qur'an. The problem for Lewis may have been that Islam simply does not uphold what he calls "The Law of General Beneficence": One is not to be charitable except to fellow believers. The unpleasant fact is that Islam simply does not teach the Golden Rule.[8] Jesus's dictum that "whatever you wish that men would do to you, do so to them" (Matthew 7:12) appears in virtually every religious tradition on the planet—except Islam. The Qur'an and Hadith make such a sharp distinction between believers and unbelievers that there is no room for any commandment of general beneficence. Unbelievers are to be questioned, suspected, resisted, and fought. That is all. Not tolerated. Never loved.

This is what sets Islam sharply apart from other religious traditions. It is impossible to imagine Sheikh Tabandeh's unembarrassed justification for punishing those who kill unbelievers less harshly than those who kill believers in any modern religious teaching, other than Islam.

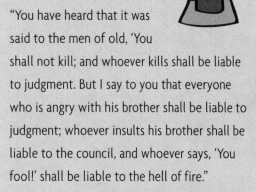

Muhammad vs. Jesus

"You have heard that it was said to the men of old, 'You shall not kill; and whoever kills shall be liable to judgment. But I say to you that everyone who is angry with his brother shall be liable to judgment; whoever insults his brother shall be liable to the council, and whoever says, 'You fool!' shall be liable to the hell of fire."

Jesus (Matthew 5:21–22)

"Therefore, when ye meet the unbelievers in fight, smite at their necks; at length, when ye have thoroughly subdued them, bind a bond firmly on them: thereafter is the time for either generosity or ransom, until the war lays down its burdens.... But those who are slain in the Way of Allah, He will never let their deeds be lost."

Qur'an 47:4

PC Myth: Islam forbids the killing of the innocent

In the wake of the September 11 attacks, many Muslim spokesmen and Middle East analysts in the West assured us that Islam forbids taking innocent life, and that to the vast majority of Muslims around the world,

A Book You're Not Supposed to Read

Umdat al-Salik, translated by Nuh Ha Mim Keller into English as *Reliance of the Traveller: A Classic Manual of Islamic Sacred Law:* Amana Publications, 1994. This is a Shafi'i legal manual intended as a handy guide to Islamic law for lay Muslims. It is endorsed by Al-Azhar University, Sunni Islam's most revered authority: Al-Azhar's Islamic Research Academy certifies that this book "conforms to the practice and faith of the orthodox Sunni community."[10]

Osama bin Laden's murder of three thousand people in the World Trade Center towers was not fulfilling the requirements of Islamic jihad, but a crime against humanity.

Yet Islamic law is not clear-cut in its condemnation of the killing of non-combatants. It prohibits the killing of women and children "unless they are fighting against the Muslims."[9] This has been widely interpreted as allowing civilians to be killed if they are perceived as somehow aiding the war effort. This is one basis for the common assertion that there are no civilians in Israel. Some Muslim leaders have argued for that on the basis that everyone, simply by virtue of being in Israel, is trespassing on Muslim land and is thus at war with Islam. Others, like the internationally famous Sheikh Yusuf al-Qaradawi, are more nuanced: "Israeli women are not like women in our society because Israeli women are militarised. Secondly, I consider this type of martyrdom operation as indication of justice of Allah almighty. Allah is just. Through his infinite wisdom he has given the weak what the strong do not possess and that is the ability to turn their bodies into bombs like the Palestinians do."[11]

Chapter 7

HOW ALLAH KILLED SCIENCE

The flowering of Islamic culture is the stuff of legend. Muslims invented algebra, the zero, and the astrolabe (an ancient navigational instrument). They blazed new trails in agriculture. They preserved Aristotelian philosophy while Europe blundered through the Dark Ages. In virtually every field, the Islamic empires of bygone days far outstripped the achievements of their non-Muslim contemporaries in Europe and elsewhere.

Or did they?

Well, not quite. Unless copying counts.

What about art and music?

We hear a great deal about Islamic literature—or at least a lot about Sufi poet Jalaluddin Rumi (1207–1273) and *The Thousand and One Nights*. There is also the Persian poet Abu Nuwas (762–814), whose heterodox views on homosexuality we discus in chapter eight; al-Mutanabbi (915–965), whose surname means "one who pretends to be a prophet"; the heterodox Turkish Sufi Nesimi (d. 1417); and Persian epic poet Hakim Abu al-Qasim Mansur Firdowsi (935–1020), who set the history of Persia to verse. For his sources, he used Christian and Zoroastrian chronicles, which have long since been lost.

Guess what?

- The much-ballyhooed "Golden Age" of Islamic culture was largely inspired by non-Muslims.

- Core elements of Islamic belief militated against scientific and cultural advancement.

- Only Judaism and Christianity, not Islam, provide a viable basis for scientific inquiry.

Many of these men were open Islamic heretics; few seem to have taken inspiration from Islam itself, with the possible exception of Farid ud-Din Attar's twelfth-century allegory *The Conference of the Birds.* They left behind many great works, but most of these are notable not for their Islamic character but for their lack of it. However, to credit the inspirational power of Islam would be tantamount to crediting the Soviet system for the works of Mandelstam, Sakharov, or even Solzhenitsyn.

But what about Islamic achievement in other artistic fields? Where are the Muslim Beethovens or Michelangelos? Where can one listen to the Islamic equivalent of Mozart's 20th Piano Concerto or savor the Islamic *Mona Lisa* or *Pietá*?

Don't waste too much time looking. There is music and art in Islamic countries, and some Muslims were responsible for impressive musical and artistic achievements, but it was always in spite of Islam; nothing comparable to Western musical and artistic traditions developed, because Islamic law outlaws both music and artistic renderings of the human form. In music, there is nothing like Bach's B Minor Mass or gospel in Islam, for above all, musical creativity has no place in religion.

Islamic law invokes Muhammad himself in forbidding musical instruments, quoting several ahadith:

> Allah Mighty and Majestic sent me as a guidance and mercy to believers and commanded me to do away with musical instruments, flutes, strings, crucifixes, and the affair of the pre-Islamic period of ignorance. On the Day of Resurrection, Allah will pour molten lead into the ears of whoever sits listening to a songstress. Song makes hypocrisy grow in the heart as water does herbage. "This Community will experience the swallowing up of some people by the earth, metamorphosis of some into animals, and being rained upon with stones." Someone asked, "When will this be, O Messenger of Allah?" and he said,

"When songstresses and musical instruments appear and wine is held to be lawful." There will be peoples of my Community who will hold fornication, silk, wine, and musical instruments to be lawful.[1]

These are not ancient laws that are universally ignored today, like some old American colonial ordinance against spitting on the sidewalk. Iran's Ayatollah Khomeini spoke vehemently about the evils of music—and not just rock and roll or rap, but all music:

Music corrupts the minds of our youth. There is no difference between music and opium. Both create lethargy in different ways. If you want your country to be independent, then ban music. Music is treason to our nation and to our youth.[2]

And art? Islam's prohibition of representational art is even more absolute. Muhammad said: "Angels do not enter a house wherein there is a dog or some images (or pictures etc.) of living creatures (a human being or an animal etc.)."[3] Not encouraging words for a budding Caravaggio.

Of course, Western museums will go to great lengths to display what they can of enamel or calligraphy in order to give Islamic art its due (and, of course, the architectural and artistic marvels inside mosques can't be transplanted from their settings), but compared to the Western artistic tradition, only the most blinkered multiculturalist would not admit that it's pretty slim pickings.

PC Myth: Islam was once the foundation of a great cultural and scientific flowering

In fact, Islam was not the foundation of much significant cultural or scientific development at all. It is undeniable that there was a great cultural and scientific flowering in the Islamic world in the Middle Ages, but there is no indication that any of this flowering actually came as a result of Islam itself. In fact, there is considerable evidence that it did notcome from Islam, but from the non-Muslims who served their Muslim masters in various capacities.

The architectural design of mosques, for example, a source of pride among Muslims, was copied from the shape and structure of Byzantine churches. (And of course, the construction of domes and arches was developed over a thousand years before the advent of Islam.) The seventh-century Dome of the Rock, considered today to have been the first great mosque, was not only copied from Byzantine models, but was built by Byzantine craftsmen. Islamic architectural innovations, interestingly enough, arose from military necessity. A historian of Islamic art and architecture, Oleg Grabar, explains, "Whatever its social or personal function, there hardly exists a major monument of Islamic architecture that does not reflect power in some fashion. . . . Ostentation is rarely absent from architecture and ostentation is almost always an expression of power. . . . For instance, in eleventh-century Cairo or fourteenth-century Granada the gates were built with an unusual number of different techniques of vaulting. Squinches coexist with pendentives, barrel vaults with cross vaults, simple semicircular arches with pointed or horseshoe arches. . . . It is possible that certain innovations in Islamic vaulting techniques, especially the elaboration of squinches and cross vaults, were the direct result of the importance of military architecture, for which strength and the prevention of fires, so common in wooden roofs and ceilings, were major objectives."[4]

There are plenty of other examples. The astrolabe was developed, if not perfected, long before Muhammad was born. Avicenna (980–1037), Averroes (1128–1198), and other Muslim philosophers built on the work of the pagan Greek Aristotle. And Christians preserved Aristotle's work from the ravages of the Dark Ages such as the fifth-century priest Probus of Antioch, who introduced Aristotle to the Arabic-speaking world.[5] The

Christian Huneyn ibn Ishaq (809–873) translated many works by Aristotle, Galen, Plato, and Hippocrates into Syriac, which his son then translated into Arabic.[6] The Jacobite (Syrian) Christian Yahya ibn 'Adi (893–974) also translated works of philosophy into Arabic and wrote his own; his treatise *The Reformation of Morals* has occasionally been erroneously attributed to several of his Muslim contemporaries. His student, a Christian named Abu 'Ali 'Isa ibn Zur'a (943–1008), also made Arabic translations of Aristotle and other Greek writers from Syriac. The first Arabic-language medical treatise was written by a Christian priest and translated into Arabic by a Jewish doctor in 683. The first hospital in Baghdad during the heyday of the Abbasid caliphate was built by a Nestorian Christian, Jabrail ibn Bakhtishu.[7] Assyrian Christians founded a pioneering medical school at Gundeshapur in Persia. The world's first university may not have been the Muslims' Al-Azhar in Cairo, as is often claimed, but the Assyrian School of Nisibis.

There is no shame in any of this. No culture exists in a vacuum. Every culture builds on the achievements of other cultures and borrows from those with which it is in contact. But the historical record simply doesn't support the idea that Islam inspired a culture that outstripped others. There was a time when Islamic culture was more advanced than that of Europeans, but that superiority corresponds exactly to the period when Muslims were able to draw on and advance the achievements of Byzantine and other civilizations. After all, the seventh-century Muslim invaders of Persia were so uncivilized, relative to those they had conquered, that they exchanged gold (which they had never seen) for silver (which they had) and used camphor, a substance entirely new to them, in cooking.[8] Are we to believe that these rough men entered their new surroundings with daring new artistic and architectural plans tucked under their arms?

But when they had taken what they could from Byzantium and Persia, and sufficient numbers of Jews and Christians had been converted to

Islam or thoroughly subdued, Islam went into a period of intellectual stagnation from which it has not yet emerged. Even more nagging is the question of why, if Islam really did reach such a high level of cultural attainment, it went into such a precipitous and lingering decline.

What happened to the Golden Age?

It's true: Muslims once led the rest of the world in various intellectual endeavors, notably mathematics and science. But there was such a decline after this "Golden Age" that of the age itself there is scarcely any trace left in the Islamic world.

Winston Churchill on Islam:

"How dreadful are the curses which Mohammedanism lays on its votaries! Besides the fanatical frenzy, which is as dangerous in a man as hydrophobia in a dog, there is this fearful fatalistic apathy. Improvident habits, slovenly systems of agriculture, sluggish methods of commerce, and insecurity of property exist wherever the followers of the Prophet rule or live. A degraded sensualism deprives this life of its grace and refinement; the next of its dignity and sanctity. The fact that in Mohammedan law every woman must belong to some man as his absolute property—either as a child, a wife, or a concubine—must delay the final extinction of slavery until the faith of Islam has ceased to be a great power among men.

"Individual Moslems may show splendid qualities. Thousands become the brave and loyal soldiers of the Queen: all know how to die. But the influence of the religion paralyses the social development of those who follow it. No stronger retrograde force exists in the world. Far from being moribund, Mohammedanism is a militant and proselytising faith. It has already spread throughout Central Africa, raising fearless warriors at every step; and were it not that Christianity is sheltered in the strong arms of science—the science against which it had vainly struggled—the civilisation of modern Europe might fall, as fell the civilisation of ancient Rome."

Take, for example, the medical sciences. Muslims established the first pharmacies and were the first to require standards of knowledge and competence from doctors and pharmacists, enforced by an examination.[9] At the time of the fifth Abbasid caliph, Harun al-Rashid (763–809), the first hospital was established in Baghdad, and many more followed. Yet it was not a Muslim, but a Belgian physician and researcher, Andreas Vesalius (1514–1564), who paved the way for modern medical advances by publishing the first accurate description of human internal organs, *De Humani Corporis Fabrica* (On the Fabric of the Human Body) in 1543. Why? Because Vesalius was able to dissect human bodies, while that practice was forbidden in Islam. What's more, Vesalius's book is filled with detailed anatomical drawings—but also forbidden in Islam are artistic representations of the human body.

In mathematics, it's the same story. Abu Ja'far Muhammad ibn Musa al-Khwarizmi (780–850) was a pioneering mathematician whose treatise on algebra, once translated from Arabic, introduced generations of Europeans to the rarified joys of that branch of mathematics. But in fact, the principles upon which al-Khwarizmi worked were discovered centuries before he was born—including the zero, which is often attributed to Muslims. Even what we know today as "Arabic numerals" did not originate in Arabia, but in pre-Islamic India—and they are not used in the Arabic language today. Nonetheless, there is no denying that al-Khwarizmi was influential. The word *algebra* itself comes from the first word of the title of his treatise *Al-Jabr wa-al-Muqabilah*; and the word *algorithm* is derived from his name. Al-Khwarizmi's work opened up new avenues of mathematical and scientific exploration in Europe, so why didn't it do the same in the Islamic world? The results are palpable: Europeans ultimately used algebra, in conjunction with other discoveries, to make significant technological advances; Muslims did not. Why?

One answer is that Europe had a long-standing intellectual tradition that made such innovations possible, while the Islamic world did not. This

Muhammad vs. Jesus

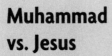

"No one is good but God alone."

Jesus (Mark 10:18)

"The Jews say: 'Allah's hand is chained.' May their own hands be chained! May they be cursed for what they say! By no means. His hands are both outstretched: He bestows as He will"

Qur'an 5:64

The idea that Allah's hand is "not chained" is a reflection of his absolute freedom and sovereignty. If God is good, as Jesus says, His goodness may be discernable in the consistency of creation; but in Islam, even to call Allah good would be to bind him.

even included making use of Arabic works in ways that Muslims themselves did not: Aristotle, along with his Muslim commentators Avicenna and Averroes, were studied in European universities in the twelfth century and after, while in the Islamic world their work was largely ignored and certainly not taught in schools, which concentrated then, as now, mostly on memorization and study of the Qur'an. There were other notable Islamic philosophers; why were Avicenna and Averroes read in the West, but anomalies in their own traditions? Why wasn't philosophy even taught in Islamic schools in those days?

Much of the responsibility for this must be laid at the feet of the Sufi Abu Hamid al-Ghazali (1058–1128). Although he was a great thinker, he nevertheless became the chief spokesman for a streak of anti-intellectualism that stifled much Islamic philosophical and scientific thought. Some philosophers, al-Ghazali noted, were a bit too hesitant to embrace the revealed truths of the Qur'an: Abu Yusuf Yaqub ibn Ishaq al-Sabbah al-Kindi (801–873), for example, had suggested that religion and philosophy were two separate but equal paths to truth.[10] In other words, philosophers need not pay attention or homage to the Qur'an, with its self-serving prophet and bordello Paradise. Abu Bakr ar-Razi (864–930), known in the West as Rhazes, even went so far as to say that *only* philosophy leads to the highest truth.[11] Other Muslim philosophers pursued similarly dangerous lines of inquiry.

In his *Incoherence of the Philosophers,* al-Ghazali accordingly accused Muslim philosophers of "denial of revealed laws and religious confessions" and "rejection of the details of religious and sectarian [teaching], believing them to be man-made laws and embellished tricks."[12] He accused the Muslim philosophers al-Farabi and Avicenna of challenging "the [very] principles of religion."[13]

At the end of *The Incoherence of the Philosophers,* al-Ghazali asks a rhetorical question about the philosophers: "Do you then say conclusively that they are infidels and *that the killing of those who uphold their beliefs is obligatory?*"[14] He answers: "Pronouncing them infidels is necessary in three questions": their teachings that the world existed eternally, that Allah does not know particular things, but only universals, and that there is no resurrection of the body. Thus, by the dictates of Islamic law, killing them was "obligatory." This is hardly the way to encourage a healthy philosophical tradition. There were Muslim philosophers after al-Ghazali, but they never achieved the stature of Avicenna. Averroes, (also called Abul-Waleed Muhammad Ibn Rushd) answered al-Ghazali in a book called *Incoherence of the Incoherence,* insisting that philosophers need not kowtow to theologians, but the damage was done. The Golden Age of Islamic philosophy, such as it were, was over.

Al-Ghazali's attack on the philosophers was a sophisticated manifestation of a tendency that has always hindered intellectual development in the Islamic world:

There is a prevailing assumption that the Qur'an is the perfect book, and no other book is needed. With the Qur'an the perfect book and Islamic society the perfect civilization, too many Muslims didn't think they needed knowledge that came from any other source—certainly not from infidels.

Allah kills science

But the main *coup de grace* to Islamic scientific and philosophical inquiry may have come from the Qur'an itself. The holy book of Islam portrays Allah as absolutely sovereign and bound by nothing. This sovereignty was so absolute that it precluded a key assumption that helped foster the development of science in Europe: Jews and Christians believe that God is good, and that His goodness is consistent. Therefore, He created the universe according to rational laws that can be discovered, making scientific investigation worthwhile. Saint Thomas Aquinas explains:

> Since the principles of certain sciences—of logic, geometry, and arithmetic, for instance—are derived exclusively from the formal principals of things, upon which their essence depends, it follows that God cannot make the contraries of these principles;He cannot make the genus not to be predicable of the species, nor lines drawn from a circle's center to its circumference not to be equal, nor the three angles of a rectilinear triangle not to be equal to two right angles.[15]

But in Islam, Allah is absolutely free. Al-Ghazali and others took issue with the very idea that there were laws of nature; that would be blasphemy, a denial of Allah's freedom.[16] To say that he created the universe according to consistent, rational laws, or that he "cannot" do something—as Aquinas affirms here—would be to bind his absolute sovereignty. His will controls all, but it is inscrutable.

Thus modern science developed in Christian Europe rather than in the House of Islam. In the Islamic world, Allah killed science.

But all is not lost: Some things for which we can thank Islam

All this doesn't mean, however, that Islam cannot be given some credit for intellectual, scientific, or artistic attainment. In fact, we can credit the House of Islam with two landmark achievements: the opening of the New World and the Renaissance in Europe.

Every schoolchild knows, or used to know, that in 1492 Christopher Columbus sailed the ocean blue and discovered America while searching for a new, westward sea route to Asia. And why was he searching for a new route to Asia? Because the fall of Constantinople to the Muslims in 1453 closed the trade routes to the East. This was devastating for European tradesmen, who had until then traveled to Asia for spices and other goods by land. Columbus's voyage was trying to ease the plight of these merchants by bypassing the Muslims altogether and making it possible for Europeans to reach India by sea. So the bellicosity and intransigence of Islam ultimately opened the Americas for Europe.

A Book You're Not Supposed to Read

The Rise of Early Modern Science: Islam, China and the West, by Toby E. Huff; Cambridge: Cambridge University Press, 2nd edition, 2003. Huff explains why it was not by accident that modern science didn't develop in the Islamic world or China, but in the West.

Another consequence of the fall of Constantinople, and the long, slow death of the Byzantine Empire that preceded it, was the emigration of Greek intellectuals to Western Europe. Muslim territorial expansion at Byzantine expense led so many Greeks to seek refuge in the West that Western universities were filled with Platonists and Aristotelians to an unprecedented extent. This led to the rediscovery of classical philosophy and literature, and to an intellectual and cultural flowering the like of which the world had never seen (and hasn't again). It may be that the decline and fall of Byzantium was a greater Muslim contribution to the history of philosophy and intellectual life in the Western world than the Arabic preservation of Aristotle.

Of course, both of these aren't really Islamic "achievements." They are consequences of the applications of the violent doctrines of Islam we explored earlier. But in terms of their real effects upon the world at large, they amount to more than a whole stack of Islamic philosophical treatises and a boatload of calligraphy.

Chapter 8

THE LURE OF ISLAMIC PARADISE

However strange it may seem to Westerners, the much-publicized virgins promised to Islamic martyrs in Paradise is no myth or distortion of Islamic theology. Muhammad painted a picture of a frankly material and lushly sensual Paradise for his followers—containing everything a seventh-century Arabian desert-dweller could possibly dream of: gold and fine material things, fruits, wine, water, women . . . and boys.

Of course, not everyone was buying into this, even during the Prophet's salad days. During one engagement against the Quraysh (the Battle of the Trench), Muhammad asked his followers: "Who is a man who will go up and see for us how the enemy is doing and then come back?" He promised to ask Allah that that spy "may be my companion in paradise." Yet he found no volunteers, requiring him finally to assign the mission to one of his men.[1]

Still, the promise of Paradise was one of the principal means by which Muhammad motivated his followers. It made fighting in jihads a win-win proposition: If a Muslim warrior was victorious, he enjoyed booty on earth; if he was killed, he enjoyed virtually identical rewards in the afterlife—on a much grander scale. During the Battle of Badr, Muhammad urged on the Muslims with promises of Paradise: "By God in whose hand is the soul of Muhammad, no man will be slain this day fighting against

Guess what?

- The Qur'an describes Paradise in terms that make it clear that it is a place merely to indulge one's physical appetites.

- September 11 hijacker Muhammad Atta packed a "paradise wedding suit" into his luggage on that fateful day.

- Paradise is guaranteed only to those who "slay and are slain" for Allah.

them with steadfast courage advancing not retreating but God will cause him to enter Paradise."

One of his warriors, 'Umayr bin al-Humam, who had been sitting near by munching on dates, was excited by this. "Fine, fine!" he exclaimed. "Is there nothing between me and my entering Paradise save to be killed by these men?" He flung away his dates, rushed into battle, and quickly met the death he had been seeking.[2]

What's behind Door Number One

In Paradise, 'Umayr bin al-Humam expected to be adorned "with bracelets of gold and pearls" (Qur'an 22:23) and "dressed in fine silk and in rich brocade" (Qur'an 44:53). Then he would recline "on green cushions and rich carpets of beauty" (Qur'an 55:76), sit on "thrones encrusted with gold and precious stones" (Qur'an 56:15), and share in "dishes and goblets of gold"—on which would be "all that the souls could desire, all that their eyes could delight in," including an "abundance of fruit" (Qur'an 43:71, 73) including "dates and pomegranates" (Qur'an 55:68). For the carnivorous, there would be "the flesh of fowls, any that they may desire" (Qur'an 56:21).

To those who lived their entire lives in the desert, water was a precious commodity—and the Qur'an promises it in abundance in Paradise. Paradise itself consists of "gardens, with rivers flowing beneath" (Qur'an 3:198; cf. 3:136; 13:35; 15:45; 22:23). In it are "two springs pouring forth water in continuous abundance" (Qur'an 55:66).

And not only water: Paradise would offer a variety of beverages. Besides "rivers of water incorruptible," there would be "rivers of milk of which the taste never changes; rivers of wine, a joy to those who drink; and rivers of honey pure and clear" (Qur'an 47:15).

Wine? But aren't alcoholic drinks forbidden to Muslims? Doesn't the Qur'an say that "strong drink" is "Satan's handiwork" (5:90)? How, then, can Satan's handiwork be found in Paradise?

Well, the wine in Paradise is different, you see. It is "free from headiness," so that those who drink it will not "suffer intoxication therefrom" (Qur'an 37:47).

All this would be presented to those blessed of Allah in a perfect climate-controlled environment: "Reclining in the Garden on raised thrones, they will see there neither the sun's excessive heat nor the moon's excessive cold. And the shades of the Garden will come low over them, and the bunches of fruit, there, will hang low in humility" (Qur'an 76:13-14).

The food and comforts would never run out: "its food is everlasting, and its shade" (Qur'an 13:35).

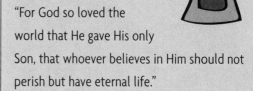

Muhammad vs. Jesus

"For God so loved the world that He gave His only Son, that whoever believes in Him should not perish but have eternal life."

John 3:16

"Allah hath purchased of the believers their persons and their goods; for theirs in return is the garden of Paradise: they fight in His cause, and slay and are slain: a promise binding on Him in truth…"

Qur'an 9:111

The joy of sex

But 'Umayr bin al-Humam probably wasn't concerned with all that, as attractive as it may have seemed. For he knew that waiting for him in Paradise were "voluptuous women of equal age" (Qur'an 78:31): "those of modest gaze, with lovely eyes" (Qur'an 37:48), "fair women with beautiful, big, and lustrous eyes" (Qur'an 44:54), "like unto rubies and coral" (Qur'an 55:58) to whom he would be "joined" (Qur'an 52:20). These women would be "maidens, chaste, restraining their glances, whom no man or Jinn [spirit being] before them has touched" (Qur'an 55:56). Allah "made them virgins" (Qur'an 56:36), and according to Islamic tradition, they would remain virgins forever.

Just Like Today: Suicide bombers and Paradise

The promise of Paradise to those who "slay and are slain" for Allah is the principal justification for suicide bombings: The bombers are laying claim to this promise by slaying Allah's enemies and being slain in the process.

Of course, Muslim spokesmen in America have been quick to point out that the Qur'an forbids suicide: "O ye who believe! Eat not up your property among yourselves in vanities.... Nor kill or destroy yourselves" (Qur'an 4:29–30). Muhammad adds in a hadith: "He who commits suicide by throttling shall keep on throttling himself in the Hell-fire forever, and he who commits suicide by stabbing himself shall keep on stabbing himself in the Hell-fire."[3]

But the influential Islamic scholar Sheikh Yusaf al-Qaradawi, who has been hailed as a "reformist" by Islamic scholar John Esposito, summed up the more common view. The prohibitions against suicide do not apply to suicide bombers, because their intention is not to kill themselves but the enemies of Allah: "It's not suicide, it is martyrdom in the name of God, Islamic theologians and jurisprudents have debated this issue. Referring to it as a form of jihad, under the title of jeopardising the life of the mujahideen. It is allowed to jeopardise your soul and cross the path of the enemy and be killed."[4]

Umm Nidal, the mother of Hamas suicide attacker Muhammad Farhat, saw her son's murderous death in the same way—as a great victory: "Jihad is a [religious] commandment imposed upon us," she explained. "We must instill this idea in our sons' souls, all the time.... What we see every day—massacres, destruction, bombing [of] homes—strengthened, in the souls of my sons, especially Muhammad, the love of Jihad and martyrdom.... Allah be praised, I am a Muslim and I believe in Jihad. Jihad is one of the elements of the faith and this is what encouraged me to sacrifice Muhammad in Jihad for the sake of Allah. My son was not destroyed, he is not dead; he is living a happier life than I."

Umm Nidal continued: "Because I love my son, I encouraged him to die a martyr's death for the sake of Allah.... Jihad is a religious obligation incumbent upon us, and we must carry it out."[5]

But Paradise would not be a bore for Muslims with different proclivities. Allah also promised his blessed that in Paradise, "round about them will serve, devoted to them, young male servants handsome as pearls well-guarded" (Qur'an 52:24), "youths of perpetual freshness" (Qur'an 56:17): "if thou seest them, thou wouldst think them scattered pearls" (Qur'an 76:19).

But surely the Qur'an isn't condoning homosexuality, is it? After all, it depicts Lot telling the people of Sodom: "For ye practise your lusts on men in preference to women: ye are indeed a people transgressing beyond bounds" (7:81) and "of all the creatures in the world, will ye approach males, and leave those whom Allah has created for you to be your mates? Nay, ye are a people transgressing all limits!" (26:165). A hadith commands that "if a man who is not married is seized committing sodomy, he will be stoned to death."[6] Another hadith has Muhammad saying: "Kill the one who sodomizes and the one who lets it be done to him."[7] These strictures have worked their way into Islamic legal codes, such that two Saudis were so anxious to avoid a flogging or prison term that they murdered a Pakistani who witnessed their "shameful acts" by running over him with a car, smashing his head in with a rock, and setting him on fire.[8]

A Book You're Not Supposed to Read

Islamikaze: Manifestations of Islamic Martyrology by Raphael Israeli; London: Frank Cass Publishers, 2003, is an exhaustive and enthralling treatment of what motivates Islamic suicide bombers.

It's all here: the oppression of women and non-Muslims, the brutal punishments, the double standards, and more—laid out clearly and precisely without a trace of self-consciousness or embarrassment. It's hair-raising—and enlightening—reading.

But the pearl-like youths of Paradise have given rise to a strange double-mindedness about homosexuality in Islam. The great poet Abu Nuwas openly glorified homosexuality in his notorious poem the *Perfumed Garden*:

O the joy of sodomy! So now be sodomites, you Arabs. Turn not away from it—therein is wondrous pleasure. Take some coy lad with kiss-curls twisting on his temple and ride him as he stands like some gazelle standing to her mate—A lad whom all can see girt with sword and belt not like your whore who has to go veiled. Make for smooth-faced boys and do your very best to mount them, for women are the mounts of the devils![9]

This paradoxical attitude toward homosexuality runs through Islamic history. Even the Ottoman sultan Mehmed II, the conqueror of Constantinople, was open about this proclivity. While the conquered city was still smoldering, Mehmed turned his mind away from wars and battles and demanded that the famously handsome teenage son of a Byzantine official, Lukas Notaras, be brought to him. Notaras went to the sultan and

Just Like Today: Paradise still lures young men

"The Americans love Pepsi-Cola, we love death," crowed Maulana Inyadullah of al Qaeda.[10] Muslims love death because Allah commands them to value the joys of Paradise over those of this world: "Those who love the life of this world more than the hereafter, who hinder men from the path of Allah and seek therein something crooked: they are astray by a long distance" (Qur'an 14:3).

As lurid as they are, the joys of Islamic Paradise have a definite and continuing appeal—an appeal felt most sharply, perhaps, by teenage boys. In 2004, a fourteen-year-old would-be Palestinian suicide bomber told the Israeli troops who disarmed him: "Blowing myself up is the only chance I've got to have sex with seventy-two virgins in the Garden of Eden."[11] Another fourteen-year-old explained how a jihadist recruiter enticed him to join the jihad in Iraq: "He told me about paradise, about virgins, about Islam."[12]

told him he would rather see his sons killed before his eyes than turned over to Mehmed's pleasures. Mehmed obliged him, and then had Notaras himself beheaded.[13]

How to gain entry into Paradise

As we have seen, the Qur'an's surest guarantee of Paradise is given to those who "slay and are slain" for Allah: "for theirs in return is the garden of Paradise . . . a promise binding on Him in truth" (Qur'an 9:111). Muhammad also proclaimed: "Know that Paradise is under the shades of swords (*Jihad* in Allah's cause)."[14] It assures those on earth that those who die for Allah are not dead, but more alive than ever: "And say not of those who are slain in the way of Allah: 'They are dead.' Nay, they are living, though ye perceive it not" (Qur'an 2:154).

The Assassins and the lure of Paradise

Around the time of the Crusades there flourished a notorious sect of Ismaili Shi'ite Muslims known as the Assassins. Although they did not invent political assassination, by murdering numerous key figures that opposed their movement, they introduced it on a large scale into the politics of the Islamic world and the Crusades themselves. After carrying out these murders, the Assassins almost always placidly allowed themselves to be caught, although at that time this meant certain death.[15]

What enticed young men to join this sect and sacrifice their lives in this way? For one thing, the Ismailis presented themselves as the exponents of "pure Islam," which they were giving their lives to restore. But it is also possible that the lure of Islamic paradise was among these motivations. When Marco Polo traversed Asia in the late thirteenth century, he reported what he had heard "told by many people" about the shadowy leader of the Assassins, the Old Man (or Sheikh) of the Mountain:

He had had made in a valley between two mountains the biggest and most beautiful garden that was ever seen, planted with all the finest fruits in the world and containing the most splendid mansions and palaces that were ever seen, ornamented with gold and with likenesses of all that is beautiful on earth, and also four conduits, one flowing with wine, one with milk, and one with honey, and one with water. There were fair ladies there and damsels, the loveliest in the world, unrivalled at playing every sort of instrument and at singing and dancing. And he gave his men to understand that this garden was Paradise. That is why he had made it after this pattern, because Mahomet assured the Saracens that those who go to Paradise will have beautiful women to their hearts' content to do their bidding, and will find there rivers of wine and milk and honey and water.... No one ever entered the garden except those whom he wished to make Assassins.[16]

It is likely that this description is more legend than fact. But Muslim warriors throughout history have been motivated by Islamic Paradise. Even September 11 hijacker Muhammad Atta packed a "paradise wedding suit" into his luggage on that fateful day, although he was unable to change into it because the airline required him to check all but one carry-on item. A letter found in Atta's bags spoke of "marriage" with the "women of paradise ... dressed in their most beautiful clothing."[17]

Chapter 9

ISLAM—SPREAD BY
THE SWORD? YOU BET.

Virtually all Westerners have learned to apologize for the Crusades, but less noted is the fact that the Crusades have an Islamic counterpart for which no one is apologizing and of which few are even aware. The first large-scale contact of Muslims with the Western world came not with the Crusades, but 450 years before them. When the forces of Islam united the scattered tribes of Arabia into a single community, the newly Islamic Arabia was surrounded by predominantly Christian lands—notably the Byzantine imperial holdings of Syria and Egypt, as well as the venerable Christian lands of North Africa. Four of Christendom's five principal cities—Constantinople, Alexandria, Antioch, and Jerusalem—lay within striking distance of Arabia. The Byzantine Empire's great rival, Persia, also had a significant Christian population.

But for centuries now, the Middle East, North Africa, and Persia (Iran) have been regarded as the heart of the Islamic world. Did this transformation take place through preaching and the conversion of hearts and minds? Not at all: The sword spread Islam. Under Islamic rule, the non-Muslim majorities of those regions were gradually whittled down to the tiny minorities they are today, through repression, discrimination, and harassment that made conversion to Islam the only path to a better life.

Guess what?

- What is known today as the "Islamic world" was created by a series of brutal conquests of non-Muslim lands.

- These were wars of religious imperialism, not self-defense.

- The early spread of Islam and that of Christianity sharply contrast in that Islam spread by force and Christianity didn't.

PC Myth: Early Muslims had no bellicose designs on neighboring lands

Toward the end of Muhammad's life, after his successful expedition against the pagan Hawazin and the Thaqif tribes, whom he defeated at Hunayn (a valley near Mecca), he attempted to move beyond Arabia, beginning an expedition against the Byzantines in Tabuk. He also contacted the Byzantine emperor, Heraclius, and other rulers in the region, by letter: "the Prophet of Allah wrote to Chosroes (King of Persia), Caesar (Emperor of Rome) [that is, Heraclius], Negus (King of Abyssinia) and every (other) despot inviting them to Allah, the Exalted."[1] He exhorted them to "embrace Islam and you will be safe."[2]

None did, and Muhammad's warning proved accurate: None of them were safe. Not long after Muhammad's death, the Muslims invaded the Byzantine Empire—fired up by Muhammad's promise that "the first army amongst my followers who will invade Caesar's city [Constantinople] will be forgiven their sins."[3]

In 635, just three years after Muhammad died, Damascus, the city where Saint Paul was heading when he experienced his dramatic conversion to Christianity, fell to the invading Muslims. In 636, the caliph Umar, who ruled and expanded the empire of Islam from 634 to 644, took al-Basrah in Iraq. Umar gave instructions to his lieutenant 'Utbah ibn Ghazwan in words that echoed the Prophet Muhammad's triple choice for unbelievers: "Summon the people to God; those who respond to your call, accept it from them, but those who refuse must pay the poll tax out of humiliation and lowliness. If they refuse this, it is the sword without leniency. Fear God with regard to what you have been entrusted."[4]

Antioch, where the disciples of Jesus were first called "Christians" (Acts 11:26), fell the next year. It was Jerusalem's turn two years later, in 638. Like Damascus and Antioch, Jerusalem was a Christian city at that time. It was the unhappy task of Sophronius, the patriarch of Jerusalem, to hand over the city to the conquering Umar. The caliph stood happily on the site of Solomon's Temple, from which he may have believed that the Prophet Muhammad, his old master, once ascended into Paradise (cf. Qur'an 17:1, a verse that has inspired centuries of debate as to its precise meaning). Sophronius, watching in deep sorrow nearby, recalled a Bible verse: "Behold the abomination of desolation, spoken of by Daniel the prophet."[5]

PC Myth: The native Christians of the Middle East and North Africa welcomed Muslims as liberators

Many modern analysts of the Crusades and Christian-Muslim relations in general seem to think that Sophronius said, "Welcome, liberator!" According to conventional wisdom, Byzantine rule was so oppressive on the Christians in the Middle East and North Africa, and Egyptians in particular, that they couldn't wait to give them the bum's rush and open their arms to the Muslims who liberated them from this oppression. But, in fact, the Muslims conquered and held Egypt only in the face of great resistance. In December 639, the general 'Amr began the invasion of Egypt; in November 642, Alexandria fell and virtually all of Egypt was in Muslim hands. But this swift conquest was not uncontested, and the Muslims met resistance with brutality. In one Egyptian town they set a pattern of behavior that they followed all over the country. According to a contemporary observer:

> Then the Muslims arrived in Nikiou. There was not one single soldier to resist them. They seized the town and slaughtered everyone they met in the street and in the churches—men, women and children, sparing nobody. Then they went to other places, pillaged and killed all the inhabitants they found.... But let us now say no more, for it is impossible to describe the

horrors the Muslims committed when they occupied the island of Nikiou.

Not only were many native Christians killed—others were enslaved:

> Amr oppressed Egypt.... He took considerable booty from this country and a large number of prisoners.... The Muslims returned to their country with booty and captives. The patriarch Cyrus felt deep grief at the calamities in Egypt, because Amr, who was of barbarian origin, showed no mercy in his treatment of the Egyptians and did not fulfill the covenants which had been agreed with him.[6]

Christian Armenia also fell to the Muslims amid similar butcheries: "The enemy's army rushed in and butchered the inhabitants of the town by the sword.... After a few days' rest, the Ismaelites [Arabs] went back whence they had come, dragging after them a host of captives, numbering thirty-five thousand."[7]

The same pattern prevailed when the Muslims reached Cilicia and Caesarea of Cappadocia in 650. According to a Medieval account:

> They [the Taiyaye, or Muslim Arabs] moved into Cilicia and took prisoners... and when Mu'awiya arrived he ordered all the inhabitantsto be put to the sword; he placed guards so that no one escaped. Aftergathering up all the wealth of the town, they set to torturing the leadersto make them show them things [treasures] that had been hidden. The Taiyaye led everyone into slavery—men and women, boys and girls—and they committed much debauchery in that unfortunate town; theywickedly committed immoralities inside churches.[8]

Caliph Umar made a telling admission in a message to an underling: "Do you think," he asked, "that these vast countries, Syria, Mesopotamia,

Kufa, Basra, Misr [Egypt] do not have to be covered with troops who must be well paid?"[9]

Why did these areas have to be "covered with" troops, if the inhabitants welcomed the invaders and lived with them in friendship?

PC Myth: Early jihad warriors were merely defending Muslim lands from their non-Muslim neighbors

The Muslim armies swept quickly over huge regions that had never threatened them—and probably hadn't even heard of them until the invaders arrived. Around the same time Egypt, the Middle East, and Armenia were falling to the Muslims, Europe was not exempt: Other Muslim forces carried out raids on Cyprus, Rhodes, Crete, and Sicily. They carried off booty and thousands of slaves. These were but preludes to the first great Muslim sieges of what was then the grandest city of Eastern Christendom and one of the greatest in the world: Constantinople. Muslim armies laid siege in 668 (and for several years thereafter) and 717. Both sieges failed, but they made it abundantly clear that the House of Islam was continuing its policy of bloody imperialism toward Christendom.

Muslim warriors did all this in obedience to the commands of their god and his prophet. One Muslim leader of that era put it this way: "The Great God says in the Koran: 'O true believers, when you encounter the unbelievers, strike off their heads.' The above command of the Great God is a great command and must be respected and followed."[11] He was referring, of course, to the Qur'an: "When you meet the unbelievers in the battlefield, strike off their heads and, when you have laid them low, bind your captives firmly" (47:4).

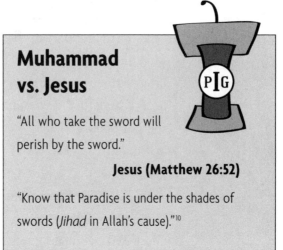

Muhammad vs. Jesus

"All who take the sword will perish by the sword."

Jesus (Matthew 26:52)

"Know that Paradise is under the shades of swords (*Jihad* in Allah's cause)."[10]

French president Jacques Chirac has remarked, "Europe owes as much to Islam as it does to Christianity."[12] But this is like saying that the hen owes as much to the fox as it does to Farmer John. For Europe in the eighth century would soon know just how seriously the Muslims took the commands of Allah about meeting the unbelievers on the battlefield. The Muslims swept rapidly through Christian North Africa, and by 711 they were in a position to invade Spain. Christian Europe was beset from both the East and the West. The campaign went well—so well, in fact, that the Muslim commander, Tarik, exceeded his orders and pressed his victorious army forward. When he was upbraided by the North African emir, Musa, and asked why he had kept going so far into Christian Spain in defiance of orders, Tarik replied simply, "To serve Islam."[13]

He served it so well that by 715 the Muslims were close to conquering all of Spain (which they held, of course, for over seven hundred years), and began to press into France. Charles Martel, "the Hammer," stopped them in 732 at the city of Tours.

Despite this defeat, the Muslims didn't give up. In 792, the ruler of Muslim Spain, Hisham, called for a new expedition into France. Muslims around the world enthusiastically responded to his call to jihad, and the army that gathered was able to do a good deal of damage—but ultimately did not prevail.

Nonetheless, it is important to note that Hisham's call was religiously based—and that it antedates the Crusades, which are supposed to mark the beginning of Christian-Muslim hostility, by just over three hundred years. Some fifty years later, in 848, another Muslim army invaded France and wreaked considerable havoc. But over time, their fervor faded. In the course of the Muslim occupation, many of the occupiers were converted to Christianity, and the force dissipated.

Somewhat earlier, in 827, the warriors of jihad set their sights on Sicily and Italy. The commander of the invading force was a noted scholar of the Qur'an who forthrightly cast the expedition as a religious war. They pillaged and looted Christian churches, all through these lands, terrorizing monks and violating nuns. By 846, they had reached Rome, where they exacted a promise of tribute from the pope. While their hold on Italy was never strong, they held Sicily until 1091—when the Normans drove them out.

In Spain, of course, the *reconquista* began to slowly chip away at Muslim domains, until 1492, when the Christians had entirely recaptured the nation. However, as battles raged in Spain, the Muslims continued to press Christendom's eastern flank. The Seljuk Turks decisively defeated the forces of the Byzantine Empire at the Armenian town of Manzikert in 1071, paving the way for the Muslim occupation of virtually all of Asia Minor—some of the central and most well-known lands of Christendom. Henceforth Christians would suffer second-class dhimmi status in the great Christian cities to which Paul addressed many of his canonical epistles. It is against the backdrop of all this, as we shall see, that Pope Urban II called the first Crusade in 1095.

Just Like Today: Islam must be spread by force

Some of the modern-day Islamic thinkers who are most revered today by jihad terrorists taught (in no uncertain terms) that Islam must impose itself by force upon non-Muslims—not as a religion, for that would violate the Qur'an's dictum that "there is no compulsion in religion" (Qur'an 2:256)—but as a system of laws and societal norms. They taught that Muslims must fight to impose Islamic law on non-Muslim states, relegating its citizens to dhimmi status or worse.

Not only West, but East

Muslim forces pressed eastward as well as westward, mounting a sea invasion of India as early as 634. Land invaders pressed into what are now Afghanistan, Pakistan, and India beginning in the eighth century, making slow but steady progress. Historian Sita Ram Goel observes that by 1206, the Muslim invaders had conquered "the Punjab, Sindh, Delhi, and the Doab up to Kanauj."[14] Later waves expanded these holdings to the Ganges and beyond.

Because Muslims considered the Hindus pagans who weren't even entitled to the "protections" of dhimmi status, they treated them with particular brutality. Sita Ram Goel observes that the Muslim invaders of India paid no respect to codes of warfare that had prevailed there for centuries:

> Islamic imperialism came with a different code—the Sunnah [tradition] of the Prophet. It required its warriors to fall upon the helpless civil population after a decisive victory had been won on the battlefield. It required them to sack and burn down villages and towns after the defenders had died fighting or had fled. The cows, the Brahmins, and the Bhikshus invited their special attention in mass murders of non-combatants. The temples and monasteries were their special targets in an orgy of pillage and arson. Those whom they did not kill, they captured and sold as slaves. The magnitude of the booty looted even from the bodies of the dead, was a measure of the success of the military mission. And they did all this as *mujahids* (holy warriors) and *ghazis* (*kafir* [unbeliever]-killers) in the service of Allah and his Last Prophet.[15]

What did the Muslims want?

What was the ultimate goal of this seemingly endless warfare? It is clear from the commands of the Qur'an and the Prophet, who told his followers that Allah had commanded him, "to fight against the people until they testify that none has the right to be worshipped but Allah and that Muhammad is the Messenger of Allah."[16] No Islamic sect has ever renounced the proposition that Islamic law must reign supreme over the entire world, and that Muslims must, under certain circumstances, take up arms to this end. They stopped waging large-scale jihads after 1683 not because they had reformed or rejected the doctrines that motivated them, but because the Islamic world had grown too weak to continue—a situation that began to change in recent times with the discovery of oil in the Middle East.

The Egyptian Qur'an commentator and Muslim Brotherhood theorist Sayyid Qutb (1906–1966) emphasized this clearly:

A Book You're Not Supposed to Read

Jihad In the West: Muslim Conquests from the 7th to the 21st Centuries by Paul Fregosi; New York: Prometheus Books, 1998, is a popular, highly readable account of the depredations of jihad in the Western world and a vivid illustration of the posture of war that the Islamic world has maintained toward Christendom and the post-Christian West since its earliest days.

> It is not the function of Islam to compromise with the concepts of Jahiliyya [the society of unbelievers] which are current in the world or to co-exist in the same land together with a jahili system. . . . Islam cannot accept any mixing with Jahiliyyah. Either Islam will remain, or Jahiliyyah; no half-half situation is possible. Command belongs to Allah, or otherwise to Jahiliyyah; Allah's Shari'ah [law] will prevail, or else people's desires: "And if they do not respond to you, then know that they only follow their own lusts. And who is more astray than one who follows his own lusts, without guidance from Allah? Verily! Allah guides not the people who are disobedient." [Qur'an 28:50] . . . *The foremost duty of Islam is to depose Jahiliyyah from the leadership of man*, with the intention of raising human beings to that high position which Allah has chosen for him.[17] (Emphasis added)

Likewise, Sayyid Abul Ala Maududi (1903–1979), founder of the Pakistani political party Jamaat-e-Islami, declared that non-Muslims have "absolutely no right to seize the reins of power in any part of God's earth nor to direct the collective affairs of human beings according to their own misconceived doctrines." If they do, "the believers would be under an obligation to do their utmost to dislodge them from political power and to make them live in subservience to the Islamic way of life."[18]

Do their utmost, even to the point of strapping on bombs and blowing themselves up in crowded buses or restaurants, or hijacking airplanes and flying them into office towers.

PC Myth: Christianity and Islam spread in pretty much the same way

This is one of many moral equivalence arguments made today—they're so common that it seems as if some people cannot bring themselves to acknowledge that there could be anything negative about Islam unless they take pains to point out that the same negative thing exists in Christianity. And it's certainly true that no group, religious or unreligious, has a monopoly on either misdeeds or virtue—but it doesn't follow that all religious traditions are equal either in the nature of their teachings or in the capacity of those teachings to inspire violence.

For nearly the first three centuries of its existence, Christianity was outlawed and subject to sporadic persecution by Roman authorities. Not only was the religion *not* spread by violence, but the lists of Christian martyrs are filled with the names of people subjected to violence *because* they became Christians. In contrast, by the time of Muhammad's death, the Muslims faced no organized or sustained opposition, and yet continued to take up the sword for their faith.

In the early days of Christianity, the Church sent missionaries to preach to non-believers and convince them of the truth of their faith. The ancient Christian nations of Europe all remember the Christian missionaries who brought the faith to them: Saint Patrick in Ireland; Saint Augustine of Canterbury in England; Saints Cyril and Methodius in Central and Eastern Europe; and others like them. They were priests and monks—not military men. Muslims, by contrast, put armies in the field that faced non-Muslim forces and offered them Muhammad's triple choice of conversion, subjugation, or death. They drew their largest numbers of converts from among conquered dhimmi populations that saw the embrace of Islam as their only path to a livable existence. Given all the depredations of dhimmitude, it is hardly surprising that many dhimmis ultimately chose Islam.

Today, many Muslims today hotly deny that Islam spread by force, and point out that forced conversion is forbidden in Islam. That is absolutely true: What spread by force was the political and social hegemony of the Islamic system. Conversions to Islam followed the imposition of that system as the dhimmis began to feel their misery.

Part II

THE CRUSADES

Chapter 10

WHY THE CRUSADES
WERE CALLED

The Crusaders' sack of Jerusalem in 1099, according to journalist Amin Maalouf in *The Crusades Through Arab Eyes*, was the "starting point of a millennial hostility between Islam and the West."[1] Islamic scholar and apologist John Esposito is a bit more expansive—he blames the Crusades ("so-called holy wars") in general for disrupting a pluralistic civilization: "Five centuries of peaceful coexistence elapsed before political events and an imperial-papal power play led to centuries-long series of so-called holy wars that pitted Christendom against Islam and left an enduring legacy of misunderstanding and distrust."[2]

Maalouf doesn't seem to consider whether "millennial hostility" may have begun with the Prophet Muhammad's veiled threat, issued over 450 years before the Crusaders entered Jerusalem, to neighboring non-Muslim leaders to "embrace Islam and you will be safe."[3] Nor does he discuss the possibility that Muslims may have stoked that "millennial hostility" by seizing Christian lands—which amounted to two-thirds of what had formerly been the Christian world—centuries before the Crusades. Esposito's "five centuries of peaceful coexistence" were exemplified, he says, by the Muslim conquest of Jerusalem in 638: "churches and the Christian population were left unmolested."[4] But he doesn't mention Sophronius' Christmas sermon for 634, when he complained of the Muslims'

Guess what?

- The Crusades were *not* acts of unprovoked aggression by Europe against the Islamic world, but were a delayed response to centuries of Muslim aggression, which grew fiercer than ever in the eleventh century.

- These were wars for the recapture of Christian lands and the defense of Christians, *not* religious imperialism.

- The Crusades were not called in order to convert Muslims or anyone else to Christianity by force.

"savage, barbarous, and bloody sword" and of how difficult that sword had made life for the Christians.[5]

PC Myth: The Crusades were an unprovoked attack by Europe against the Islamic world

Wrong. The conquest of Jerusalem in 638 stood at the beginning of centuries of Muslim aggression, and Christians in the Holy Land faced an escalating spiral of persecution. A few examples: Early in the eighth century, sixty Christian pilgrims from Amorium were crucified; around the same time, the Muslim governor of Caesarea seized a group of pilgrims from Iconium and had them all executed as spies—except for a small number who converted to Islam; and Muslims demanded money from pilgrims, threatening to ransack the Church of the Resurrection if they didn't pay. Later in the eighth century, a Muslim ruler banned displays of the cross in Jerusalem. He also increased the anti-religious tax (jizya) that Christians had to pay and forbade Christians to engage in religious instruction of others, even their own children.

Brutal subordination and violence became the rules of the day for Christians in the Holy Land. In 772, the caliph al-Mansur ordered the hands of Christians and Jews in Jerusalem to be stamped with a distinctive symbol. Conversions to Christianity were dealt with particularly harshly. In 789, Muslims beheaded a

---

Muhammad vs. Jesus

"Blessed are the pure in heart, for they shall see God. Blessed are the peacemakers, for they shall be called sons of God. Blessed are those who are persecuted for righteousness' sake, for theirs is the kingdom of heaven."

Jesus (Matthew 5:8–10)

"Allah assigns for a person who participates in (holy battles) in Allah's Cause and nothing causes him to do so except belief in Allah and His Messengers, that he will be recompensed by Allah either with a reward, or booty (if he survives) or will be admitted to Paradise (if he is killed in the battle as a martyr)."[6]

---

monk who had converted from Islam and plundered the Bethlehem monastery of Saint Theodosius, killing many more monks. Other monasteries in the region suffered the same fate. Early in the ninth century, the persecutions grew so severe that large numbers of Christians fled to Constantinople and other Christian cities. More persecutions in 923 saw additional churches destroyed, and in 937, Muslims went on a Palm Sunday rampage in Jerusalem, plundering and destroying the Church of Calvary and the Church of the Resurrection.[7]

In reaction to this persecution of Christians, the Byzantines moved from a defensive policy toward the Muslims to the offensive position of trying to recapture some of their lost territories. In the 960s, General Nicephorus Phocas (a future Byzantine emperor) carried out a series of successful campaigns against the Muslims, recapturing Crete, Cilicia, Cyprus, and even parts of Syria. In 969, he recaptured the ancient Christian city of Antioch. The Byzantines extended this campaign into Syria in the 970s.[8]

In Islamic theology, if any land has ever belonged to the House of Islam, it belongs forever—and Muslims must wage war to regain control over it. In 974, faced with a string of losses to the Byzantines, the Abbasid (Sunni) caliph in Baghdad declared jihad. This followed yearly jihad campaigns against the Byzantines launched by Saif al-Dawla, ruler of the Shi'ite Hamdanid dynasty in Aleppo from 944 to 967. Saif al-Dawla appealed to Muslims to fight the Byzantines on the pretext that they were taking lands that belonged to the House of Islam. This appeal was so successful that Muslim warriors from as far off as Central Asia joined the jihads.[9]

However, Sunni/Shi'ite disunity ultimately hampered Islamic jihad efforts, and in 1001 the Byzantine emperor Basil II concluded a ten-year truce with the Fatimid (Shi'ite) caliph.[10]

Basil, however, soon learned that to conclude such truces was futile. In 1004, the sixth Fatimid caliph, Abu 'Ali al-Mansur al-Hakim (985–1021), turned violently against the faith of his Christian mother and uncles (two of whom were patriarchs), ordering the destruction of churches, the burning of crosses, and the seizure of church property. He moved against the Jews with similar ferocity. Over the next ten years, thirty thousand churches were destroyed, and untold numbers of Christians converted to Islam simply to save their lives. In 1009, al-Hakim gave his most spectacular anti-Christian order: He commanded that the Church of the Holy Sepulcher in Jerusalem be destroyed, along with several other churches (including the Church of the Resurrection). The Church of the Holy Sepulcher, rebuilt by the Byzantines in the seventh century after the Persians burned an earlier version, marks the traditional site of Christ's burial; it also served as a model for the Al-Aqsa Mosque. Al-Hakim commanded that the tomb within be cut down to the bedrock. He ordered Christians to wear heavy crosses around their necks (and for Jews, heavy blocks of wood in the shape of a calf). He piled on other humiliating decrees, culminating in the order that they accept Islam or leave his dominions.[11]

The erratic caliph ultimately relaxed his persecution of non-Muslims and even returned much of the property he had seized from the Church.[12] A partial cause of al-Hakim's changed attitude was probably his increasingly tenuous connection to Islamic orthodoxy. In 1021, he disappeared under mysterious circumstances; some of his followers proclaimed him divine and founded a sect based on this mystery and other esoteric teachings of a Muslim cleric, Muhammad ibn Isma'il al-Darazi (after whom the Druze sect is named).[13] Thanks to al-Hakim's change of policy, which continued after his death, the Byzantines were allowed to rebuild the Church of the Holy Sepulcher in 1027.[14]

Nevertheless, Christians were in a precarious position, and pilgrims remained under threat. In 1056, the Muslims expelled three hundred Christians from Jerusalem and forbade European Christians from entering the Church of the Holy Sepulcher.[15] When the fierce and fanatical Seljuk Turks swept down from Central Asia, they enforced a new Islamic rigor, making life increasingly difficult for both native Christians and pilgrims (whose pilgrimages they blocked). After they crushed the Byzantines at Manzikert in 1071 and took the Byzantine emperor Romanus IV Diogenes prisoner, all of Asia Minor was open to them, and their advance was virtually unstoppable. In 1076, they conquered Syria; in 1077, Jerusalem. The Seljuk emir Atsiz bin Uwaq promised not to harm the inhabitants of Jerusalem, but once his men had entered the city, they murdered three thousand people.[16] The Seljuks established the sultanate of Rum (Rome, referring to the New Rome, Constantinople) in Nicaea that same year, perilously close to Constantinople itself; from there they continued to threaten the Byzantines and harass the Christians all over their new domains.

The Christian empire of Byzantium, which before Islam's wars of conquest had ruled over a vast expanse including southern Italy, North Africa, the Middle East, and Arabia, was reduced to little more than Greece. It looked as if its death at the hands of the Seljuks was imminent. The Church of Constantinople considered the popes schismatic and had squabbled with them for centuries, but the new emperor Alexius I Comnenus (1081–1118), swallowed his pride and appealed for help. And that is how the First Crusade came about: It was a response to the Byzantine Emperor's call for help.

PC Myth: The Crusades were an early example of the West's predatory imperialism

Predatory imperialism? Hardly. Pope Urban II, who called for the First Crusade at the Council of Clermont in 1095, was calling for a defensive action—one that was long overdue. As he explained, he was calling for the Crusade because without any defensive action, "the faithful of God will be much more widely attacked" by the Turks and other Muslim forces. After admonishing his flock to keep peace among themselves, he turned their attention to the East:

For your brethren who live in the east are in urgent need of your help, and you must hasten to give them the aid which has often been promised them. For, as the most of you have heard, the Turks and Arabs have attacked them and have conquered the territory of Romania [the Greek empire] as far west as the shore of the Mediterranean and the Hellespont, which is called the Arm of St. George. They have occupied more and more of the lands of those Christians, and have overcome them in seven battles. They have killed and captured many, and have destroyed the churches and devastated the empire. If you permit them to continue thus for awhile with impunity, the faithful of God will be much more widely attacked by them. On this account I, or rather the Lord, beseech you as Christ's heralds to publish this everywhere and to persuade all people of whatever rank, foot-soldiers and knights, poor and rich, to carry aid promptly to those Christians and to destroy that vile race from the lands of our friends. . . . Moreover, Christ commands it.[17]

Note that the pope says nothing about conversion or conquest. A call to "destroy that vile race from the lands of our friends" falls harshly on modern ears; however, it was not an exhortation for mass extermination, but one to remove Islamic rule from lands that had been Christian. Another summary of the pope's speech at Clermont reports that Urban spoke of an "imminent peril threatening you and all the faithful which has brought us hither."

From the confines of Jerusalem and from the city of Constantinople a grievous report has gone forth and has repeatedly been brought to our ears; namely, that a race from the kingdom of the Persians, an accursed race, a race wholly alienated from God, "a generation that set not their heart aright and whose spirit was not steadfast with God," violently invaded the lands

Just Like Today: Defenders of Islam?

In Islamic law, jihad is obligatory whenever a Muslim territory is attacked: "When non-Muslims invade a Muslim country or near to one, . . . jihad is personally obligatory upon the inhabitants of that country, who must repel the non-Muslims with whatever they can."[18]

The call to jihad has occurred throughout the history of Islam. When the Hamdanid ruler Seyf al-Dawla waged annual jihad campaigns against the Byzantines in the mid-tenth century, Muslims came from far and wide to participate. They came because, in their view, the Byzantines were waging aggressive wars to seize Muslim lands. Later, during the First Crusade, a poet exhorted Muslims to respond: "Do you not owe an obligation to God and Islam, defending thereby young men and old? Respond to God! Woe to you! Respond!"[19] The venerable Islamic jurist most beloved of today's jihadists, Ibn Taymiyya (Taqi al-Din Ahmad Ibn Taymiyya, 1263–1328) considered jihad an absolute: "If the enemy wants to attack the Muslims, then repelling him becomes a duty for all those under attack and for the others in order to help them."[20]

Some other examples of calls to jihad during the last hundred years: In 1914, the Ottoman caliph Sultan Mehmet V issued a *fatwa* (religious ruling) calling for jihad at the outbreak of World War I; in 2003, a Chechen jihadist group announced: "When the enemy entered a territory, a city or a village where Muslims are living, then everybody is obligated to go to war;"[21] in 2003, the Islamic Center for Research at Al-Azhar University in Cairo issued a declaration: "It is in accordance with logic and with Islamic religious law that if the enemy raids the land of the Muslims, Jihad becomes an individual's commandment, applying to every Muslim man and woman, because our Muslim nation will be subject to a new Crusader invasion targeting the land, honor, belief, and homeland;"[22] and when Sheikh Omar Bakri Muhammad, the notorious London-based jihadist imam, said in late 2002, "when the enemy enters Muslim land, such as Palestine, Chechnya, Kosova [sic] or Kashmir," "all Muslims living within travelling distance of the aggression" must fight, with all possible support from Muslims worldwide.[23]

of those Christians and has depopulated them by pillage and fire. They have led away a part of the captives into their own country, and a part have they have killed by cruel tortures. They have either destroyed the churches of God or appropriated them for the rites of their own religion. They destroy the altars, after having defiled them with their uncleanness. . . . The

Just Like Today: Jihadists from all over

As they have done throughout history, Muslim warriors travel long distances in order to participate in the latest jihads. In the 1990s, the Balkans became a favored destination for veterans of the jihad wars in Afghanistan and Chechnya. A prominent jihad commander in Bosnia, Abu Abdel Aziz, explained that he went there after meeting with several Islamic authorities in Saudi Arabia. They "all support," he said, "the religious dictum that 'the fighting in Bosnia is a fight to make the word of Allah supreme and protect the chastity of Muslims.' It is because Allah said (in his holy book), 'Yet, if they ask you for succor against religious persecution, it is your duty to give [them] this succor.' (Lit. 'to succor them in religion,' Qur'an, al-Anfal, 8:72). It is then our (religious) duty to defend our Muslim brethren wherever they are, as long as they are persecuted because they are Muslims and not for any other reason."[24]

Before, during, and after the 2003 war in Iraq, jihadists streamed into that country from all over the world—including some unexpected places; a German security official noted in late 2003 that "since the end of the war, there has been a large movement of people motivated by Islamic extremism from Germany and the rest of Europe toward Iraq."[25]

kingdom of the Greeks is now dismembered by them and has been deprived of territory so vast in extent that it could be traversed in two months' time. . . . This royal city, however, situated at the center of the earth, is now held captive by the enemies of Christ and is subjected, by those who do not know God, to the worship the heathen. She seeks, therefore, and desires to be liberated and ceases not to implore you to come to her aid. From you especially she asks succor, because as we have already said, God has conferred upon you above all other nations great glory in arms.[26]

The pope's call invoked the Muslim destruction of the Church of the Holy Sepulcher: "Let the holy sepulcher of our Lord and Saviour, which is possessed by unclean nations, especially arouse you, and the holy places which are now treated with ignominy and irreverently polluted with the filth of the unclean."[27]

The Crusades came together as pilgrimages: Christians from Europe made their way to the Holy Land for religious purposes, with the intention to defend themselves if their way was blocked and they were attacked. Many took religious vows. Particularly at the outset, many soldiers left for the Holy Land—and most of the participants in this "People's Crusade" were unceremoniously massacred by the Turks in Western Asia Minor in August 1096.

PC Myth: The Crusades were fought by Westerners greedy for gain

Of course, not every Crusader's motives were pure. More than once, many fell from the high ideals of Christian pilgrims. But the PC dogma that the Crusades were unprovoked, imperialist actions against a peaceful, indigenous Muslim population is simply historically inaccurate and reflects distaste for Western civilization rather than genuine historical research.

Pope Urban didn't envision the Crusades as a chance for gain. He decreed that lands recovered from the Muslims would belong to Alexius Comnenus and the Byzantine Empire. The pope saw the Crusades as an act of sacrifice rather than profit.[28]

Crusading was, in fact, prohibitively expensive. Crusaders sold their property to raise money for their long journey to the Holy Land, and did so knowing they might not return.

A typical example of a Crusader was Godfrey of Bouillon, the Duke of Lower Lorraine, and one of the more prominent European lords who "took the cross" (as joining the Crusade was known). He sold off many properties in order to finance his trip, but he clearly planned to come home, rather than settle in the Middle East, because he did not give up his title or all his holdings.[29]

Recent studies of Crusaders' documents reveal that the vast majority of them were not "second sons" looking for a profit and estates in the Middle East. Most were, like Godfrey, lords of their own estates, men with a great deal to lose.[30] Certainly some Crusaders did very well for themselves after the First Crusade. Fulcher of Chartres writes, "Those who were poor there, here God makes rich. Those who had few coins, here possess countless besants; and those who had not had a villa, here, by the gift of God, already possess a city."[31] But most who did return to Europe came back with nothing material to show for their efforts.

PC Myth: The Crusades were fought to convert Muslims to Christianity by force

To hear some PC types tell it, the Crusaders swept into the Middle East, swords in hand, and set about killing every "infidel" they saw, except those they forced to convert to Christianity. But this is lurid, politically motivated fantasy. Glaringly absent from every report about Pope Urban's address at the Council of Claremont is any command to convert Muslims. The pope's only preoccupation is to defend Christian pilgrims and recapture Christian lands. It was not until over a hundred years after the First Crusade (in the thirteenth century) that European Christians made any organized attempt to convert Muslims to Christianity, when the Franciscans began missionary work among Muslims in lands held by the Crusaders. This effort was largely unsuccessful.

A Book You're Not Supposed to Read

The New Concise History of the Crusades by Thomas F. Madden; Lanham, MD: Rowman & Littlefield, 2005, is a briskly told page-turner that dispels innumerable PC myths about why the Crusades were fought, who fought them, and what happened during each one.

When the Crusaders were victorious and established kingdoms and principalities in the Middle East, they generally let the Muslims in their domains live in peace, practice their religion freely, build new mosques and schools, and maintain their own religious tribunals. Some have compared their status to that of the dhimmis in Muslim lands; they retained a certain measure of autonomy, but were subject to unfavorable taxation rates and other restrictions. It is likely that the Crusaders adopted some of the dhimmi laws already in place, but they did not subject Jews or Muslims to dress codes. So Jews and Muslims could avoid day-to-day discrimination and harassment.[32] This was the opposite of Muslim practice. The key difference is that the dhimma was never part of Christian doctrine and law, as it has been and remains part of Islam.

What's more, the Spanish Muslim Ibn Jubayr (1145–1217), who traversed the Mediterranean on his way to Mecca in the early 1180s, found that Muslims had it better in the lands controlled by the Crusaders than they did in Islamic lands. Those lands were more orderly and better managed than those under Muslim rule, so that even Muslims preferred to live in the Crusader realms:

> Upon leaving Tibnin (near Tyre), we passed through an unbroken skein of farms and villages whose lands were efficiently cultivated. The inhabitants were all Muslims, but they live in

comfort with the Franj [Franks, or Crusaders]—may God preserve them from temptation! Their dwellings belong to them and all their property is unmolested. All the regions controlled by the Franj in Syria are subject to this same system: the landed domains, villages, and farms have remained in the hands of the Muslims. Now, doubt invests the heart of a great number of these men when they compare their lot to that of their brothers living in Muslim territory. Indeed, the latter suffer from the injustice of their coreligionists, whereas the Franj act with equity.[33]

So much for the contention that the Crusaders were barbarians attacking a far superior and more advanced civilization.

Chapter 11

THE CRUSADES: MYTH AND REALITY

It is often said: "The Crusaders marched across Europe to the Middle East. Once there, they pillaged and murdered Muslim and Jewish men, women, and children indiscriminately, and forced the survivors to convert to Christianity. Awash in pools of blood, they established European proto-colonies in the Levant, inspiring and setting a pattern for legions of later colonialists. They were the setting for the world's first mass killings, and are a blot on the history of the Catholic Church, Europe, and Western civilization. So horrifying were they that Pope John Paul II ultimately apologized to the Islamic world for the Crusades."

Any truth?

No. Virtually every assertion in this paraphrase, though routinely made by numerous "experts," is wrong.

PC Myth: The Crusaders established European colonies in the Middle East

As the Crusaders made their way east in response to Pope Urban's call, their principal leaders met with Byzantine emperor Alexius Comnenus. He prevailed upon them to agree individually, in accord with Urban's wishes, that any lands they conquered would revert to the Byzantine Empire. The Crusaders changed their minds about this after the siege of Antioch in 1098. As the siege dragged on through the winter and Muslim

Guess what?

● The Crusades were *not* early manifestations of European colonialism in the Middle East.

● The Crusader massacre of Jews and Muslims in Jerusalem in 1099 was a terrible atrocity, but it was nothing unusual according to the rules of warfare of the time.

● The Crusades were not called in order to target Jews as well as Muslims.

armies advanced north from Jerusalem, the Crusaders waited for the Byzantine emperor to arrive with troops. But the emperor had received a report that the Crusaders' situation in Antioch was hopeless and turned back his forces. The Crusaders felt betrayed and became enraged. After they overcame immense odds and took Antioch, they renounced their agreements with Alexius and began to establish their own governments.

These were not, however, colonial arrangements. The Crusader states simply would not have been recognizable as colonies to someone familiar with Virginia, Australia, or the Dutch East Indies in later centuries. Broadly, a colony is a land that is ruled by a far-off power. But the Crusader states were not ruled from Western Europe; the governments they established did not answer to any Western power. Nor did the Crusader rulers siphon off the wealth of their lands and send it back to Europe. They had no economic arrangements with any European country. The Crusaders established their states in order to provide permanent protection for Christians in the Holy Land.

In fact, many Crusaders ceased to think of themselves as Europeans. The chronicler Fulcher of Chartres wrote:

> Consider, I pray, and reflect how in our time God has transferred the West into the East. For we who were Occidentals now have been made Orientals. He who was a Roman or a Frank is now a Galilaean, or an inhabitant of Palestine. One who was a citizen of Rheims or of Chartres now has been made a citizen of Tyre or of Antioch. We have already forgotten the places of our birth; already they have become unknown to many of us, or, at least, are unmentioned. Some already possess here homes and servants which they have received through inheritance. Some have taken wives not merely of their own people, but Syrians, or Armenians, or even Saracens who have received the grace of baptism. Some have with them father-in-law, or daughter-in-law, or son-in-law, or stepson, or step-father.

There are here, too, grandchildren and great-grandchildren. One cultivates vines, another the fields. The one and the other use mutually the speech and the idioms of the different languages. Different languages, now made common, become known to both races, and faith unites those whose forefathers were strangers. As it is written, "The lion and the ox shall eat straw together." Those who were strangers are now natives; and he who was a sojourner now has become a resident.[1]

At the same time, another feature of colonialism, large-scale emigration from the home country, did not materialize. No streams of settlers came from Europe to settle in the Crusader states.

PC Myth: The capture of Jerusalem was unique in medieval history and caused Muslim mistrust of the West

After a five-week siege, the Crusaders entered Jerusalem on July 15, 1099. An anonymous contemporary account by a Christian has seared what happened next into the memory of the world:

> One of our knights, Letholdus by name, climbed on to the wall of the city. When he reached the top, all the defenders of the city quickly fled along the walls and through the city. Our men followed and pursued them, killing and hacking, as far as the temple of Solomon, and there there was such a slaughter that our men were up to their ankles in the enemy's blood.
>
> The emir who commanded the tower of David surrendered to the Count [of St. Gilles] and opened the gate where pilgrims used to pay tribute. Entering the city, our pilgrims pursued and killed the Saracens up to the temple of Solomon. There the Saracens assembled and resisted fiercely all day, so that the whole temple flowed with their blood. At last the pagans

were overcome and our men seized many men and women in the temple, killing them or keeping them alive as they saw fit. On the roof of the temple there was a great crowd of pagans of both sexes, to whom Tancred and Gaston de Beert gave their banners [to provide them with protection]. Then the crusaders scattered throughout the city, seizing gold and silver, horses and mules, and houses full of all sorts of goods. Afterwards our men went rejoicing and weeping for joy to adore the sepulchre of our Saviour Jesus and there discharged their debt to Him.[2]

It is jarring to our modern sensibilities to read a positive account of such a wanton massacre; such is the difference between the attitudes and assumptions of those days and our own. Similarly, three principal Crusade leaders, Archbishop Daimbert; Godfrey, Duke of Bouillon; and Raymond, Count of Toulouse; boasted to Pope Paschal II in September 1099 about the Crusaders' Jerusalem exploits: "And if you desire to know what was done with the enemy who were found there, know that in Solomon's porch and in his temple our men rode in the blood of the Saracens up to the knees of their horses."[3] Significantly, Godfrey himself, one of the most respected Crusade leaders, did not participate in the slaughter; perhaps he was more aware than the rank-and-file soldiers of what a betrayal this behavior represented to the Crusaders' principles.

Balderic, a bishop and author of an early twelfth-century history of Jerusalem, reports that the Crusaders killed between twenty and thirty thousand people in the city.[4] That is likely exaggerated, but Muslim sources put the number even higher. Although the earliest Muslim sources do not specify a death count, Ibn al-Jawzi, writing about a hundred years after the event, says that the Crusaders "killed more than seventy thousand Muslims" in Jerusalem. Ibn al-Athir, a contemporary of Saladin, the Muslim leader who gained impressive victories over the Crusaders late in the twelfth century, offers the same number.[5] The fifteenth-century historian Ibn Taghribirdi records one hundred thousand. So the story of this massacre has grown over the centuries, to the point where a former president of the United States, Bill Clinton, recounted at a leading Catholic university, Georgetown, in November 2001, that the Crusaders murdered not just every Muslim warrior or even every Muslim male, but "every woman and child who was Muslim on the Temple mound" until the blood was running not just up to their ankles, as the Christian chronicler had it, but as Daimbert, Godfrey, and Raymond have boasted: "up to their knees."[6]

This atrocity, this outrage, was—we have been told time and again—the "starting point of a millennial hostility between Islam and the West."[7] It might be more accurate to say that it was the start of a millennium of anti-Western grievance mongering and propaganda. The Crusaders' sack of Jerusalem was a heinous crime—particularly in light of the religious and moral principles they professed to uphold. However, by the military standards of the day, it was not out of the ordinary. In those days, it was a generally accepted principle of warfare that if a city under siege resisted capture, it could be sacked, and if it did not resist, mercy would be shown. Some accounts say that the Crusaders promised the inhabitants of Jerusalem that they would be spared, but reneged on this promise. Others tell us that they did allow many Jews and Muslims to leave the city in safety. Count Raymond gave a personal guarantee of safety to the Fatimid governor of Jerusalem, Iftikar al-Daulah.[8] In the mind of a Crusader, when such guarantees were issued, those who remained in the city would have been more likely to be identified with the resistance—and their lives forfeited.[9]

And what about those ankle- or knee-deep rivers of blood? This was a rhetorical flourish. When the Christian chronicler and Crusade leaders boasted of this, everyone would have considered it an embellishment. In fact, such rivers were not even remotely possible. There weren't enough people in Jerusalem to bleed that much, even if its population had swelled with refugees from the surrounding regions. The fact that the sack of Jerusalem was not out of the ordinary probably accounts for the laconic nature of the earliest Muslim accounts of the incident. Around 1160, two Syrian chroniclers, al-'Azimi and Ibn al-Qalanisi, wrote separately of the sack. Neither one offered an estimate of the numbers killed. Al-'Azimi said only that the Crusaders "turned to Jerusalem and conquered it from the hands of the Egyptians. Godfrey took it. They burned the Church of the Jews." Ibn al-Qalanisi added a bit more detail: "The Franks stormed the town and gained possession of it. A number of the townsfolk fled to the sanctuary and a great host were killed. The Jews assembled in the synagogue, and the Franks burned it over their heads. The sanctuary was surrendered to them on guarantee of safety on 22 Sha'ban [July 14] of this year, and they destroyed the shrines and the tomb of Abraham."[10] It wasn't until later that Muslim writers realized the propaganda value of stressing (and inflating) the death totals.

In any event, it is a matter of record that Muslim armies frequently behaved in exactly the same way when entering a conquered city. This is not to excuse the Crusaders' conduct by pointing to similar incidents and suggesting that "everybody does it," as Islamic apologists frequently do today when confronted with the realities of modern jihad terrorism. One atrocity does not excuse another. But it does illustrate that the Crusaders' behavior in Jerusalem was consistent with that of other armies of the period—since all states subscribed to the same notions of siege and resistance.

Indeed, in 1148, Muslim commander Nur ed-Din did not hesitate to order the killing of every Christian in Aleppo. In 1268, when the jihad forces of the Mamluk sultan Baybars took Antioch from the Crusaders, Baybars was annoyed to find that the Crusader ruler, Count Bohemond VI, had already left the city. He wrote to Bohemond to make sure he knew what his men had done in Antioch:

You would have seen your knights prostrate beneath the horses' hooves, your houses stormed by pillagers and ransacked by looters, your wealth weighed by the quintal, your women sold four at a time and bought for a dinar of your own money! You would have seen the crosses in your churches smashed, the pages of the false Testaments scattered, the Patriarchs' tombs overturned. You would have seen your Muslim enemy trampling on the place where you celebrate the Mass, cutting the throats of monks, priests and deacons upon the altars, bringing sudden death to the Patriarchs and slavery to the royal princes. You would have seen fire running through your palaces, your dead burned in this world before going down to the fires of the next, your palace lying unrecognizable, the Church of St. Paul and that of the Cathedral of St. Peter pulled down and destroyed; then you would have said, "Would that I were dust, and that no letter had ever brought me such tidings!"[11]

Most notorious of all may be the jihadists' entry into Constantinople on May 29, 1453, when they—like the Crusaders in Jerusalem in 1099—finally broke through a prolonged resistance to their siege. Here the rivers of blood ran again, as historian Steven Runciman notes. The Muslim soldiers "slew everyone that they met in the streets, men, women, and children without discrimination. The blood ran in rivers down the steep streets from the heights of Petra toward the Golden Horn. But soon the lust for slaughter was assuaged. The soldiers realized that captives and precious objects would bring them greater profit."[12]

Like Crusaders, who violated the sanctuary of both synagogue and mosque, Muslims raided monasteries and convents, emptying them of their inhabitants, and plundered private houses. They entered the Hagia Sophia, which for nearly a thousand years had been the grandest church in Christendom. The faithful had gathered within its hallowed walls to pray during the city's last agony. The Muslims halted the celebration of Orthros (morning prayer), while the priests, according to legend, took the sacred vessels and disappeared into the cathedral's eastern wall, through which they shall return to complete the divine service one day. Muslim men then killed the elderly and weak and led the rest off into slavery.

When the slaughter and pillaging was finished, the Ottoman sultan Mehmet II ordered an Islamic scholar to mount the high pulpit of the Hagia Sophia and declare that there was no God but Allah, and Muhammad was his prophet. The magnificent old church was turned into a mosque; hundreds of other churches in Constantinople and elsewhere suffered the same fate. Millions of Christians joined the wretched ranks of the dhimmis; others were enslaved and many martyred.

PC Myth: The Muslim leader Saladin was more merciful and magnanimous than the Crusaders

One of the most famous figures of the Crusades is the Muslim warrior Saladin, who reunited much of the Islamic world and inflicted great damage on the Crusaders. In our age, Saladin has become the prototype of the tolerant, magnanimous Muslim warrior, historical "proof" of the nobility of Islam and even of its superiority to wicked, Western, colonialist Christianity. In *The Crusades Through Arab Eyes*, Amin Maalouf portrays the Crusaders as little more than savages, even gorging themselves on the flesh of those they have murdered. But Saladin! "He was always affable with visitors, insisting that they stay to eat, treating them with full honours, even if they were infidels, and satisfying all their requests. He could not bear to let someone who had come to him depart disappointed, and there were those who did not hesitate to take advantage of this quality. One day, during a truce with the Franj [Franks], the 'Brins,' lord of Antioch, arrived unexpectedly at Saladin's tent and asked him to return a district that the sultan had taken four years earlier. And he agreed!"[13] The lovable lug! If asked, he might have given away the entire Holy Land!

In one sense it's true: Saladin set out to conquer Jerusalem in 1187 because Crusaders under the command of Reynald of Chatillon were taking a page from the Prophet Muhammad's book and raiding caravans, in this case, Muslim caravans. The Christian rulers of Jerusalem ordered Reynald to stop because they knew that his actions endangered the very survival of their kingdom. Yet he persisted; finally, Saladin, who had

Just Like Today: The moral double standard

Bill Clinton suggested that the sack of Jerusalem in 1099 was the ultimate cause of the September 11 attacks. Yet the Muslims' sack of Constantinople in 1453 does not burn in anyone's memory. No president has pointed to it as the root cause of any modern-day terrorist acts. Indeed, it is less well known today than another sack of Constantinople: the one perpetrated by misguided Crusaders in 1204.

This is one illustration of the strange, unacknowledged moral double standard that PC types use when evaluating behavior by Westerners and non-Westerners: Any number of massacres and atrocities can be forgiven non-Western, non-white, non-Christian people, but misdeeds by Christian (or even post-Christian) Westerners remain seared in the world's collective memory. The Abu Ghraib prison scandals received horrified attention worldwide in 2004 and 2005, often from the same people who glossed over or ignored worse evils of Saddam Hussein, Osama bin Laden, and Hamas. It's a tacit admission of a fact that the PC establishment stoutly denies in every other case: Christianity does teach a higher moral standard than Islam, and more is expected not only of observant Christians, but of those who have imbibed these high principles by living in the societies molded by them.

been looking for a reason to go to war with the Christians, found one in Reynald's raids.[14]

A lot is made of the fact that when Saladin recaptured Jerusalem for the Muslims in October 1187, he treated the Christians with magnanimity—in sharp contrast to the behavior of the Crusaders in 1099. However, the real Saladin was not the proto-multiculturalist, early version of Nelson Mandela that he is made out to be today. When his forces decisively defeated the Crusaders at Hattin on July 4, 1187, he ordered the mass execution of his Christian opponents. According to his secretary, Imad ed-Din, Saladin "ordered that they should be beheaded [in accordance with Qur'an 47:4, "When you meet the unbelievers on the battlefield, strike their necks"], choosing to have them dead rather than in prison. With him was a whole band of scholars and Sufis and a certain number of devout men and ascetics; each begged to be allowed to kill one of them, and drew his sword and rolled back his sleeve. Saladin, his face joyful, was sitting on his dais; the unbelievers showed black despair."[15]

Also, when Saladin and his men entered Jerusalem later that year, their magnanimity was actually pragmatism. He had initially planned to put all the Christians in the city to death. However, when the Christian commander inside Jerusalem, Balian of Ibelin, threatened in turn to destroy the city and kill all the Muslims there before Saladin could get inside, Saladin relented—although once inside the city, he did enslave many of the Christians who could not afford to buy their way out.[16]

PC Myth: Crusades were called against Jews in addition to Muslims

It is unfortunately true that Crusaders targeted Jews on several occasions. Some groups of Crusaders allowed themselves to be diverted from the mission Pope Urban had given them. Stirred up by anti-Semitic preachers, one contingent of men who were making their way east for the First Crusade instead turned to terrorize Jews in Europe, massacring many. Count

Emicho of Leiningen and his followers advanced through the Rhineland, killing and plundering Jews in five German cities: Speyer, Worms, Mainz, Trier, and Cologne. Some of the bishops in those areas tried to prevent these massacres, and eventually Count Emicho and his followers met their end when he tried to extend his pogrom into Hungary. However, the damage was done; news of his exploits spread to the Middle East and led many Jews to ally with the Muslims and fight against the Crusaders when they arrived. Fifty years later, another group in the Rhineland, bound for the Second Crusade, began massacring Jews again.

Muhammad vs. Jesus

"Blessed are the merciful, for they shall obtain mercy.... For if you love those who love you, what reward have you? Do not even the tax collectors do the same? And if you salute only your brethren, what more are you doing than others?"

Jesus (Matthew 5:7, 46–7)

"Muhammad is Allah's Apostle. Those who follow him are ruthless to the unbelievers but merciful to one another."

Qur'an 48:29

All this was inexcusable, as well as being an incalculable error of judgment. The Crusaders would have been much wiser to see the Jews, fellow dhimmis, as their natural allies in the resistance to the Islamic jihad. The Muslims treated Jews and Christians more or less the same way: badly. It is unfortunate that neither group ever saw the other as a companion in the sufferings of dhimmitude and a fellow fighter against its oppressions. However, even today, eight centuries after the last Crusade, that kind of thinking is rare, so it is perhaps unfair to expect it of the Crusaders.

In any case, was the mistreatment of Jews a fundamental feature of the Crusades in general? Not according to the historical record. Pope Urban's call for the First Crusade at the Council of Claremont says nothing about Jews, and churchmen were Emicho's most formidable opponents. In fact, Urban himself condemned Emicho's attacks. Bernard of Clairvaux, one of the chief organizers of the Second Crusade, went to the Rhineland and

A Book You're Not Supposed to Read

The Crusades: The World's Debate by Hilaire Belloc; 1937, republished by Tan Books, 1992.

Belloc presents an arresting prophecy:

"In the major thing of all, Religion, we have fallen back and Islam has in the main preserved its soul....We are divided in the face of a Mohammedan world, divided in every way—divided by separate independent national rivalries, by the warring interests of possessions and dispossessed—and that division cannot be remedied because the cement which once held our civilization together, the Christian cement, has crumbled. Perhaps before [these lines] appear in print the rapidly developing situation in the Near East will have marked some notable change. Perhaps that change will be deferred, but change there will be, continuous and great. Nor does it seem probable that at the end of such a change, especially if the process be prolonged, Islam will be the loser."[19]

personally stopped the persecution of the Jews, declaring: "Ask anyone who knows the Sacred Scriptures what he finds foretold of the Jews in the Psalm. 'Not for their destruction do I pray,' it says."[17] Popes and bishops repeatedly called for the mistreatment of the Jews to end.

Yet even after the sack of Jerusalem and massacre of the Jews, during the Crusader period Jews in the Middle East generally preferred to live in areas controlled by the Franks, despite the undeniable hostility the Christians from Europe had for them.[18] They knew all too well that what was in store for them in Muslim lands was even worse.

PC Myth: The Crusades were bloodier than the Islamic jihads

The Crusaders massacred in Jerusalem; Saladin and his Muslim troops didn't. This has become emblematic of conventional wisdom regarding the Crusades: Yes, the Muslims conquered, but the inhabitants of the lands they seized welcomed their conquest. They were just and magnanimous toward religious minorities in those lands. The Crusaders, by contrast, were bloody, rapacious, and merciless.

We have shown this conventional wisdom to be completely false. Saladin only refrained from massacring the inhabitants of Jerusalem for pragmatic reasons, and Muslim conquerors easily matched and exceeded the cruelty of the Crusaders in Jerusalem on many occasions. The Muslim conquerors were not welcomed, but were tenaciously resisted and met resistance with extreme brutality. Once in power, they instituted severe repressive measures against religious minorities.

Did the pope apologize for the Crusades?

"Alright," you may say, "but despite everything you're saying, the Crusades are still a blot on the record of Western civilization. After all, even Pope John Paul II apologized for them. Why would he have done that if they weren't regarded negatively today?"

There is no doubt that the belief that Pope John Paul II apologized for the Crusades is widespread. When he died, the *Washington Post* reminded its readers "during his long reign, Pope John Paul II apologized to Muslims for the Crusades, to Jews for anti-Semitism, to Orthodox Christians for the sacking of Constantinople, to Italians for the Vatican's associations with the Mafia and to scientists for the persecution of Galileo."[20]

A broad list, but John Paul II never apologized for the Crusades. The closest he came was on March 12, 2000, the "Day of Pardon." During his homily, he said, "We cannot fail to recognize *the infidelities to the Gospel committed by some of our brethren*, especially during the second millennium. Let us ask pardon for the divisions which have occurred among Christians, for the violence some have used in the service of the truth and for the distrustful and hostile attitudes sometimes taken towards the followers of other religions."[21] This is hardly a clear apology for the Crusades. Anyway, given the true history of the Crusades, such an apology would not have been warranted.

The Crusaders do not deserve the opprobrium of the world, but—as we shall see—the world's gratitude.

Chapter 12

WHAT THE CRUSADES ACCOMPLISHED—AND WHAT THEY DIDN'T

There were many crusades, but when historians refer to "the Crusades" they generally mean a series of seven campaigns by troops from Western Europe against Muslims in the Holy Land. The First Crusade was called in 1095 and began in 1099; the Seventh Crusade ended in 1250. The last Crusader cities fell to the Muslims in 1291.

1. The First Crusade (1098–1099) was the most successful: The Crusaders captured Jerusalem and established several states in the Middle East.

2. The Second Crusade (1146–1148) was an unsuccessful— indeed, disastrous—attempt to recapture a Crusader state, Edessa, which had been conquered by the Muslims in 1144. At first, it was diverted to a successful operation to recapture Lisbon from the Muslims in 1147; then, when it finally arrived in the East, most of this army of Crusaders was crushed in Asia Minor in December 1147—before it ever reached the Holy Land.

3. The Third Crusade (1188–1192) was called by Pope Gregory VIII in the wake of Saladin's capture of Jerusalem and destruction of the Crusader forces at Hattin in 1187. This Crusade was dominated by strong personalities who were often at odds with one another: Emperor Frederick Barbarossa, King Richard the

Guess what?

- After the Crusades, the Muslims resumed their attempts to conquer Europe by jihad.

- Christians were as responsible as Muslims for the Islamic conquest of Eastern Europe: They made short-sighted and ultimately disastrous alliances with jihad forces.

- Western leaders who think non-Muslims can "win hearts and minds" among Islamic jihadists are similarly naïve and shortsighted.

Lionhearted of England, and King Philip of France. They did not manage to retake Jerusalem, but they did strengthen Outremer, the Crusader state that stretched along the coast of the Levant.

4. The Fourth Crusade (1201–1204) was disastrously diverted by a claimant to the Byzantine throne, who convinced the Crusaders to come to Constantinople to help him press his claim. The Crusaders ended up sacking the great city, shocking the Christian world. They established a Latin kingdom in Constantinople, earning the everlasting enmity of the Byzantines and further weakening the already fragile Byzantine Empire.

5. The Fifth Crusade (1218–1221) focused on Egypt. The Crusaders hoped that by breaking Egyptian power, they could recapture Jerusalem. They besieged Damietta, a city on the Nile Delta that was the gateway to Egypt's great cities, Cairo and Alexandria. As the siege dragged on, the Egyptian sultan al-Kamil grew increasingly worried and twice offered the Crusaders a restored kingdom of Jerusalem if they would just leave Egypt. The Crusaders refused and ultimately took Damietta; however, infighting and disunity ultimately doomed this Crusade. The Crusaders concluded an eight-year truce with al-Kamil and abandoned Damietta in exchange for the True Cross (a relic of the cross used to crucify Jesus), which Saladin had captured.

6. The Sixth Crusade (1228–1229) was essentially a continuation of the Fifth. After years of delaying his Crusader vow, the Holy Roman Emperor Frederick II was excommunicated by the pope; however, he still made his way to the Holy Land. The mere prospect of another Crusade seemed to frighten al-Kamil, who was also distracted by his attempt to conquer Damascus. He offered the Crusaders a ten-year truce, by which they would regain Jerusalem, Bethlehem, and Nazareth. However, Frederick

agreed to leave Jerusalem defenseless and allowed Muslims to remain there without restriction. This made it all but inevitable that the Muslims would eventually retake the city. This they did in 1244, killing large numbers of Christians and burning numerous churches, including the Church of the Holy Sepulcher.

7. The Seventh Crusade (1248–1250) was the best-equipped and best-organized of all the Crusades. It was led by the pious French king Louis IX. He again set his sights on Egypt, and captured Damietta. However, when attempting to take Cairo, the Crusaders were defeated at Mansourah; shortly thereafter, Louis himself was captured. He was ultimately ransomed and returned to Europe after a brief period in the Crusader center of Acre. He even attempted another crusade later, but accomplished little.

The Crusader kingdom lasted a few more decades. Antioch, where the Crusaders established their first kingdom in 1098, fell to the warriors of jihad in 1268. In 1291, the Muslims took Acre, devastating the Crusader army in the process. The rest of the Christian cities of Outremer fell soon afterward. There were other attempts in Europe to mount Crusades, but they came to little or nothing. The Crusader presence in the Middle East was no more, and would never be restored.

Making deals with the Mongols

Just as the last cities of Outremer were facing extinction, an offer of help came from a most unlikely source: Arghun, the Mongol ruler of Persia and client of the great conqueror Kublai Khan, sent an emissary to Europe in 1287. Arghun was not simply eccentric; the Mongols had been at odds with the Muslims for quite some time. In 1258, Hulagu Khan, the brother of Kublai Khan, toppled the Abbasid caliphate. Two years later, a Christian Mongol leader named Kitbuka seized Damascus and Aleppo for the

Mongols. Arghun wanted to raise interest among the Christian kings of Europe in making common cause to wrest the Holy Land from the Muslims once and for all. Arghun was a Buddhist; his best friend was the leader, or Catholicos, of the Nestorian Church, a Christian sect that had broken with the great Church of the Empire in 431. His vizier, meanwhile, was a Jew. Arghun seemed to hold every religion in high regard except Islam. He came to power in Persia by toppling the Muslim ruler Ahmed (a convert from Nestorian Christianity) after Ahmed made attempts to join forces with the Mamluks in Cairo.

Ahmed had written to Pope Honorius IV in 1285 to suggest an alliance, but when the pope did not answer, the Mongol ruler sent Rabban Sauma, a Nestorian Christian from deep in the heart of Central Asia, to Europe to discuss the matter personally with the pope and the Christian kings. Sawma's journey was one of the most remarkable in the ancient world: He started out from Trebizond and traveled all the way to Bordeaux to meet with King Edward I of England. Along the way, he met the Byzantine Emperor Andronicus in Constantinople (to whom he referred as "King Basileus," or King King, demonstrating that thirteenth-century translators weren't infallible); traveled to Naples, Rome (where Honorius IV had just died and a new pope had not yet been chosen), and Genoa; went on to Paris, where he dined with King Philip IV of France; met with Edward I in Bordeaux; and returned to Rome for a triumphant meeting with Pope Nicholas IV.

All the European leaders liked Rabban Sauma's proposal of a Mongol-Christian alliance to free the Holy Land. Philip IV offered to march to Jerusalem himself at the head of a Crusader army. Edward I was likewise enthusiastic: Sauma was proposing an alliance that the king himself had called for in the past. Pope Nicholas showered Sauma, Arghun, and the Nestorian Catholicos with gifts. But what none of these men, or anyone else in Europe, could decide was a date for this grand new Crusade. Their enthusiasm remained vague, their promises non-specific.

The crowned heads of Europe were too disunited and distracted with challenges at home to take up the Mongols' offer; perhaps they were also suspicious of a non-Christian king who wanted to wage war to liberate the Christian Holy Land. They may have feared that once they helped the wolf devour the Muslims, the wolf would turn on them. But in any case, it was an opportunity missed. Dissatisfied with the results of Rabban Sauma's journey, Arghun sent another emissary, Buscarel of Gisolf, to Europe in 1289. He asked Philip IV and Edward I for help, offering to take Jerusalem jointly with soldiers sent by the Christian kings; he would then hand the city over to the Crusaders. Edward's answer, which is the only one that survives, was polite but non-committal. Dismayed, Arghun tried yet again in 1291, but by then Outremer had fallen. By the time the emissaries returned, Arghun himself was dead.[1]

Certainly, if the pope and the Christian kings had concluded an alliance with Arghun, the Crusaders might have been able to retake Jerusalem and reestablish a significant presence in the Holy Land. This would probably have postponed, at the very least, the Muslim march into Eastern Europe that commenced with a fury in the century following the final destruction of Outremer. But the leaders of Europe were distracted and shortsighted, so preoccupied with relatively insignificant squabbles at home that they did not realize just how much was at stake. Had they fully recognized the ultimate goals of the jihad warriors, they almost certainly would have been more open to an alliance with Arghun.

But there was considerable evidence that they had no real understanding of those goals at all.

Making deals with the Muslims

The jihad was now a seven-hundred-year-old project that advanced with Muslim strength and grew quiescent with Muslim weakness, but was never abandoned or repudiated by any Muslim leader or sect. But that did not mean that they were unwilling to enter into agreements with the Christians. The English historian Matthew of Paris reported that in 1238, Muslim envoys visited France and England, hoping to gain support for a common action against the Mongols—a fact that opens a new perspective on the modern Muslim and PC view that the Crusaders were nothing more than "rapists" of Islamic land.[2]

With the end of Crusader activity in the Holy Land, the jihad gained new energy. Some of this new energy was handed to them by shortsighted Christians: In 1345, in one notorious instance, the Byzantine emperor John VI Cantacuzenus asked for help from the Turks in a dynastic dispute.

This was by no means the first time that Christians had concluded agreements with the Muslims. John VI was following ample precedent. One of the principal sources of enmity between Eastern and Western Christians during earlier Crusades was the Byzantines' willingness to conclude pacts with the enemies of Christianity. Alexius I Comnenus enraged the earliest Crusaders by engaging in negotiations with Egypt. Another Byzantine emperor, Manuel I Comnenus (1143–1180), likewise earned the contempt of the Crusaders for dealing with the Turks, and many blamed him for the disaster of the Second Crusade. Later, of course, Emperor Frederick II and other Crusaders entered into pacts with the warriors of jihad themselves. But according to Islamic law, Muslims may only conclude truces during jihad warfare with non-Muslims when they are in a position of weakness and need time to gather strength to fight again. Those who concluded agreements with the Crusaders did not lose sight of this principle and never entered into a pact that ultimately weakened the Muslims' position.

The invitation from John VI was a prime example of Christian shortsightedness. The Muslims arrived in Europe to help him, crossing over the Dardanelles in 1348 and occupying Gallipoli in 1354. In 1357, they captured the imposing Byzantine fortress of Adrianople. In 1359, Sultan Murad I founded the janissary corps, a crack force of young men who were seized from their Christian families as boys, enslaved, and forcibly converted to Islam. According to historian Godfrey Goodwin, "No child might be recruited who was converted to Islam other than by his own free will—if the choice between life and death may be called free will."[3]

The janissaries became the Ottoman Empire's most formidable warriors against Christianity. The collection of boys for this corps became an annual event in some places: Christian fathers were forced to appear in the town squares with their sons; the Muslims took the strongest and brightest young men, who never saw their homes again unless they happened to be part of a Muslim fighting force sent to that area.

Just Like Today: Winning hearts and minds

When a deadly tsunami hit South Asia in December 2004, Secretary of State Colin Powell expressed hope that the aid the United States was giving to countries hit by the tsunami would turn the tide of anti-American sentiment in the Muslim world.

However, it was more than a year and a half before Powell's statement that the South African mufti Ebrahim Desai, the imam of an "Ask the Imam" feature on a Muslim question-and-answer website, made a statement which, had Powell known of it, might have diminished his confidence in the religious effect of the aid. A questioner asked if the West should receive praise from Muslims for sending troops to Bosnia and condemning the killing of Muslims elsewhere. Desai's answer was brief: "In simple the Kuffaar [unbelievers] can never be trusted for any possible good they do. They have their own interest at heart."[4]

One man's opinion? Sure. But it is an opinion with deep roots in Islamic tradition, and it would therefore be naïve to dismiss it as simply Desai's own mean-spiritedness. The Qur'an tells believers not to "take for friends or helpers unbelievers rather than believers. If any do that, in nothing will there be help from Allah; except by way of precaution, that ye may guard yourselves from them" (Qur'an 3:28). Did John VI Cantacuzenes or Powell know of the existence of that verse?

Muhammad vs. Jesus

"The hour is coming when whoever kills you will think he is offering service to God."

Jesus (John 16:2)

"Fight those who believe not in Allah nor the Last Day, nor hold that forbidden which hath been forbidden by Allah and His Messenger, nor acknowledge the religion of Truth, even if they are of the People of the Book [Jews and Christians], until they pay the Jizya with willing submission, and feel themselves subdued."

Qur'an 9:29

The Muslims were in Europe to stay, and in the ensuing years they resumed the jihad. With Europe disunited and distracted, they were able to seize ever larger tracts of European land: Greece, Bulgaria, Serbia, Macedonia, Albania, Croatia, and more. On June 15, 1389, they engaged Christian forces in battle at Kosovo. On the night before the battle, the grand vizier opened the Koran at random seeking inspiration. His eyes fell upon the verse that said, "Oh Prophet, fight the hypocrites and unbelievers." "These Christian dogs are unbelievers and hypocrites," he said. "We fight them."[5]

Fight them he did, and prevailed against a stronger, larger force, making June 15 a day of mourning for Serbs ever after.

The advance into Eastern Europe was just beginning—arguably, it was the shortsightedness of John VI that had opened the door. What did John know about the motives and goals of the Turks? How aware was he of the jihad imperative that led them to accept his request for help and then, once in Europe, continue warfare against the Christians? Perhaps he thought that the theology and legal superstructure of jihad was just theory, and in reality Muslims were men with whom one could bargain. He might have thought that sophisticated men could reach an understanding across cultural and religious divides. He might even have thought that his invitation to the Muslims would show his goodwill, winning over their hearts and minds and stopping the assault against imperial domains.

He would not have been the first European statesman to think so, or the last.

The jihad in Eastern Europe

What did the Europeans do in the face of the Islamic onslaught? They continued to call Crusades, but instead of fighting over Jerusalem or Damietta, they found themselves fighting the jihadists ever closer to home and finally in Europe itself, with their backs increasingly against the wall. The kingdom of Jerusalem became the kingdom of Cyprus, whose king retained the title King of Jerusalem. But that title was now fiction. One king of Cyprus, Peter I (1359–1369), tried to gather support in Europe for a new Crusade, and actually seized Alexandria in 1365. But he had to withdraw after receiving no help from a Europe distracted by its internal problems. In 1426, Cyprus itself fell to the jihad of the Egyptian Mamluks.

The Crusaders were pushed relentlessly westward. A large Crusader force was defeated in Nicopolis, a town on the Danube, in 1395. All of Europe now lay open to the Turks, with virtually nothing standing in the way of their conquest of Rome, Paris, or even London. It looked as though the Muslims' attempt to conquer Europe was finally going to succeed. It had begun seven hundred years earlier, when the jihad armies first besieged Constantinople and entered Spain, and had been fueled over all those centuries by the theology and legal superstructure of jihad as mandated by the Qur'an and the words and deeds of the Prophet Muhammad. For the first time in over a thousand years, since before the Roman Emperor Constantine proclaimed himself a Christian and legalized Christianity, the smart money was on the complete disappearance of Christianity—and the relegation of virtually every Christian in the world to dhimmi status.

Help from an unlikely quarter

But then arose a most unlikely source of aid for Christendom: the Mongols. These were not the pagan Mongols of a century before, hoping to

A Book You're Not Supposed to Read

Hatred's Kingdom by Dore Gold; Washington, DC: Regnery, 2003, traces the history and development of the violent Wahhabi sect in Saudi Arabia. Gold's history demonstrates the foolhardiness of entering into lasting accords with Islamic states that regard bonds with any non-Muslim state not as genuine alliances between equals, but as temporary arrangements that are useful only as long as they strengthen the Muslims, and not a minute longer.

make common cause with the Christians against the Muslims. These Mongols were Muslims. Tamerlane ("Timur the Lame," 1336–1405), the bloody conqueror of Central Asia, was probably a member of the Naqshbandi Sufi sect of Islam.[6] This is noteworthy because the Sufis are often presented today as a peaceful, tolerant sect of Islam; however, their history is full of jihad (e.g., Chechnya).

A direct descendant of Genghis Khan, Tamerlane began to attack the Muslim lands of the Middle East. Faced with immense losses, the Mamluk and Ottoman Turkish jihadists were forced to divert their attention from Europe. But Tamerlane didn't appear all that interested in Europe either, although his victories were enough to compel the Byzantine Emperor John I to pay him tribute. After crushing the Ottomans at Ankara in 1402, Tamerlane turned his attention to China, leaving Muslims in the West too weak to continue the jihad against Europe. A Muslim had, in effect, saved Christendom.

The respite, however, was only temporary. The Ottoman sultan Murad II (1421–1451) set his sights on the jewel of Christendom, Constantinople. He laid siege to its land walls in 1422, but could not break through them. He didn't give up, though; he took Thessalonica in 1430 and blockaded Constantinople. Byzantine emperor John VIII appealed to Rome for help and even agreed to a reunion between the Catholic and Orthodox Churches on Western terms at the Council of Florence, hoping to persuade Westerners to come to the aid of the diminished Empire. Pope Eugenius IV duly called a Crusade, and an army assembled from the Eastern European states of Poland, Wallachia, and Hungary. However, the last hopes for Constantinople were dashed when Murad soundly defeated a Crusader army of thirty thousand at Varna, Hungary, in November 1444. Although in reaching Varna, the Crusaders had entered Turkish territory (the Muslims had conquered the town in 1391), it was a far cry from the days when the Crusaders established their own kingdoms in Antioch and Jerusalem and struck fear in the heart of the Sultan in Cairo.

After the disaster of Varna, it was only a matter of time before Constantinople fell. The end came on Tuesday, May 29, 1453. After weeks of resistance, the great city finally fell to an overwhelming Muslim force—which, as we have seen, brutally massacred those inside.

Even then the jihadist advance was not over. The Turks besieged Belgrade in 1456 and even tried to get to Rome, but at this point they were turned back. Finally, the tide was starting to change. The Muslims were turned away from Malta in the sixteenth century and failed in their first siege of Vienna in 1529. Later, they defeated the Poles in 1672 and seized large portions of the Ukraine, but they lost what they had gained fewer than ten years later. Finally, they besieged Vienna again, only to be turned back by Poland's King Jan III Sobieski and thirty thousand Polish hussars on a day that marks the high point of Muslim expansion in Europe: September 11, 1683.

The Crusades had accomplished nothing of what they had set out to do, and would go down in history as one of the West's most spectacular failures.

But were they really?

Chapter 13

WHAT IF THE CRUSADES HAD NEVER HAPPENED?

If the Crusades had never taken place, what kind of a world would we live in today? Would there be peace, understanding, and goodwill between Christians and Muslims? Would the Islamic world be free of the suspicion and often downright paranoia with which it regards so much that comes from the West? After all, Amin Maalouf says, "there can be no doubt that the schism between these two worlds dates from the Crusades, deeply felt by the Arabs, even today, as an act of rape."[1]

Or would the world be different in other, quite unexpected ways? Do the words "St. Peter's Mosque in Rome" mean anything to you?

PC Myth: The Crusades accomplished nothing

Faced with the Muslims' continued pursuit of jihad even into the heart of Europe, the Crusaders' inability to establish any lasting states or continued presence in the Holy Land, and the enmity that the Crusades undoubtedly sowed not only between Christians and Muslims, but between Eastern and Western Christians, most historians have deemed the Crusades a failure.

After all, their objective was to protect Christian pilgrims in the Holy Land. They originally established the Crusader states for this reason. But after the Second Crusade, those states were immensely diminished, and

Guess what?

◈ Although the Crusades failed in their primary objective, they played a key role in staving off the jihad conquest of Europe.

◈ The peoples who lived in the "tolerant, pluralistic Islamic societies" of old dwindled down to tiny, harassed, despised minorities.

◈ Islamic distaste for unbelievers is a constant of Islamic history and persists today.

A Book You're Not Supposed to Read

The splendidly titled *The Monks of Kublai Khan Emperor of China, or The History of the Life and Travels of Rabban Sawma, Envoy and Plenipotentiary of the Mongol Khans to the Kings of Europe, and Markos Who As Mar Yahbh-Allaha III Became Patriarch of the Nestorian Church in Asia*, translated by Sir E. A. Wallis Budge. First published in London in 1928, this book is long out of print and is just the sort of book that modern-day PC academics want to make sure stays that way. However, the Assyrian International News Agency has done a splendid service by making it available online at http://www.aina.org/books/mokk/mokk.htm#c72. The whole story is here, from the rise and glory of the Nestorians to the monstrous persecutions that destroyed Christianity in Central Asia. It also tells the story of the remarkable journey of Rabban Sawma, the emissary of the Mongol ruler Arghun, to Europe to try to get support from the European kings for a joint operation against the Muslims. It's indefatigably researched, elegant, and eloquently told.

remained so; after 1291, they were gone. Nor did the Crusaders prevent Islamic warriors from crossing into Europe.

However, it is significant that the level of Islamic adventurism in Europe dropped off significantly during the era of the Crusades. The conquest of Spain, the Middle East, and North Africa, as well as the first siege of Constantinople, all took place well before the First Crusade. The battles of Kosovo and Varna, which heralded a resurgent Islamic expansionism in Eastern Europe, took place after the collapse of the last Crusader holdings in the Middle East.

So what did the Crusades accomplish? They bought Europe time—time that might have meant the difference between her demise and dhimmitude and her rise and return to glory. If Godfrey of Bouillon, Richard the Lionhearted, and countless others hadn't risked their lives to uphold the honor of Christ and His Church thousands of miles from home, the jihadists would almost certainly have swept across Europe much sooner. Not only did the Crusader armies keep them tied down at a crucial period, fighting for Antioch and Ascalon instead of Varna and Vienna, they also brought together armies that would not have existed otherwise. Pope Urban's call united men around a cause; had that cause not existed or been publicized throughout Europe, many of these men would not have been warriors at all. They would have been ill-equipped to repel a Muslim invasion of their homeland.

The Crusades, then, were the ultimate reason why Edward Gibbon's vision of "the interpretation of the Koran" being "taught in the schools of Oxford" did not come true.

This is not a small matter. It is from Christian Europe, after all, no matter how reluctant the PC establishment is to acknowledge it, that most philosophical and scientific exploration, as well as technological advancement, have sprung. We have already seen one key reason why science developed in the Christian world rather than the Muslim world: Christians believed in a coherent and consistent universe governed by a good God; Muslims believed in a universe governed by a God whose will was so absolute as to preclude coherence and consistency.

But the implications of this all-important philosophical difference could not have worked themselves out without freedom. That freedom was not available to Christians or any other non-Muslims who had the misfortune to live under Muslim rule. In fact, any people who came under Muslim rule throughout history were ultimately reduced—no matter how extensive their numbers and grand their achievements before the Muslim conquest— to the status of a tiny and culturally derivative minority. Of course, few con- quered peoples have ever escaped this fate. The only people who have escaped Muslim dhimmitude have been those who were successful in resisting Islamic jihad: the Christians of Europe and the Hindus of India.

Others were not so fortunate.

Case study: The Zoroastrians

Would it really have been so bad if the Muslims had conquered Europe? After all, the Christians would still have been able to practice their reli- gion. They would just have had to put up with a little discrimination, right?

Although "a little discrimination" is all that most Islamic apologists will acknowledge about dhimmitude, the long-term effects of the dhimma were much more damaging for non-Muslims. Even centuries after the Muslim conquest of Egypt, the Coptic Christians maintained an overwhelming majority there. Yet today the Copts amount to just 10 percent, or less, of the Egyptian population.

It's the same story with every non-Muslim group that has fallen completely under Islamic rule.

The Zoroastrians, or Parsis, are followers of the Persian priest and prophet Zoroaster, or Zarathustra (628–551 B.C.). Before the advent of Islam, Zoroastrianism was for a long period the official religion of Persia (modern-day Iran), and was the dominant religion when the Persian Empire spanned from the Aegean Sea to the Indus River. Zoroastrians were commonly found from Persia to China. But after the Muslim conquest of Persia, Zoroastrians were given dhimmi status and subjected to cruel persecutions, which often included forced conversions. Many fled to India to escape Muslim rule, only to fall prey to the warriors of jihad again when the Muslims started to advance into India.

The suffering of the Zoroastrians under Islam was strikingly similar to that of Christians and Jews under Islam farther to the West, and it continued well into modern times (even to this very day under the Iranian mullahocracy). In 1905, a missionary named Napier Malcolm published a book in which he related his adventures among the Zoroastrians in the Persian town of Yezd.

> Up to 1895 no Parsi (Zoroastrian) was allowed to carry an umbrella. Even during the time that I was in Yezd they could not carry one in town. Up to 1895 there was a strong prohibition upon eye-glasses and spectacles; up to 1885 they were prevented from wearing rings; their girdles had to be made of rough canvas, but after 1885 any white material was permitted.

Up to 1896 the Parsis were obliged to twist their turbans instead of folding them. Up to 1898 only brown, grey, and yellow were allowed for the *qaba* [outer coat] or *arkhaluq* [under coat] (body garments), but after that all colors were permitted except blue, black, bright red, or green. There was also a prohibition against white stockings, and up to about 1880 the Parsis had to wear a special kind of peculiarly hideous shoe with a broad, turned-up toe. Up to 1885 they had to wear a torn cap. Up to 1880 they had to wear tight knickers, self-colored, instead of trousers. Up to 1891 all Zoroastrians had to walk in town, and even in the desert they had to dismount if they met a Mussulman of any rank whatsoever. During the time that I was in Yezd they were allowed to ride in the desert, and only had to dismount if they met a big Mussulman. There were other similar dress restrictions too numerous and trifling to mention.

Then the houses of both the Parsis and the Jews, with the surrounding walls, had to be built so low that the top could be reached by a Mussulman with his hand extended; they might, however, dig down below the level of the road.... Up to about 1860 Parsis could not engage in trade. They used to hide things in their cellar rooms, and sell them secretly. They can now trade in the caravanserais or hostelries, but not in the bazaars, nor may they trade in linen drapery. Up to 1870 they were not permitted to have a school for their children.

The amount of the *jaziya*, or tax upon infidels, differed according to the wealth of the individual Parsi, but it was never less than two *tomans* [10,000 dinars]. A *toman* is now worth about three shillings and eight pence, but it used to be worth much more. Even now, when money has much depreciated, it represents a laborer's wage for ten days. The money must be paid on the spot, when the *farrash* [literally, a carpet sweeper. Really a servant, chiefly outdoor], who was acting as collector, met the man. The farrash was at liberty to do what he liked when collecting the jaziya. The man was not even allowed to go home and fetch the money, but was beaten at once until it was given. About 1865 a farrash collecting this tax tied a man to a dog, and gave a blow to each in turn.

About 1891 a mujtahid caught a Zoroastrian merchant wearing white stockings in one of the public squares of the town. He ordered the man to be beaten and the stockings taken off. About 1860 a man of seventy went to the bazaars in white trousers of rough canvas. They hit him about a good deal, took off his trousers, and sent him home with them under his arm. Sometimes Parsis would be made to stand on one leg in a mujtahid's house until they consented to pay a considerable sum of money.[2]

What is the effect of being made to live this way over a long period? The answer is in the numbers: After nearly 1,400 years of living as dhimmis and experiencing the true nature of Islamic tolerance, Zoroastrians today make up less than 2 percent of the population of Iran (and even less than that in India, where they fled for refuge). In Afghanistan, where Zoroastrianism also once thrived, Zoroastrians today are virtually nonexistent. This is no surprise: Conversion to Islam was often the only way these persecuted people could have any hope of living a decent life.

If the Crusaders had not held off the Muslims, and Islamic jihads had ultimately finished off Christendom, would Christians in Europe have become a tiny minority, like their coreligionists in the Middle East (where Christianity was once the dominant religion) and the Zoroastrians? Would the achievements of European Christian civilization be treated no better than trash, as Islamic societies generally tend to regard the "pre-Islamic period of ignorance" in their histories?

Just Like Today:
Sistani equates unbelievers with excrement

The distaste that Muslims have for unbelievers, who are called the "vilest of creatures" in the Qur'an (98:6), is not a thing of the past. The Iraqi Shi'ite leader Grand Ayatollah Sayyid Ali Husayni Sistani, who has been hailed by many in the West as a reformer, a moderate, and a hope for democracy in Iraq and the Middle East at large, makes it quite clear in his religious rulings that the Islamic contempt for unbelievers is still very much in effect. This is the perspective that caused the Zoroastrians to dwindle from a vibrant majority to a tiny and despised minority. Among Sistani's voluminous rulings on all manner of questions concerning Islamic law is this illuminating little list:

The following ten things are essentially najis [unclean]:

1. Urine
2. Fæces
3. Semen
4. Dead body
5. Blood
6. Dog
7. Pig
8. Kafir [unbeliever]
9. Alcoholic liquors
10. The sweat of an animal who persistently eats najasat [i.e., unclean things].[3]

Sistani adds, "the entire body of a Kafir, including his hair and nails, and all liquid substances of his body, are najis."

Double standard alert: Sistani is respected throughout the Western world. But imagine the international outcry if, say, Jerry Falwell said that non-Christians were on the level of pigs, feces, and dog sweat.

Would the ideas of the equality of rights and dignity for all people, which grew out of Christianity and which conflict with Islamic law in numerous ways, be known today in Europe or the Americas?

Case study: The Assyrians

It's the same story with the Assyrian Church of the East. This is the ancient Church of Edessa, the city that was to become the center of the first Latin kingdom established by the Crusaders. In the fourth and fifth centuries, this church's ties with churches farther to the West grew

Just Like Today: Christian persecution in Iraq

In 775, the seat of the Assyrian Church was moved from the Persian city of Seleucia-Ctesiphon to Baghdad, and there it has been ever since. However, the increasingly unfavorable situation for Christians in the Middle East today, with the resurgence of jihadist Islam, has led the current Catholicos, Mar Dinkha IV, to live in Chicago since 1980. Patriarch Emmanuel Delly, leader of the Chaldean Catholics (a group of Assyrians who restored communion with the Church of Rome centuries ago), has remained in Baghdad—only to see jihad terrorists target Christians for special persecution all over Iraq after the fall of Saddam Hussein. Saddam's government was relatively secular; jihadists hope to ultimately establish a government that will follow Sharia rules more rigorously. Christians who operate liquor stores have therefore been targeted, in line with dhimmi laws forbidding Christians to "display wine" or sell it in places where Muslims may buy it.[4] Christian women have been threatened to wear hijab, the Islamic head covering—or else.[5] Many Christians have been killed, and thousands have fled the country. In September 2004, Iraqi columnist Majid Aziza observed that "it is difficult to recall a period in which Christian Arabs were in greater danger than today."[6]

Considering Tamerlane, that is saying a great deal.

increasingly strained, until in 424 the Church of the East finally declared in a synod that its leader, the Catholicos of Seleucia-Ctesiphon (the Persian capital), was not subject to the churches of Rome or Antioch, and was equal to them in authority. Later, the Assyrians adopted the view of Christ articulated by Nestorius, patriarch of Constantinople, who had been deposed as a heretic by the third Ecumenical Council in Ephesus in 431. This further alienated the Assyrians from both Byzantine and Latin Christians. After 424, the Assyrians had little or no contact with the great Churches of Constantinople and Rome for centuries.

During those centuries, the Assyrians proved to be some of the most energetic missionaries Christianity has ever known. At one point in time, the Nestorian Church stretched all the way from the Mediterranean to the Pacific Ocean. Nestorian Christians could be found all across Central Asia, as well as in the Byzantine Empire, and particularly in the Middle East and Egypt. At their height, the Assyrians had metropolitan sees in Azerbaijan, Syria, Jerusalem, Beijing, Tibet, India, Samarkand, Edessa, and Arabia (at Sana in Yemen), as well as churches from Aden to Bombay and Shanghai. The Nestorian missionary Alopen took the Gospel into China in 635; the first church in China was completed three years later. By the eighth century, there were enough Nestorians in China to establish several dioceses there; one Chinese emperor called Christianity "the luminous doctrine" and fostered its growth.

However, storm clouds were forming on the horizon. Late in the seventh century, the caliph Muawiya II (683–684) began a persecution and destroyed many churches after the Catholicos refused his demand for gold. The persecution continued under the caliph Abd al-Malik (685–705). The Abbasid caliph al-Mahdi (775–786) noticed that the Assyrians had built new churches since the Muslim conquest, in violation of dhimmi laws; he ordered them destroyed. He apparently thought that the Christians had violated the terms of the dhimma, the contract of protection; five thousand Christians in Syria were given the choice of conversion to Islam or death. Al-Mahdi's successor, Harun al-Rashid (786–809), ordered the destruction of still more churches. Half a century later, the caliph al-Mutawakkil (847–861) began an active persecution of the Church. Rioters and plundering mobs targeted Christians in Baghdad and its environs several times during the ninth and tenth centuries. Many of the churches destroyed and Christians victimized were Assyrian. Meanwhile, in China, a new emperor initiated a persecution so fierce that by 981 Nestorian missionaries visiting China found an utterly decimated Church. Nonetheless, the Assyrian Church continued to attract large numbers of converts among the Turks and others and maintained a presence in China; late in the thirteenth century, a Nestorian served as governor of China's Gansu province.

Assyrians suffered again when Crusader Antioch fell to the Muslims in 1268. Many Assyrians were enslaved and their churches destroyed; an Assyrian bishop was stoned and his body displayed on the city gates as a warning to the Christians. In other attacks by Arabs, Kurds, and Mongols during the twelfth and thirteenth centuries, untold numbers of Assyrians were killed or enslaved. But the worst came from the Mongol Tamerlane, a dedicated Muslim who conducted furious jihad campaigns against the Nestorians and devastated their cities and churches. It was full-blown war against the Assyrian Christians: Tamerlane offered them conversion to Islam, dhimmitude, or death. By 1400, the vast Nestorian domains were no more; Christianity had almost completely died out in Persia, Central Asia, and China.[7]

Muhammad vs. Jesus

"And you will be hated by all for my name's sake. But he who endures to the end will be saved."

Jesus (Mark 13:13)

"There is for you an excellent example to follow in Abraham and those with him, when they said to their people: 'We are clear of you and of whatever ye worship besides Allah: we have rejected you, and there has arisen, between us and you, enmity and hatred for ever, unless ye believe in Allah and Him alone.'"

Qur'an 60:4

After this, virtually all Nestorians lived as dhimmis under Muslim rule. And like the Zoroastrians, their community dwindled down to a tiny remnant under the relentless weight of this institutionalized injustice.

If the Christians in Europe had been subjected to the same fate, it is distinctly possible that the world might never have known the works of Dante Alighieri, or Michelangelo, or Leonardo da Vinci, or Mozart, or Bach. It is likely that there would never have been an El Greco, or a Giotto, or an Olivier Messaien. A community that must expend all its energy just to survive does not easily pursue art and music.

The Crusades may have made the full flowering of European civilization possible.

Chapter 14

ISLAM AND CHRISTIANITY: EQUIVALENT TRADITIONS?

"It's not like a stupid Hollywood movie," said French actress Eva Green about English director Sir Ridley Scott's Crusades flick, *Kingdom of Heaven.*

That's true. It's, like, a stupid English movie.

"Muslims," gushed the *New York Times* after an advance showing of the new blockbuster, "are portrayed as bent on coexistence until Christian extremists ruin everything. And even when the Christians are defeated, the Muslims give them safe conduct to return to Europe." Sir Ridley, according to the *Times*, "said he hoped to demonstrate that Christians, Muslims and Jews could live together in harmony—if only fanaticism were kept at bay." Or, as Green put it, the movie is intended to move people "to be more tolerant, more open towards the Arab people."[1]

By now it should be clear: The idea that Muslims were "bent on coexistence" with non-Muslims until the Crusaders arrived is historically inaccurate—unless by "coexistence" Ridley Scott means the coexistence of oppressor and oppressed that was the dhimma. Both he and Eva Green make the PC motivations behind this movie clear: to show that what interferes with peaceful coexistence between Muslims and non-Muslims is "fanaticism," not any element in a religious tradition. The film is also intended to make us intolerant racist Westerners nicer to Arabs.

Guess what?

⬥ Most modern-day presentations of the Crusades are politically motivated, ahistorical nonsense.

⬥ The problem the world faces today is not generalized "religious fundamentalism"—it is Islamic jihad.

⬥ We will not be able to resist jihad without recovering pride in Western civilization.

But the movie is just one part of a much larger campaign to convince Westerners that Islamic civilization is equal or superior to Western civilization.

The whitewash of *Kingdom of Heaven*

Kingdom of Heaven is a classic cowboys-and-Indians story in which the Muslims are noble and heroic and the Christians are venal and violent. The script is heavy on modern-day PC clichés and fantasies of Islamic tolerance; brushing aside dhimmi laws and attitudes (of which Ridley Scott has most likely never heard), it invents a peace-and-tolerance group called the "Brotherhood of Muslims, Jews and Christians." But of course, the Christians spoiled everything. A publicist for the film explained, "They were working together. It was a strong bond until the Knights Templar caused friction between them." Ah yes, those nasty "Christian extremists."

Kingdom of Heaven was made for those who believe that all the trouble between the Islamic world and the West has been caused by Western imperialism, racism, and colonialism, and that the glorious paradigm of Islamic tolerance, which was once a beacon to the world, could be reestablished if only the wicked white men of America and Europe would be more tolerant. Ridley Scott and his team arranged advance screenings for groups like the Council on American-Islamic Relations, making sure that sensitive Muslim feelings were not hurt. It is a dream movie for the PC establishment in every way except one: It isn't true.

Professor Jonathan Riley-Smith, author of *A Short History of the Crusades* and one of the world's leading historians of the period, called the movie "rubbish," explaining that "it's not historically accurate at all" as it "depicts the Muslims as sophisticated and civilised, and the Crusaders are all brutes and barbarians. It has nothing to do with reality." Oh, and "there was never a confraternity of Muslims, Jews and Christians. That is utter nonsense."

Bertrand Russell on Islam:

"Bolshevism combines the characteristics of the French Revolution with those of the rise of Islam. Marx has taught that Communism is fatally predestined to come about; this produces a state of mind not unlike that of the early successors of Mahommet. Among religions, Bolshevism is to be reckoned with Mohammedanism rather than with Christianity and Buddhism. Christianity and Buddhism are primarily personal religions, with mystical doctrines and a love of contemplation. Mohammedanism and Bolshevism are practical, social, unspiritual, concerned to win the empire of this world."

Professor Jonathan Philips, author of *The Fourth Crusade and the Sack of Constantinople*, also dismissed the idea of the film as a true depiction of history and took issue with its portrayal of the Crusader Knights Templar as villains: "The Templars as 'baddies' is only sustainable from the Muslim perspective, and 'baddies' is the wrong way to show it anyway. They are the biggest threat to the Muslims and many end up being killed because their sworn vocation is to defend the Holy Land."[2] Saladin is, according to a film publicist, a "hero of the piece." No mention, of course, is made of his massacres at Hattin, or his plans for more of the same in Jerusalem.

Yet despite *Kingdom of Heaven*'s numerous whitewashes of history and strenuous efforts to portray the Muslims of the Crusader era in a favorable light, Islamic apologist Khaled Abou El Fadl, a professor of Islamic law at the University of California, is in a froth about the film: "In my view," he raged, "it is inevitable—I'm willing to risk my reputation on this—that after this movie is released there will be hate crimes committed directly because of it. People will go see it on a weekend and decide to teach some turbanhead a lesson." Of course, this is less an indictment of the film than of the American people.

In any event, *Kingdom of Heaven* cost over $150 million to make, features an all-star cast, and is being touted as "a fascinating history lesson."

Fascinating, maybe—but only as evidence of the lengths to which modern Westerners are willing to go to delude themselves.

PC Myth: The problem the world faces today is religious fundamentalism

Is every religious tradition equally capable of giving rise to violence? This notion, widespread as it is, would have a lot more credibility if Pat Robertson and Jerry Falwell were writing articles defending the stoning of adulterers (as did the Switzerland-based Muslim writer Hani Ramadan, who published an article in the French journal *Le Monde* in September 2002 doing just that), or calling for the killing of blasphemers (blasphemy is a capital offense in Pakistan and elsewhere in the Islamic world), or flying planes into the iconic buildings of those they considered enemies.[3]

Muhammad vs. Jesus

"And when those who were about him saw what would follow, they said, 'Lord, shall we strike with the sword?' And one of them struck the slave of the high priest and cut off his right ear. But Jesus said, 'No more of this!' And he touched his ear and healed him."

Jesus (Luke 22:49–51)

"Narrated Abu Qilaba: Anas said, 'Some people of 'Ukl or 'Uraina tribe came to Medina and its climate did not suit them. After they became healthy, they killed the shepherd of the Prophet and drove away all the camels. The news reached the Prophet early in the morning and he sent (men) in their pursuit and they were captured and brought at noon. He then ordered to cut their hands and feet (and it was done), and their eyes were branded with heated pieces of iron. They were put in Al-Harra and when they asked for water, no water was given to them.' Abu Qilaba added, 'Those people committed theft, murder, became infidels after embracing Islam and fought against Allah and His Messenger.'"[4]

That evangelical Christians do not commit these acts is one clear indication that not all "fundamentalisms" are equivalent. Contrary to the deconstructionist views that prevail on college campuses today, religions are not simply raw material that can be fashioned into absolutely anything by believers. There is considerable overlap in the behavior of religious people in all traditions. For example, they pray, meet together, and perform certain rituals. Sometimes they even commit violence in the name of their religion. But the frequency and commonality of such acts of violence—and how close they are to each religion's mainstream—is determined to a great degree by the actual teachings of each religion. Islamic apologists like to point to Timothy McVeigh and Eric Rudolph as examples of Christian terrorists, but there are three reasons why McVeigh and Rudolph are not equivalent to bin Laden and Zarqawi:

- They did not even attempt to justify their actions by reference to Christian Scripture or tradition.
- They were not acting on mainstream Christian teachings.
- There are not large Christian groups around the world dedicated to implementing the same teachings.

The difference between Osama bin Laden and Eric Rudolph is the difference between aberrant acts and aberrant teachings. Any human being with a belief system can do abominable things. But abominable acts are more likely to come in greater numbers and frequency when they are encouraged and perpetuated by religious texts and those who teach from them.

But surely you're not saying that Islam is the problem?

What is the alternative to the Ridley Scott view that "fanaticism" is causing all our troubles today? It's a view that PC types just can't understand: The problem is within Islam and will not go away, or be neutralized, until this fact is recognized.

To say that the problem is within Islam is not to say that every Muslim is the problem. As we have seen, many who identify themselves as Muslims have only a glancing acquaintance with and interest in what Islam teaches. No, to admit that global jihadist violence indicates a problem with Islam is simply to be honest: There are groups around the world that believe that it is their responsibility before God to wage war against non-Muslims and impose Islamic law, first on Muslim states and then on non-Muslim states. This is a core motivation behind terrorist violence today, and it is rooted in the teachings of the Qur'an and Sunna (Islamic tradition).

Some analysts fear that if Western authorities begin to acknowledge that America's foe in the War on Terror is not a bunch of hijackers of Islam, but people who are working from core Islamic teachings, we will soon be embroiled in a war with the entire Islamic world. This will certainly make it harder to perpetuate the sham alliances that now exist with the Saudis, the Pakistanis, and the Egyptians. But it would also allow the United States to call those putative allies to account for their allegiance to the global jihad and to give real substance to President George W. Bush's post–September 11 announcement to the world that "you're either with the terrorists or with us."

Others have shied away from admitting the deep crisis in Islam today on the pretext that it will demoralize and anger moderate Muslims. If they are genuine moderates, there is no reason why this should occur. No problem can be solved unless its source is identified. A doctor who treats persistent headaches caused by brain tumors with aspirin will not escape malpractice suits for long. If any moderate Islam project is to succeed, it will only do so by identifying the elements in Islam that give rise to violence and terrorism, and working in whatever way possible to change Muslims' understanding of those elements so that jihadist recruiters can no longer convince young men to join them by appealing to their desire to live out "pure Islam."

Whether moderate Muslims can actually succeed in changing millions of Muslims' understanding of Islam is an open question. But it has no chance whatsoever of happening unless they acknowledge why Islam creates people like bin Laden and Zarqawi.

That makes sense. Why is it so hard for people to accept?

Part of the reason why the PC establishment finds this so hard to accept is because, in their simplistic and reductionist view of the world, Westerners are "white" and Muslims are "brown." The brown peoples of the world, goes the PC myth, cannot be guilty of wrongdoing; they are forever the wronged and eternal victims. Any violence they commit is a reaction to the egregious provocations of the white man.

The most outrageous example of this may be radical lawyer Lynne Stewart, who was convicted in February 2005 of smuggling messages for the jailed Sheikh Omar Abdel Rahman, the mastermind of the 1993 World Trade Center bombing. Why did Stewart become an errand girl for bloodthirsty jihad terrorists? She explained, "To rid ourselves of the entrenched, voracious type of capitalism that is in this country that perpetuates sexism and racism, I don't think that can come nonviolently."[5] How did Stewart get the idea that Omar Abdel Rahman, a traditionalist Muslim who no doubt believes that women exist to serve men and that disobedient ones should be beaten (as per Qur'an 4:34), was a champion of the fight against sexism and racism? Well, he's fighting the "white man," isn't he?

Recovering pride in Western civilization

"Look, Dr. Yeagley, I don't see anything about my culture to be proud of. It's all nothing. My race is just nothing.... Look at your culture. Look at

American Indian tradition. Now I think that's really great. You have something to be proud of. My culture is nothing."[6]

A white American student, "Rachel," spoke these words to American Indian professor Dr. David Yeagley in 2001.

Clearly Rachel had imbibed deeply of the mindset Jesse Jackson memorably articulated in 1985: "Hey! Hey! Ho! Ho! Western Civ has got to go!" And it is virtually certain that she considers the Crusaders to have been the ultimate Dead White Males, and the Crusades to be an inexcusable exercise in Western imperialism, racism, and probably genocide. If she attended a school with "Crusaders" as its mascot, she would have been among the first to want it changed. The way the Crusades are presented in most schools these days, that's perfectly understandable. But most of what the average student today knows about the Crusades, and other topics like them, is false. Those who teach such falsehoods have a vested interest in creating Americans who speak like Rachel. She believes all these falsehoods due to decades of anti-American, anti-Western, and anti-Christian conditioning in our schools and universities.

Why the truth must be told

This is why the truth must be told about the Crusades and other elements of the historical interaction between Christianity and Islam. Americans and Europeans—as well as Christians in the Middle East and elsewhere—need to stop apologizing for past sins and recall past heroism, and recognize what Judeo-Christian civilization has brought to the world. We must look honestly at Islam and Christianity and recognize how they differ. PC censors must no longer be allowed to make it taboo to note that although human nature is everywhere the same, and people have justified violence in the name of every faith, religions are not the same.

Christianity is at the heart of Western civilization. It has formed who we are as Americans, and influenced Europeans and others around the globe for even longer. Like it or not, it has even formed those who reject the Christian faith. Christianity also shares key moral principles with Judaism—principles that pervade the West but do *not* universally carry over into Islam. These principles are the fountain from which modern ethicists have drawn the concept of universal human rights—the foundation of Western secular culture.

Yeagley observes, "The Cheyenne people have a saying: A nation is never conquered until the hearts of its women are on the ground.... When Rachel denounced her people, she did it with the serene self-confidence

A Book You're Not Supposed to Read

How the Catholic Church Built Western Civilization by Thomas E. Woods, Jr.; Washington, DC: Regnery, 2005. Here is a book that everyone in the Western world—non-Catholic as well as Catholic—should read. It vividly illustrates how many features of Western life and thought originated in the Catholic Church, and puts to rest the PC notion that all religious traditions are morally equivalent.

of a High Priestess reciting a liturgy. She said it without fear of criticism or censure. And she received none. The other students listened in silence, their eyes moving timidly back and forth between me and Rachel, as if unsure which of us constituted a higher authority.... Who had conquered Rachel's people? What had led her to disrespect them? Why did she behave like a woman of a defeated tribe?"

Why indeed? The ultimate end result, as Yeagley points out, is defeat: People who are ashamed of their own culture will not defend it.

That's why telling the truth about the Crusades, Christianity, and the West is not a matter of cultural cheerleading or religious apologetics. It's an essential element of the defense of the West against today's global jihad.

Part III

TODAY'S JIHAD

Chapter 15

THE JIHAD CONTINUES

H ere's a test. Which of these two statements is from the eleventh century, and which from the twenty-first?

"O God, raise the banner of Islam and its helper and refute polytheism by wounding its back and cutting its ropes. Help those who fight for jihad for your sake and who in obedience to you have sacrificed themselves and sold their souls to you.... Because they persist in going astray, may the eyeball of the proponents of polytheism become blind to the paths of righteousness."[1]

"We ask Allah to turn this Ramadan into a month of glory, victory, and might, to hoist high in [this month] the banner of religion, to strengthen Islam and the Muslims, to humiliate polytheism and polytheists, to wave the banner of monotheism, to firmly plant the banner of *Jihad,* and to smite the perverts and the obstinate."[2]

Islamic scholar Ibn al-Mawsilaya wrote the first paragraph late in the eleventh century. The al Qaeda Sheikh Aamer bin Abdallah al-Aamer wrote the second in 2004.

Guess what?

- Islam has not reformed or changed its traditional doctrines of jihad warfare.

- Modern-day jihad groups are working to restore the caliphate as a means to further their war with the West.

- These groups despise democracy as a Western import at odds with the caliphate and sharia.

If you failed the test, don't worry. After all, the two paragraphs are extremely similar to each other—and that is no accident. Modern-day jihad movements consciously pattern themselves after the jihad warriors of old, and frequently invoke their memories. "During the month of Ramadan," Dr. Fuad Mukheimar, secretary-general of the Egyptian Sharia Association, wrote in 2001, "a great Muslim victory was won over the Crusaders under the leadership of [Salah Al-Din] [Saladin] Al-Ayubi. His advisors counseled him to rest from the Jihad during the month of fasting, but Saladin insisted on continuing the Jihad during Ramadan because he knew . . . that fasting helps to [achieve] victory, because during Ramadan the Muslims overcome themselves through fasting, and thus their victory over their enemies is certain. Fasting gives them determination, heroism, and will-power . . . Saladin replied to his advisors, 'Life is short.' Allah learned of [Saladin's] loyalty and the loyalty of his soldiers, and gave them a decisive victory. They took the fortress of Safed, the greatest of the Crusader fortresses, in the middle of the month of fasting. [Saladin] conquered the lands of Al-Sham [Greater Syria] and purified Jerusalem of the tyranny and defilement of the Crusaders."[3] Mukheimar also referred to the Battle of Badr and other historic battles to try to rouse modern-day Muslims to imitate Muhammad and Saladin and wage jihad for themselves.

This is a principal reason why jihad terrorists routinely refer to American troops as "Crusaders." In their view, the War on Terror, which began for Americans on September 11, 2001, is only the latest installment of a conflict that has continued for over a thousand years.

What are they fighting for?

This conflict, in their view, is destined to end with the hegemony of Islam. In the words of Osama bin Laden, jihad warriors the world over are fighting, "so that Allah's Word and religion reign supreme."[4] This involves the re-establishment of full Islamic law in Muslim countries and above all, the restoration of the caliphate.

As we have seen, the caliph was (in Sunni Islam) the successor to Muhammad and the leader of the Muslim community; Kemal Ataturk's secular Turkish government abolished the caliphate in 1924. Islamic theology makes no distinction between the sacred and the secular, and for Sunni Muslims the caliph was something like a combined generalissimo and pope, although he never wielded anything comparable to the pope's spiritual authority. Michelangelo's patron, Pope Julius II, earned the dubious honor of going down in history as the "warrior pope;" by contrast, the overwhelming majority of the Prophet's successors were warrior caliphs.

Many modern jihad groups date all the woes of the Islamic world to the loss of Muslim unity that resulted, in their view, from the loss of the caliphate.

That was when our heartaches began

This exhortation from the international Muslim group Hizb ut-Tahrir indicates the depth of anguish jihadists feel at the loss of the caliphate, which they attribute to Kemal Ataturk, an "English agent":

> It was a day like this 79 years ago, and more specifically on the 3rd of March 1924 that the kuffar [unbelievers] were able to reap the fruits of their tireless efforts of plotting and planning, which they had expended for more than a hundred years. This happened when the criminal English agent, Mustafa Kemal (so-called Ataturk, the 'Father of the Turks'!) announced that the Grand National Assembly had agreed to destroy the Khilafah [caliphate]; and announced the establishment of a secular, irreligious, Turkish republic after washing his hands from

responsibility of the remaining Islamic lands which the kuffar occupied in the First World War.

Since that day the Islamic ummah has lived a life full of calamities; she was broken up into small mini states controlled by the enemies of Islam in every aspect. The Muslims were oppressed and became the object of the kuffar's derision in Kashmir, Philippines, Thailand, Chechnya, Iraq, Bosnia-Herzegovina, Afghanistan, Palestine and other lands belonging to the Muslims until what happened to the Muslims became the subject of studies and statistics. Thousands were killed, millions dispossessed and the honour of tens of thousands has been violated amongst other calamities. Anyone who reads the papers or hears the news always finds the Muslims under a state of oppression, humiliation and killings; and this is prevalent in every report.

Indeed, the ummah [global Muslim community] is not in a situation as she used to be under the banner of Islam, when she used to be ruled by the Khilafah state that united the Muslims. She was not divided as we see today by borders drawn up by the kafir colonialists or dispersed by oppressive laws of residence. The Muslim used to travel from one corner of the Muslim lands to another without anyone asking him who he was or describing him as a foreigner. When the Khilafah existed the Muslims witnessed the power of Islam through the power of the Khilafah. They led the word under the banner of the Khilafah that applied Islam and conveyed it as a message, guidance and light to the world. However, where is the Khilafah? It existed in the past, but it was destroyed and suspended as a system....

Those were critical nights in which the political entity of the Muslims was destroyed. At that time the Islamic ummah was supposed to raise its sword in the face of this treacherous agent who changed Dar al-Islam into Dar al-Kufr and realized for the kuffar a dream they had wished for a long time. However, the Islamic ummah was overwhelmed, in the worst state of decline. So the crime took place and the kuffar tightened their grasp over the Islamic lands and tore it up into pieces. They divided the one ummah into nationalities, ethnicities and tribes; they tore up the single country into homelands and regions in which they established borders and barriers. In place of a single Khilafah state they established cartoon states and installed rulers as agents to carry out the orders of their kuffar masters. They abolished the Islamic Sharee'ah from the sphere of ruling, economy, international relations, domestic transactions and the judiciary. They separated the deen from the state and confined the Islamic deen to certain rituals, like those in Christianity. They worked to destroy the Islamic culture and uproot the Islamic thoughts to plant in their place western thoughts and culture.

Only one thing will fix this problem

A new caliph and restored Islamic unity are the only things that can repair these wrongs. Allah willed, says the Hizb ut-Tahrir document, "that the Islamic ummah should reawaken again and revive from her decline and realise that her rescue is only by the re-establishment of the Khilafah."[5]

When jihad fighters streamed into Iraq in 2003, eager for a showdown with American troops, Mullah Mustapha Kreikar, leader of the Muslim terrorist group Ansar al-Islam, placed their struggle in a larger religious context (from his safe haven in Norway): "The resistance is not only a reaction to the American invasion, it is part of the continuous Islamic

John Wesley on Islam:

"Ever since the religion of Islam appeared in the world, the espousers of it...have been as wolves and tigers to all other nations, rending and tearing all that fell into their merciless paws, and grinding them with their iron teeth; that numberless cities are raised from the foundation, and only their name remaining; that many countries, which were once as the garden of God, are now a desolate wilderness; and that so many once numerous and powerful nations are vanished from the earth! Such was, and is at this day, the rage, the fury, the revenge, of these destroyers of human kind."

(from The Doctrine of Original Sin, *Works* (1841), ix. 205)

struggle since the collapse of the caliphate. All Islamic struggles since then are part of one organized effort to bring back the caliphate."[6]

The intellectual father of all modern-day Muslim radicals, the Egyptian Hasan al-Banna (1906–1949), decried the end of the caliphate because it separated "the state from religion in a country which was until recently the site of the Commander of the Faithful." Al-Banna characterized the end of the caliphate as part of a larger "Western invasion which was armed and equipped with all [the] destructive influences of money, wealth, prestige, ostentation, power and means of propaganda."[7] Al-Banna founded the first modern jihad terror organization, the Muslim Brotherhood.

Another influential Muslim theorist, Sayyid Abul A'la Maudlid (1903–1979), founder of the Pakistani hard-line party Jamaat-e-Islami (Muslim Party), envisioned a unified Islamic state that would steadily expand throughout the subcontinent and beyond: "The Muslim Party will inevitably extend invitation to the citizens of other countries to embrace the faith which holds promise of true salvation and genuine welfare for them. Even otherwise also if the Muslim Party commands adequate resources it will eliminate un-Islamic Governments and establish the power of Islamic Government in their stead." This was, according to Maudidi, exactly what Muhammad and the first caliphs did. "It is the same policy which was executed by the Holy Prophet (peace of Allah be upon him) and his successor illustrious Caliphs (may Allah be pleased with them). Arabia, where the Muslim Party was founded, was the first country which was subjugated and brought under the rule of Islam."[8]

Restoration of the caliphate and the global expansion of Islamic rule and law were also goals of Osama bin Laden and the Taliban. In 1996, Mullah Omar wrapped himself in the cloak of Muhammad, which lies in a shrine in Afghanistan, as the Taliban proclaimed him the "new caliph" and *Emir ul-Momineen*, or Commander of the Faithful. In May 2002, a U.S. official noted that their plan was to "take over the whole country" of Afghanistan, and then "expand the caliphate."[9]

Caliphate dreams in Britain— and the United States

Such views have long since come to the West. In 1999, Abu Hamza al-Masri, who was then imam of London's Finsbury Park mosque, spoke at a London conference dedicated to lamenting the seventy-fifth anniversary of the destruction of the caliphate. "Islam needs the sword," he said to shouts of "Allahu Akbar" (Allah is great) from the crowd of four hundred Muslims. "Whoever has the sword, he will have the earth."[10]

Abu Hamza was a close associate of Omar Bakri and the now-disbanded British Muslim group Al-Muhajiroun. Bakri has declared his desire to see "the black flag of Islam"—that is, the battle flag of jihad— "flying over Downing Street." Like Bakri and Al-Muhajiroun in Britain, Shaker Assem and the Islamic Liberation Party (Hizb ut-Tahrir) in Germany work to reestablish the caliphate and institute sharia. Declares Assem, "People who say there is a conflict between sharia and Western democracy are right."[11]

What about America? Let's get it straight from America's leading Muslim advocacy group, the Council on American-Islamic Relations (CAIR).

CAIR board chairman Omar Ahmad said this to a Muslim audience in 1998: "Islam isn't in America to be equal to any other faith, but to become dominant. The Koran should be the highest authority in America, and Islam the only accepted religion on earth."[12] Ahmad has since then claimed that he was misquoted, but the reporter who heard him stands by her story.[13] CAIR spokesman Ibrahim Hooper was almost as forthright as Ahmad, telling the Minneapolis *Star Tribune*: "I wouldn't want to create the impression that I wouldn't like the government of the United States to be Islamic sometime in the future. But I'm not going to do anything violent to promote that. I'm going to do it through education."[14]

Through education, not violence, you say, Mr. Hooper? Thank you, everyone feels better now.

Khomeini in Dearborn and Dallas

In November 2004, Muslims in Dearborn, Michigan, held an anti-America, anti-Israel demonstration. Protesters carried a large model of Jerusalem's Al-Aqsa Mosque and waved signs bearing slogans such as "U.S. Hands Off Muslim Land." But the most arresting image was that of two Muslim women carrying large signs featuring the face of Ayatollah Ruhollah Khomeini.

The following month, the Metroplex Organization of Muslims in North Texas held a "Tribute to the Great Islamic Visionary," Ayatollah Khomeini, in Irving, Texas, a suburb of Dallas.[15]

Khomeini, a hero? In the United States? For Muslims in America to revere him was revealing, for Khomeini's 1979 triumph in Iran embodied the idea that Islamic law was superior to all others and must be pressed by force. As Khomeini himself put it, "Islam makes it incumbent on all adult males, provided they are not disabled or incapacitated, to prepare themselves for the conquest of countries so that the writ of Islam is obeyed in every country in the world. . . . But those who study Islamic

Holy War will understand why Islam wants to conquer the whole world." The goal of this conquest would be to establish the hegemony of Islamic law. As Khomeini proclaimed: "What is the good of us [i.e., the mullahs] asking for the hand of a thief to be severed or an adulteress to be stoned to death when all we can do is recommend such punishments, having no power to implement them?"

He then delivered a notorious rebuke to the Islam-is-a-religion-of-peace crowd: "Those who know nothing of Islam pretend that Islam counsels against war. Those [who say this] are witless. Islam says: Kill all the unbelievers just as they would kill you all! Does this mean that Muslims should sit back until they are devoured by [the unbelievers]? Islam says: Kill them, put them to the sword and scatter [their armies]. . . . Islam says: Whatever good there is exists thanks to the sword and in the shadow of the sword! People cannot be made obedient except with the sword! The sword is the key to Paradise, which can be opened only for the Holy Warriors! There are hundreds of other [Qur'anic] psalms and Hadiths [sayings of the Prophet] urging Muslims to value war and to fight. Does all this mean that Islam is a religion that prevents men from waging war? I spit upon those foolish souls who make such a claim."[16]

The sharia state Khomeini envisioned was not one that guaranteed equal rights for all. In 1985, Sa'id Raja'i-Khorassani, the permanent delegate to the United Nations from the Islamic Republic of Iran, declared that "the very concept of human rights was 'a Judeo-Christian invention' and inadmissible in Islam. . . . According to Ayatollah Khomeini, one of the shah's 'most despicable sins' was the fact that Iran was one of the original group of nations that drafted and approved the Universal Declaration of Human Rights." [17]

The Dearborn and Dallas pro-Khomeini displays indicated that Khomeini's vision for society is alive in America today—and that it is dangerously naive to assume that all Muslims immediately and unquestioningly accept American pluralism and the idea of a state not governed by religious law. Just where American Muslims stand on Khomeini's doctrines—and how many stand with him—are still forbidden questions for the major media. But if the old man could have spoken from his sign in Dearborn, he might have said, "Ignore me at your own risk."

A tiny minority of extremists?

So there are some Muslims who want to establish Islamic governments in the West. Aren't they just a tiny minority? Most Muslims in the West are quite happy to live in Western society...right?

Terrorism expert Daniel Pipes estimates that 10 to 15 percent of the world's Muslims support the jihadist agenda.[18] But there are indications from various parts of the Islamic world that the actual number of supporters of today's jihad might be higher. American moderate Muslim leader Kamal Nawash said on the *O'Reilly Factor* in August 2004 that 50 percent of Muslims worldwide supported the jihad.[19] During a terrorism finance trial in New York in February 2005, Bernard Haykel, an associate professor of Islamic studies at New York University, said, "There are a billion plus Muslims in the Arab world, 90 percent of whom support Hamas"—the Islamic terrorist organization that blows up civilians in buses and restaurants to further its goal of a Palestinian sharia state.[20] Dr. Imran Waheed, the London spokesman for the international "peaceful" jihadist group Hizb ut-Tahrir, declared in May 2005, "I believe that 99 percent of Muslim people anywhere in the world want the same thing, a caliphate to rule them."[22]

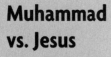

Muhammad vs. Jesus

"My kingship is not of this world; if my kingship were of this world, my servants would fight."

Jesus (John 18:36)

"I have been ordered (by Allah) to fight against the people until they testify that none has the right to be worshipped but Allah and that Muhammad is the Messenger of Allah."[21]

According to a survey conducted in Pakistan in 2004 by the Pew Research Center, "65 per cent favoured Osama and that pluralities of 47 per cent believed Palestinian suicide attacks on Israelis were justified. Forty-six per cent thought attacks on Westerners in Iraq were justified."[23]

Restoration of Muslim unity

One of the chief ills Hizb ut-Tahrir bemoans is the lack of unity among Muslims; in the good old days of the caliphate, the Muslim *umma* (community) "was not divided as we see today by borders drown up by the kafir colonialists." Jihadists see this unity as paramount partly because Saladin's victories over the Crusaders came after he was able to unite most of the Muslim world. Before Saladin, the Crusaders had been able to play the Sunni Abbasids of Baghdad off the Shi'ite Fatimids of Cairo and even entered into perfidious alliances with one against the other. But in 1171, Saladin allowed the call to prayer to resound through Cairo in the name of the Abbasid Caliph; the Fatimids were overthrown and the Islamic world reunited.[25] Some of the most resounding victories over the Crusaders only became possible on the basis of this unity, and today's jihadists have not forgotten this lesson.

A Book You're Not Supposed to Read

Milestones by Sayyid Qutb; Mother Mosque Foundation, n.d. In this slim and hard-hitting book, Qutb (1906–1966) makes it plain: "If we look at the sources and foundations of modern ways of living, it becomes clear that the whole world is steeped in *Jahiliyyah* [ignorance of the divine guidance]. This *Jahiliyyah* is based on rebellion against God's sovereignty on earth. It transfers to man one of the greatest attributes of God, namely sovereignty, and makes some men lords over others."[24]

Islam, says Qutb, in response to this wrongful deification of human beings, must "proclaim the authority and sovereignty of God" and thereby "eliminate all human kingship and to announce the rule of the Sustainer of the universe over the entire earth. In the words of the Qur'an: 'He alone is God in the heavens and in the earth.' (43:84) 'The command belongs to God alone. He commands you not to worship anyone except Him. This is the right way of life.' (12:40)"[26] In other words, Muslims must wage war until Islamic law reigns supreme all over the world.

Chapter 16

"ISLAMOPHOBIA" AND TODAY'S IDEOLOGICAL JIHAD

What have moderate Muslims done with the unmistakable evidence that jihad terrorists are working within mainstream Islamic traditions and using the Qur'an and Muhammad's example to exhort Muslims to wage war against unbelievers? Have they clearly and definitively rejected the teachings of the jihadists as being incompatible with any twenty-first-century version of Islam? Have they confronted and refuted the jihadist exegesis of the Qur'an and Islamic tradition? Have they presented an alternative vision of Islam that will be convincing enough to compete with the jihadists' "pure Islam" in the global battle for Muslim minds?

By and large, the answer to all these questions is no. Instead, "moderate" Muslims have invented "Islamophobia."

At the UN: A new word for a new tool of political manipulation

No one had heard of "Islamophobia" just a few short years ago. But a year is a long time for a well-oiled propaganda machine. Now this concept, vague and ultimately empty, is taken seriously at the highest levels. In December 2004, Kofi Annan presided over a UN seminar on "Islamophobia," explaining with his best PC straight face: "When the

Guess what?

● The UN has condemned "Islamophobia" while turning a blind eye to atrocities committed by jihadists.

● The charge of "Islamophobia" is used to intimidate and silence critics of violent jihad in Islam.

● Some groups are even trying to brand those who tell the truth about Islam and jihad as purveyors of "hate speech."

world is compelled to coin a new term to take account of increasingly widespread bigotry, that is a sad and troubling development. Such is the case with 'Islamophobia.' The word seems to have emerged in the late 1980s and early 1990s. Today, the weight of history and the fallout of recent developments have left many Muslims around the world feeling aggravated and misunderstood, concerned about the erosion of their rights and even fearing for their physical safety."

The UN's focus, not unexpectedly, stayed mostly on the aggrieved, misunderstood Muslims, with no questions raised about the Islamic roots of jihad terrorism. Nor was there any discussion of the compatibility of Islam with universally accepted ideas of human rights, as embodied in the UN's own 1948 Universal Declaration of Human Rights.

The Universal Declaration of Human Rights: Islamic responses

We have already seen that Iran's Sheikh Tabandeh published an Islamic critique of the Universal Declaration of Human Rights. The Islamic world has seen fit to formulate two major responses to this document: the 1981 Universal Islamic Declaration of Human Rights and the 1990 Cairo Declaration on Human Rights in Islam. Article 18 of the Universal Declaration of Human Rights, which we owe to the courageous Charles Malik of Lebanon, states: "Everyone has the right to freedom of thought, conscience and religion; this right includes freedom to change his religion or belief."[1]

You will find no analogous guarantee of the freedom to change one's religion in either of the Islamic declarations; indeed, as we have seen, traditional Islamic law mandates the death penalty for those who leave Islam. What's more, the Cairo declaration states: "Everyone shall have the right to advocate what is right, and propagate what is good, and warn against what is wrong and evil according to the norms of Islamic Shari'ah."[2]

By focusing on "Islamophobia" instead of the unpleasant realities of Islam, the UN dishonors past and present victims of jihad terror, and colludes with terrorists. Although this stance is born of political correctness and a putative concern to prevent vilification of innocent Muslims, it actually prevents honest attempts by Muslims and non-Muslims to address the actual sources of jihad terror and find some way to turn Muslims away from the path of violence.

What is Islamophobia, anyway?

Journalist and Islamic apologist Stephen Schwartz defines "Islamophobia" this way:

> Notwithstanding the arguments of some Westerners, Islamophobia exists; it is not a myth. Islamophobia consists of:
> - attacking the entire religion of Islam as a problem for the world
> - condemning all of Islam and its history as extremist
> - denying the active existence, in the contemporary world, of a moderate Muslim majority
> - insisting that Muslims accede to the demands of non-Muslims (based on ignorance and arrogance) for various theological changes in their religion
> - treating all conflicts involving Muslims (including, for example, that in Bosnia-Hercegovina a decade ago), as the fault of Muslims themselves
> - inciting war against Islam as a whole[3]

While there may be by this definition some Islamophobes in the world, Schwartz actually obscures more than he reveals. Does labeling as "Islamophobic" the practice of "attacking the entire religion of Islam as a problem for the world" mean that it is also Islamophobic to focus attention on the Qur'an and the Sunnah of the Prophet as motivations for terrorist activity? If so, then jihad terrorists worldwide are themselves "Islamophobic," for, as we have seen, they routinely point to jihad passages from the Qur'an and Hadith to justify their actions. Nor is a frank discussion of the doctrine of Islamic jihad equivalent to saying that the "entire religion of Islam" is a "problem for the world." No one is saying that *tayammum* (ablution with sand instead of water) or *dhikr* (a dervish religious devotion) or other elements of Islam pose a problem for the world.

Defining the condemnation of "all of Islam and its history as extremist" as "Islamophobic" is similarly problematic—and not just because of the sloppy imprecision of the word "extremist." Jihad and dhimmitude are part of Islam. Yet no commandment of any religion has ever been uniformly observed by its adherents, nor any law universally enforced. Jews and Christians in Islamic lands were able at various times and places to live with a great deal of freedom; however, this does not contradict the fact that the laws of the dhimma always remained on the books, able to be enforced by any Muslim ruler.

Likewise, while it may seem "Islamophobic" to deny "the active existence, in the contemporary world, of a moderate Muslim majority," it is also beside the point. Whether a moderate Muslim majority exists depends on how you define "moderate Muslim." Is it one who will never engage in terrorist acts? That would make moderates an overwhelming majority of Muslims worldwide. Or is a moderate one who sincerely disapproves of those terrorist acts? That would reduce the number of moderates. Or is a moderate Muslim one who actively speaks out and works against the jihadists? That would lower the number yet again. Or finally, is a moderate Muslim one who actively engages the jihadists in a theological battle, trying to convince Muslims that jihad terrorism is wrong on Islamic grounds? That would leave us with a tiny handful.

Moreover, it would be silly for anyone to treat "all conflicts involving Muslims ... as the fault of Muslims themselves," or to incite "war against

Islam as a whole." To go to war with Islam as a whole—grizzled shepherds in Kazakhstan and giggly secretaries in Jakarta as well as bin Laden and Zarqawi—would be absurd and unnecessary. But what does Schwartz really mean by saying that those who would advocate "war against Islam as a whole" are "Islamophobic?" Would that include those who recognize that Islamic jihad has been declared against Americans and who advocate resistance?

All this indicates that "Islamophobia" is virtually useless as an analytical tool. To adopt it is to accept the most virulent form of theological equivalence, and to affirm, against all the evidence, that every religious tradition is equally capable of inspiring violence. In many cases, this is part of an attempt to smear Western civilization by comparing the sins of Christians to an ideal, fictionalized Islam. To make this comparison is to deny the sensible observation of the once eminent atheist and, late in life, theist philosopher Antony Flew: "Jesus is an enormously attractive charismatic figure, which the Prophet of Islam most emphatically is not."[4] Once again, this is not base theological one-upmanship, but a realistic analysis of Islamic jihad. It also strengthens the idea that Western civilization is worth defending.

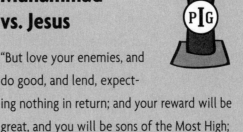

Muhammad vs. Jesus

"But love your enemies, and do good, and lend, expecting nothing in return; and your reward will be great, and you will be sons of the Most High; for he is kind to the ungrateful and the selfish."

Jesus (Luke 6:35)

"Let not the believers take for friends or helpers unbelievers rather than believers. If any do that, in nothing will there be help from Allah; except by way of precaution, that ye may guard yourselves from them."

Qur'an 3:28

"Islamophobia" as a weapon of jihad

The charge of "Islamophobia" is routinely used to shift attention away from jihad terrorists. After a rise in jihadist militancy and the arrest of eight people in Switzerland on suspicion of aiding suicide bombers in Saudi Arabia, some Muslims in Switzerland were in no mood to clean house: "As far as we're concerned," said Nadia Karmous, leader of a Muslim women's group in Switzerland, "there is no rise in Islamism, but rather an increase in Islamophobia."[5]

This pattern has recurred in recent years all over the world as "Islamophobia" has passed into the larger lexicon and become a self-perpetuating industry. In Western countries, "Islamophobia" has taken a place beside "racism," "sexism," and "homophobia." The absurdity of all this was well illustrated by a recent incident in Britain: While a crew was filming the harassment of a Muslim for a movie about "Islamophobia," two passing Brits, who didn't realize the cameras were rolling, stopped to defend the person being assaulted. Yet neither the filmmakers nor the reporters covering these events seemed to realize that this was evidence that the British were not as violent and xenophobic as the film they were creating suggested.[6]

Historian Victor Davis Hanson has ably explained the dangerous shift of focus that "Islamophobia" entails:

> There really isn't a phenomenon like "Islamophobia"—at least no more than there was a "Germanophobia" in hating Hitler or "Russophobia" in detesting Stalinism. Any unfairness or rudeness that accrues from the "security profiling" of Middle Eastern young males is dwarfed by efforts of Islamic fascists themselves—here in the U.S., in the UK, the Netherlands, France, Turkey, and Israel—to murder Westerners and blow up civilians. The real danger to thousands of innocents is not an occasional evangelical zealot or uncouth politician spouting off about Islam, but the deliberately orchestrated and very sick anti-Semitism and anti-Americanism that floods the

airways worldwide, emanating from Iran, Lebanon, and Syria, to be sure, but also from our erstwhile "allies" in Egypt, Saudi Arabia, and Qatar.[7]

Reform or denial?

Often going hand in hand with charges of Islamophobia is a strange disingenuousness on the part of Muslim reformers. In April 2005, the *Toronto Star* ran a gushing profile of Indonesian Muslim feminist Musdah Mulia, exulting that she "blames Muslims, not Islam, for gender inequity" in the Islamic world. This was one in a long series of articles that have appeared in newspapers and magazines in the Western world, which describe "true" Islam as a religion of tolerance, freedom, and pluralism. Yet the idea that "true Islam" is more akin to Quaker pacifism than to the religion of Osama bin Laden is untrue and dangerously misleading. It keeps Americans in the dark about the real motives and goals of the jihadists.

Mulia, according to journalist Haroon Siddiqui, "wears the hijab but says it's not mandated by Islam, a position augmented by a sizeable majority of Muslim women in Indonesia, indeed around the world, who don't don it and feel no less Muslim." Yet neither Siddiqui nor Mulia mention the Islamic tradition in which the Prophet Muhammad commands, "When a woman reaches the age of menstruation, it does not suit her that she displays her parts of body except . . . face and hands."[8] Nor do they mention, while noting that she "wants polygamy banned," that Mulia will face an extremely difficult battle, since the Qur'an tells men to "marry women of your choice, two or three or four" (4:3).

Musdah Mulia, exults Siddiqui, "is no Westernized secular feminist. She is an Islamic scholar, with a Ph.D. from the Institute of Islamic Studies" in Jakarta. "She teaches there part-time but her day job is director of research at the ministry of religious affairs, from where she needles the government. When her bosses issued a white paper last year updating religious laws, she wrote a 170-page critique that annoyed them and the conservatives."

Mulia was not always such a gadfly. She is the "granddaughter of a cleric, went to an Islamic boarding school and grew up in a strict environment." She offers one stinging memory of her childhood: "I could not laugh hard. My parents did not allow me to befriend non-Muslims. If I did, they ordered me to shower afterwards." But then she traveled to "other Muslim nations" and realized that "Islam had many faces. It opened my eyes. Some of what my grandfather and the ulema (clerics) had taught me was right but the rest was myth."

News flash: Islam as Muslims live it is false Islam!

So what led to her transformation? It turns out that her parents, her grandfather, the clerics, everyone had Islam all wrong, and she, Mulia, had gotten hold of the real Islam: "The more she studied Islam, the more she found it modern and radical."

So the hijab, the burka, the chador, the polygamy, the divorce that the man achieves by uttering a phrase three times, the unequal inheritance laws, the inability of women in many Muslim countries to leave the house without a male relative as escort, the ban in some Muslim countries on women even driving—all this is now, according to Mulia, un-Islamic. After all, Islam, she says, "had liberated women 1,400 years ago, well ahead of the West."

The claim that Muhammad actually improved the lot of women is curious. It is based on the allegation that women in pagan Arab society were treated terribly. But did those conditions really improve with the coming of Islam? As we have seen, even Aisha, Muhammad's beloved child bride, said, "I have not seen any woman suffering as much as the believing women."[9]

So many fighters for women's rights or wider reform in Islam are like Mulia. They cannot admit to themselves or others that Islam itself, through its religious texts, is responsible for the problems they seek to reform. They speak blandly of how the jihadists, or terrorists, or Wahhabis, or the villain du jour, have hijacked Islam, without offering any coherent program for converting these violent "misunderstanders" of Islam throughout the world into peaceful, tolerant pluralists.

Mulia does not explain how the "cultural traditions and interpretations" to which she objects arose in Islamic countries. How did Muslims in Saudi Arabia and Iran model their laws and fashion their mores other than through Islam? Beyond the basics of faith, Mulia says, most laws affecting women are man-made; "none of it came as a fax from heaven." But those who legislate in Saudi Arabia, Iran, Sudan, and Pakistan believe that they are following a "fax from heaven," namely the Qur'an. After all, what is a series of dictations by Allah to Muhammad other than a "fax from heaven"?

Like so many other self-proclaimed Islamic reformers, Mulia seems to be on the side of the angels, but she is actually helping to promote confusion about Islam. Ibn Warraq put it well: "There are moderate Muslims, but Islam itself is not moderate." Too many Muslim reformers think they must defend Islam at all costs, whatever mental contortions they have to perform in order to do so—even if it means glossing over and refusing to face the elements of Islam that jihad terrorists use to justify their actions. It is only "bad Muslims," we're told—Wahhabis, other extremists, you name it—who are responsible. Yet these very same "bad Muslims" seem to be those who most fervently accept, in every area of life, the actual teachings of Islam, while the more relaxed, unobservant, and above all non-literal minded believer treats women better and is committed to pluralism and peaceful coexistence with non-Muslims.

That is something that even Musdah Mulia and others like her cannot hide from forever.

Misrepresenting Islam

Besides the denial that unpleasant elements of Islam are "true Islam," some Muslim advocacy groups and their allies routinely brand true statements about Islam as "hate speech." In December 2004, CAIR issued a predictably venomous reaction to some observations made by former CIA official Bruce Tefft. CAIR objected to statements by Tefft such as "Islamic terrorism is based on Islam as revealed through the Qur'an," "To pretend that Islam has nothing to do with September 11 is to willfully ignore the obvious and to forever misinterpret events," and "There is no difference between Islam and Islamic fundamentalism, which is a totalitarian construct." CAIR called on the Canadian branch of the Simon Wiesenthal Center, which sponsored Tefft's address, "to condemn these Islamophobic remarks in the strongest possible terms. Characterizing Islam and its revealed text as promoting terrorism can only lead to increased anti-Muslim prejudice and intolerance."

"As an organization that says it is committed to 'fostering tolerance and understanding,'" CAIR fulminated, "the Simon Wiesenthal Center must immediately repudiate all Islamophobic rhetoric and hold its Canadian office accountable for failing to challenge the speaker's hate-filled views."[10]

Of course, in light of the fact that many Muslims advocate jihad and base their arguments on the Qur'an and Sunnah, Tefft didn't invent this connection. But instead of working to refute it through these sources, CAIR took aim at Tefft.

CAIR says that it was established in order to "promote a positive image of Islam and Muslims in America," and declares "we believe misrepresentations of Islam are most often the result of ignorance on the part of non-Muslims and reluctance on the part of Muslims to articulate their case."[11] That sounds great if you're a weepy PC type—but the cure CAIR offers may be worse than the disease.

Dhimmitude from media and officials

Whether from a fear of alarming the populace or a PC unwillingness to cause offense to Muslims, or both, authorities have on occasion been absurdly reticent about drawing conclusions from evidence that points to jihad terrorist activity in the United States.

In April 2005, firefighters conducting a routine inspection in a Brooklyn supermarket found two hundred automobile airbags and a room lined with posters of Osama bin Laden and beheadings in Iraq. An element in the airbags can be used to make pipe bombs. The owner of the building, according to the *New York Post*, "served jail time in the late 1970s and early 1980s for arson, reckless endangerment, weapons possession and conspiracy, according to the records." But officials were definite: The hidden stockpile had nothing to do with terrorism.

It doesn't? What does it have to do with, then? Macramé?

Similarly, when explosions killed fifteen people and injured over a hundred at an oil refinery in Texas City, Texas, on March 23, 2005, the FBI quickly ruled out terrorism as a possible cause.[12] When a group calling itself Qaeda al-Jihad and another Islamic group both claimed responsibility, the FBI was still dismissive.[13] But then it came to light that investigators did not visit the blast site until eight days after the explosions and after they ruled out terrorism as a possibility. A more independent-minded investigator asked, "How do you rule out one possibility when you don't have any idea what the cause is?"[14] Still later came the revelation that initial reports of a single blast were inaccurate; there were as many as five different explosions at the refinery.[15]

It may still be possible that these blasts were accidental, and that five distinct things went wrong at the refinery to cause five separate explosions at around the same time. And maybe there was no terrorist involvement. But how did the FBI know that before even investigating?

These are just two examples of a consistent pattern, as terrorism expert Daniel Pipes has documented:

- On March 1, 1994, on the Brooklyn Bridge, a Muslim named Rashid Baz started shooting at a van filled with Hasidic boys, murdering one of them.[16] FBI: It was "road rage."[17]

- On February 24, 1997, at the Empire State Building, a Muslim named Ali Abu Kamal started shooting at tourists, killing one and wounding six before killing himself.[18] New York mayor Rudolph Giuliani informed the public that he had "many, many enemies in his mind."[19]

- On July 4, 2002, at the Los Angeles International Airport counter of El Al, the Israeli national airline, a Muslim named Hesham Mohamed Ali Hadayet started shooting at people. He killed two. The FBI initially said that "there's nothing to indicate terrorism." However, after it came to light that Hadayet may have been involved with al Qaeda and was known for his hatred for Israel, the FBI finally did classify this as a terrorist act.[20]

- The Beltway snipers, John Muhammad and Lee Malvo, who were linked to eighteen shootings and ten murders in the Washington, D.C. area in October 2002, were two converts to Islam. Before they were caught investigators ascribed the crimes to an "angry white man;" the perpetrators turned out to be two black men. After they were caught, the media persistently referred to John Muhammad as John Williams, ignoring his conversion to Islam and consequent name change. And even after Malvo's drawings of Osama bin Laden (whom he labeled a "servant of Allah") and ramblings about "jihad" were revealed, authorities continued to downplay the possibility that the shootings had anything to do with Islam or terrorism.[21]

🌸 On August 6, 2003, in Houston, a Muslim named Mohammed Ali Alayed slashed the throat of his friend Ariel Sellouk, a Jew. Alayed had broken off his friendship with Sellouk when he began to become more devout in his Islam. On the night of the murder, Alayed called Sellouk and they went out to a bar together before going back to Alayed's apartment, where Alayed killed his friend. The two were not seen arguing at the bar. Although Alayed killed Sellouk after the fashion of jihadist murders in Iraq and went to a mosque after committing the murder, authorities said they "could not find any evidence that Sellouk . . . was killed because of his race or religion."[22]

A Book You're Not Supposed to Read

The Raft of Mohammed by Jean-Pierre Péroncel-Hugoz; St. Paul, MN: Paragon House, 1988. Besides vividly detailing the prejudice against non-Muslims that is rampant in the Islamic world, Péroncel-Hugoz devastatingly describes the intellectual dhimmitude of numerous American and European writers, politicians, and other public figures. He shows how eager PC Westerners are to believe the best about Islam—and even to exchange fact for fantasy in order to do so.

There are many similar examples: When a Muslim named El Sayyid Nosair murdered Israeli political activist Meir Kahane in New York City on November 5, 1990, authorities ascribed the killing not to jihad but to Nosair's depression; and when a co-pilot crashed EgyptAir flight 990 on October 31, 1999, killing 217 people, officials posited no link to terrorism, although the co-pilot exclaimed, "I rely on Allah" eleven times as he crashed the plane.[23]

Are officials trying to not alarm Americans? Or are they trying to protect innocent Muslims from backlash? Whatever their motivations, they are keeping Americans in the dark about the true nature and extent of the jihadist terror threat.

Chapter 17

CRITICIZING ISLAM MAY BE HAZARDOUS TO YOUR HEALTH

The window of free speech in America is closing—at least regarding Islam.

The whitewashing of Islam and jihad goes farther than tendentious propaganda. Honest investigations of the causes of Islamic terrorism are increasingly termed "hate speech" by the PC establishment. CAIR has filed numerous lawsuits against those who say things about Islam that it doesn't like—making for a chilling effect on those who speak the truth about the religion. "There's no doubt that CAIR understands this," notes *National Review*'s John Derbyshire. "They have Saudi oil money behind them and finance is no issue at all to them. They essentially have infinite funds. They will shut up everyone. On the topic of Islam, free speech is dead."[1]

Meanwhile, Islamic jihadists have their own methods of silencing critics, as the murder of Theo van Gogh last year on the streets of Amsterdam illustrates.

The chilling of free speech in America: FOX's *24* and CAIR

24 is a FOX TV drama about terrorism. Episodes have featured Bosnian terrorists, German terrorists, South American terrorists, and terrorists

Guess what?

- One Australian state has outlawed speaking the truth about Islam...and Great Britain and other countries are contemplating similar laws.

- Violent Islamic intimidation has come to the West: Filmmaker Theo van Gogh was murdered on an Amsterdam street for allegedly offending Muslims.

- Converts from Islam to Christianity must live in fear even in the United States.

from a Halliburton-like conglomerate. And, most famously, *24* featured Muslim terrorists—or at least terrorists with a vaguely Middle Eastern aspect. But while no Bosnians, Germans, South Americans, or Halliburton execs contacted the network to complain about the way they were portrayed on the show, when FOX ventured into Islamic terror territory, the network immediately aroused CAIR's ire.

Sabiha Khan of CAIR's Anaheim chapter worried that *24*'s Muslim terrorists would "contribute to an atmosphere that it's okay to harm and discriminate against Muslims. This could actually hurt real-life people."[2] CAIR scheduled a meeting with FOX executives in Los Angeles to air its concerns.

Meanwhile, IslamOnline, a popular Muslim news portal run from Qatar, had its own ideas of who was behind *24*'s introduction of Muslim terrorists: FOX Entertainment Group, it said, was "part of Jewish billionaire Rupert Murdoch's News Corporation." It asserted that *24*'s new plot direction was "hailed by Jewish groups and lobbyists as a bid to reveal Muslims' 'true nature,'" and noted that "Jewish writer Daniel Pipes wrote in the Israeli *Jerusalem Post* and the American *New York Post* hoping FOX would not bow to Muslim objections on the series."[3]

IslamOnline dropped "Jewish" from in front of "billionaire Rupert Murdoch" when informed that Murdoch is not, in fact, Jewish, but the implication of the article is still clear: *24*'s introduction of Muslim terrorist characters was yet another in a long line of Jewish conspiracies. It is frequently a bit of knee-jerk paranoia on the part of the defenders of Islamic jihad that anyone who opposes them must be Jewish. This paranoia about the Jews is nourished by the Qur'an's portrayal of them as crafty, untrustworthy, and accursed. And, of course, jihadists today would have us believe that the trouble between Muslims and non-Muslims is all because of Israel.

But the shadowy "Jewish groups and lobbyists" evidently dropped FOX's puppet strings, because even before network execs met with CAIR, the producers of *24* removed some material from the show that they were afraid might stereotype Muslims. FOX also agreed to distribute CAIR's public service announcement about American Muslims to their affiliates, although the affiliates were not bound to run it.

Dealing with the devil

But why was FOX playing ball with CAIR in the first place? Were the execs who met with CAIR representatives aware that three of its officials have been arrested for various terrorist-related activities? Yes, said a FOX source, that is a matter of public record. Are they aware that CAIR founder Nihad Awad helped establish the organization after working at the Islamic Association for Palestine (IAP), where he was public relations director—and that former FBI counterterrorism official Oliver Revell has called the IAP "a front organization for Hamas that engages in propaganda for Islamic militants"?[4] Did they know that Awad himself has declared, "I am in support of the Hamas movement"?[5] Well, yes, said the source, they were aware of allegations that CAIR had some links, however tenuous, with Hamas, but they judged the organization's complaints on their merits. That's what FOX always does, he said; it considers not the source of a complaint, but the worthiness of the complaint itself.

So if the Ku Klux Klan called FOX with a complaint, that complaint would be judged on its merits, not on its source?

Death knell for the West?

In December 2004, two Christian pastors in Australia were found guilty of religious vilification of Muslims. Although the decision was based on religious hatred laws that are currently on the books in only one Australian state, the greater consideration that such laws are receiving by legislatures all over the Western world makes this a threat to us all. For example, Tony Blair's government introduced a bill banning "Incitement to Religious Hatred," shamelessly pandering to the growing Muslim voter bloc in Britain. It proved too controversial and was dropped in April 2005, but it is still very much a live issue and could become law in Britain in the near future.[6] The Australian case shows the end result of such laws.

One of the pastors, Daniel Scot, is Pakistani. He fled his native land seventeen years ago when he ran afoul of the notorious Section 295(c) of the penal code, which mandates death or life in prison for anyone who blasphemes "the sacred name of the holy Prophet Muhammad." It's a treacherously elastic statute that is often used to snare Christians who find themselves charged with blasphemy if they are cornered and made to state they don't believe Muhammad was a prophet.

Scot went to Australia, where he encountered the Australian state of Victoria's new religious vilification laws. Judge Michael Higgins of the Victorian Civil and Administrative Tribunal found him guilty of vilify-ing Islam in a seminar hosted by his group, Catch the Fire Ministries. The judge noted that during the seminar, Scot stated "the Quran pro-motes violence, killing and looting." In light of Qur'anic passages such as 9:5, 2:191, 9:29, 47:4, 5:33 and many others, this cannot seriously be a matter of dispute. As we know, Muslims have pointed to verses in the Bible that they claim are equivalent in violence and offensiveness, or have claimed that the great majority of Muslims don't take such verses literally. However, it takes a peculiarly strong resistance to the truth to deny that such verses exist, and to charge anyone who points them out with religious vilification.

Yet Higgins wasn't finished. He also scored Scot for contending that the Qur'an "treats women badly; they are to be treated like a field to plough, 'use her as you wish,'" and that in it, "domestic violence in general is encouraged.'"[7] He charged Scot with saying that the Qur'an directs that "a thief's hand is cut off for stealing." Yet the idea of the field and "use her as you wish" are from Sura 2:223 of the Qur'an. Husbands are told to beat their disobedient wives in 4:34. Amputation for theft is prescribed in 5:38. What Qur'an is Higgins reading?

Higgins not only got the Qur'an wrong, but was also mistaken about Scot's own statements. The judge charged that Scot called Muslims "demons," but according to human rights activist Mark Durie, who was deeply involved in the case, "Scot said at one point in the seminar that in the Qur'an there were jinn (spirit beings) which became Muslims in response to the message of Islam. However, in his summary the judge appears to interpret this as Scot saying that Muslims are demons. So 'Some demons are Muslims' becomes 'Muslims are demons'!"[8]

A predetermined outcome

There are some hints that the outcome of the case was predetermined. When, during the trial, Scot began to read Qur'anic verses that discriminate against women, a lawyer for the Islamic Council of Victoria, the organization that brought the suit, stopped him: Reading the verses aloud, she said, would in itself be religious vilification. Dismayed, Scot replied, "How can it be vilifying to Muslims in the room when I am just reading from the Qur'an?"[9]

With religious vilification laws now coming to Britain and undoubtedly elsewhere in the West, Scot's question rings out with global implications and must be answered. If it is inciting hatred against Muslims when non-Muslims simply explore what Islam and the Qur'an actually teach, then there cannot be a reasonable public discussion of Islam. Such legal protections actually make Muslims a separate class, beyond criticism, precisely at the moment when the West needs to examine the implications of having admitted people with greater allegiance to Islamic law than to pluralism, freedom, and democracy.

To criticize is not to incite

The courageous ex-Muslim Ibn Warraq calls on Muslims to "admit the role of the Qur'an in the propagation of violence." If they do not, how can there be an end to jihad terrorism? What will keep jihadists from continuing to use the Qur'an to recruit more terrorists, right under the noses of fatuous Westerners like Judge Higgins, who would prefer to pretend otherwise?

When Judge Higgins signed the guilty verdict on Daniel Scot, he may have been signing the death warrant not just for Victoria state, but for a free Australia, and—if his example is followed elsewhere—the entire Western world.

The murder of Theo van Gogh

An event in Holland a month before Higgins's verdict was even more ominous: On November 2, 2004, Theo van Gogh was shot dead by a Muslim on an Amsterdam street because of a film he had made. His assailant was a Dutch Moroccan who was wearing traditional Islamic clothing. After shooting van Gogh several times, he stabbed him repeatedly, slit his throat with a butcher knife, and left a note on the body containing verses from the Qur'an and threats to several public figures who had opposed the flood of Muslim immigrants into the Netherlands. Yet Dutch prime minister Jan Peter Balkenende said, "Nothing is known about the motive" of the killer.[10]

Others were not quite so cautious. A Dutch student said, "This has to end, once and for all. You cannot just kill people on the street in a brutal way when you disagree with them." Job Cohen, the mayor of Amsterdam,

declared, "We will show loud and clear that freedom of speech is important to us."[11]

Eight weeks earlier, van Gogh's film *Submission* had aired on Dutch TV.
The brainchild of an ex-Muslim member of the Dutch parliament, Ayaan
Hirsi Ali, *Submission* decried the mistreatment of Muslim women, featuring images of battered women wearing transparent robes that exposed
their breasts, with verses from the Qur'an written on their bodies.

Insulting? In poor taste? That was probably the intention. Van Gogh,
the great-grandson of Vincent van Gogh's brother ("dear Theo"), was a
well-known and controversial gadfly on the Dutch scene; in the past, he
had attacked Jews and Christians with enough vehemence to elicit for-
mal complaints. But after *Submission*, the death threats started to come.
Van Gogh, in the eyes of many Dutch Muslims, had blasphemed Islam—
an offense that brought the death penalty. The filmmaker was uncon-
cerned. The film itself, he said, was "the best protection I could have. It's
not something I worry about."[12]

Van Gogh was not the first

Van Gogh's death shows that everyone who values freedom should
worry because murder committed by a Muslim enraged at "blasphemy"
is not new. Nor is it a relic of the distant past. In 1947, Islamic radicals
murdered Iranian lawyer Ahmad Kasravi in court; Kasravi was there to
defend himself against charges that he had attacked Islam. Four years
later, members of the same radical Muslim group, Fadayan-e Islam,
assassinated Iranian prime minister Haji-Ali Razmara after a group of
Muslim clerics issued a fatwa calling for his death. In 1992, Egyptian
writer Faraj Foda was murdered by Muslims enraged at his "apostasy"
from Islam—another offense for which traditional Islamic law prescribes
the death penalty. Foda's countryman, the Nobel Prize–winning novel-
ist Naguib Mahfouz, was stabbed in 1994 after accusations of blasphemy.

Under Pakistan's blasphemy laws, many non-Muslims have been arrested, tortured, and sentenced to die on the slimmest of evidence. And of course, there is Ayatollah Khomeini's notorious death fatwa against author Salman Rushdie.

But for such things to happen in Iran and Egypt, two countries where Islamic radicalism is widespread, is one thing; to have a "blasphemer" brutally murdered on the streets of Amsterdam in broad daylight is another. For thirty years, Europe has encouraged massive immigration from Muslim nations; Muslims now account for 5 percent of Holland's population, and that number is growing rapidly. But it is still largely taboo in Europe—as in America—to raise any questions about how ready that population is to accept Western pluralism. When Dutch politician Pim Fortuyn tried to raise some of those questions in 2002, he was vilified by the PC establishment as a right-wing racist—in line with the continuing tendency of the Western media to frame questions regarding Islam in racial terms, despite the fact that the intransigence of radical Islam is found among all races. And Fortuyn himself, of course, was ultimately murdered by a Dutch assailant who "did it for Dutch Muslims."[13]

The costs of maintaining the PC myths

The deaths of Fortuyn and van Gogh indicate that the cost of maintaining the taboo against criticizing Islam is growing ever higher. One of the prerequisites of peaceful coexistence of beliefs in a secular society is freedom of speech—particularly the freedom to question, to dissent, even to ridicule. Multiculturalism is heading toward contradiction: If one group is able to demand that its tenets remain above criticism, it is no longer equal, but has embarked on the path of hegemony. Must all other groups tolerate that group in the name of political correctness?

It is long past due for such considerations to become part of the public debate in Western countries. To what extent are Muslim immigrants in Western countries willing to set aside Islamic strictures on questioning, criticizing, and leaving Islam?

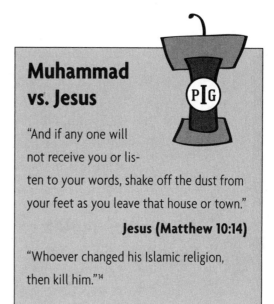

Muhammad vs. Jesus

"And if any one will not receive you or listen to your words, shake off the dust from your feet as you leave that house or town."

Jesus (Matthew 10:14)

"Whoever changed his Islamic religion, then kill him."[14]

After van Gogh was killed, thousands of people took to the streets of Amsterdam to pay him homage. Among them was a Muslim woman who stated, "I didn't really agree with van Gogh but he was a person who used his freedom of expression." She held up a sign reading "Muslims Against Violence," explaining, "I decided that as a Muslim and a Moroccan I should take up my responsibility to show that we do not support this act."[15]

But the traditional Muslim view is, unfortunately, alive and well; it was firmly restated several years ago by Pakistan's Federal Sharia Court: "The penalty for contempt of the Holy Prophet . . . is death and nothing else."[16] No one knows how many Muslims in Europe and America hold the views of the Moroccan woman at the rally, and how many would side with Pakistan's Sharia Court—and the killer of Theo van Gogh.

If Western countries continue, out of ignorance, fear, or narrow self-interest, to refuse to find out, there will be many more incidents like the bloody scene in Amsterdam in November 2004.

Living in fear of being a Christian— in Falls Church, Virginia

That couldn't happen in America, right? Wrong. At a conference held in September 2004, security was tight because of death threats from people holding the same ideology as the killer of Theo van Gogh. The conference was held not in Qom or Karachi, but just outside Washington, D.C., in Falls Church, Virginia.

That's right: In America in 2004, converts from Islam to Christianity spoke publicly only under assumed names, for fear of becoming the newest victims of the global jihad. The conference was called the "Muslim Background Believers Convention," a Christian gathering sponsored by several groups, including the Baptist General Association of Virginia. The *Washington Times* noted that "the convention kept the registration and entrance process under tight security to protect the participants, many of whom say they face death threats or ostracism from their families for leaving the Islamic faith."[17]

A Book You're Not Supposed to Read

23 Years: A Study of the Prophetic Career of Mohammad, by 'Ali Dashti; Costa Mesa, CA: Mazda Publishers, 1994. 'Ali Dashti (1896–1982) was an Iranian Muslim who had the courage to look honestly at Muhammad's career and write openly about the Prophet's violence, the non-miraculous character and moral defects of the Qur'an, and much more. For this, although he was over eighty, he was imprisoned, tortured, and ultimately murdered by thugs in the employ of the Islamic Republic of Iran.

If you leave Islam, you must die

Why did they have to take this extraordinary precaution? Because, as we have seen, in traditional Islamic law, when a Muslim converts to another faith, it can bring a death sentence. This is not, mind you, "extremist" Islam. It is the Islamic *mainstream*, based on a statement of Muhammad: "Whoever changed his Islamic religion, then kill him."[18] It's also based on a statement of the Qur'an: "But whoever of you recants and dies an unbeliever, his works shall come to nothing in this world and the next, and they are the companions of the fire for ever" (Qur'an 2:217). This has been widely interpreted by traditional Muslim commentators as giving sanction to the death penalty for apostates—which they derive from the verse's assertion that the apostate's work will "come to nothing in this world" as well as the next.

When converts are not killed, they are otherwise pressured. The organizer of the conference has felt this firsthand: "I was called by my embassy and told I'd better repent or I could not go back home with my family." Another convert reported that she had not yet told her family that she had become a Christian. "I know they're going to disown me," she said, "if they don't kill me." In a free America, you say?

What happens when the law looks the other way

These people have to live in fear because of the long-entrenched and continuing unwillingness on the part of American authorities to face up to the realities of Islam. Law enforcement officials either haven't known or haven't cared that Islam mandates the death penalty for those who leave the religion. If they knew that this provision even existed, they probably assumed that Muslims who settled in the United States would discard it and accept the values of American society.

Many have, but an unknown number haven't, and it is time this fact is acknowledged. This is especially tough for Westerners, however, since the concept of apostasy is so foreign to today's secular society. Although the Falls Church converts are Christians, this is not solely a Christian issue. Freedom of conscience should be a concern of everyone who professes an interest in human rights. The human rights organizations should be the first to defend these people. American government and law enforcement officials should rush to their aid in the name of freedom.

But because of the PC stranglehold on discussion of Islam, and because shady groups like CAIR have managed to claim victim status for American Muslims, neither the rights groups nor the government have yet noticed that the converts even exist.

Chapter 18

THE CRUSADE WE MUST FIGHT TODAY

When asked at the end of Pope John Paul II's long pontificate if the Catholic Church might change its stance on Islam, Archbishop Michael Fitzgerald, president of the Pontifical Council for Inter-Religious Dialogue, replied, "There may be a greater insistence on religious liberty. But I don't think we're going to go to war. The times of the Crusades are over."[1]

This surely goes without saying. Despite the fevered fantasies of jihadists around the world, the Crusades of the history books are definitely over. But the jihad that the Crusaders faced is not over. The thousand-year-old Muslim dream of an Islamic Europe is definitely not over. In fact, in a certain sense, it is now closer to fulfillment than at any time in history.

The Islamization of Europe

Will tourists in Paris in the year 2105 take a moment to visit the "mosque of Notre Dame" and the "Eiffel Minaret?" Through massive immigration and official dhimmitude from European leaders, Muslims are accomplishing today what they failed to do at the time of the Crusaders: conquer Europe. How quickly is Europe being Islamized? So quickly that even historian Bernard Lewis, who has continued throughout his honor-filled career to be disingenuous about Islamic radicalism and terrorism,

Guess what?

- Europe could be Islamic by the end of the twenty-first century.

- In order to defeat the international jihadist threat, the U.S. must reconfigure its alliances on the basis of where countries stand on Islamic jihad.

- Converts from Islam to Christianity must live in fear even in the United States.

forthrightly told the German newspaper *Die Welt*: "Europe will be Islamic by the end of the century."[2]

Or maybe sooner: If demographic trends continue, France, Holland, and other Western European nations could have Muslim majorities by middle of this century. Meanwhile, these growing Muslim minorities are increasingly assertive and disruptive. Consider some recent indicators from other European nations:

- Sweden's third-largest city, Malmö, has become a Middle East outpost in Scandinavia. A quarter of the city's population is now Muslim, and that number is rapidly growing. Nor are the Muslims of Malmö inclined to be peaceful and tolerant. Even the police are afraid: "If we park our car it will be damaged—so we have to go very often in two vehicles, one just to protect the other vehicle," reported a police officer in Malmö. Meanwhile, Swedish ambulance drivers will not enter some areas of Malmö unless police accompany them.[3]

- The Nordgårdsskolen in Aarhus, Denmark, has become the first Dane-free school. The students now come entirely from Denmark's fastest-growing constituency: Muslim immigrants.[4]

- Also in Denmark, the Qur'an is now required reading for all upper-secondary school students.[5] There should be nothing wrong with requiring students to read the Qur'an, but given the current ascendancy of political correctness on the Continent, it is unlikely that critical perspectives will be included.

- Pakistani Muslim leader Qazi Hussain Ahmed gave an address at the Islamic Cultural Center in Oslo. He was allowed into the country despite that fact that, according to Norway's *Aftenposten*, he "has earlier made flattering comments about Osama bin Laden, and his party, Jamaat-e-

Islami, also has hailed al-Qaeda members as heroes."[6] In Norway, he declined to answer questions about whether he thought homosexuals should be killed.[7]

Elsewhere in Europe, jihad is taking a more violent form. Dutch officials have uncovered at least fifteen separate terrorist plots, all aimed at punishing the Netherlands for its 1,300 peacekeeping troops in Iraq.[8] And in Spain, Moroccan Muslims, including several suspected participants in the March 11 Madrid bombings, took control of a wing in a Spanish prison in fall 2004. From there, they broadcast Muslim prayers at high volume, physically intimidated non-Muslim prisoners, hung portraits of Osama bin Laden, and boasted, "We are going to win the holy war." What was the guards' response? They asked the ringleaders to please lower the volume on the prayers.[9]

What Europe has long sown it is now reaping. In her book *Eurabia,* Bat Ye'or, the pioneering historian of dhimmitude, chronicles how this has come to pass. Europe, she explains, began thirty years ago to travel down a path of appeasement, accommodation, and cultural abdication in pursuit of shortsighted political and economic benefits. She observes that today, "Europe has evolved from a Judeo-Christian civilization, with important post-Enlightenment/secular elements, to a 'civilization of dhimmitude,' i.e., Eurabia: a secular-Muslim transitional society with its traditional Judeo-Christian mores rapidly disappearing."[10]

If Western Europe does become Islamized, as demographic trends suggest, before too long America will be facing a world that is drastically different and more forbidding than it is today.

What is to be done?

Archbishop Fitzgerald is right; the time of the Crusades is long past. The idea that a modern pope would summon Christians to a military defense of the Holy Land or anything else against Muslims is inconceivable. It is even more inconceivable that a significant portion of the Western world would respond to such a call. Not only is the West riven with a disunity that makes the fissures of Crusader times seem like love fests, but there is little or no unanimity of outlook and purpose. While America fights a war on terror that has included the toppling of Saddam Hussein and the occupation of Iraq, France and Germany have pursued a different strategy, attempting to establish the European Union as a global counterweight to the United States—a strategy that involves close cooperation with the Arab League.

The situation in Europe has grown quite grave, and something must be done. It may be that the world needs a new Crusade, though of a kind different from those led by Richard the Lionhearted and Godfrey of Bouillon. We have seen in this book that the Crusades were primarily an act of defense against the encroachment of Islam. In that sense a new Crusade is not only possible but desirable.

Am I calling for a war between Christianity and Islam? Certainly not. What I am calling for is a general recognition that we are already in a war between two vastly different ideas of how to govern states and order societies, and that in this struggle the West has nothing to apologize for and a great deal to defend. Indeed, the struggle against sharia is nothing less than a struggle for universal human rights, a concept that originated in the West and is denied by Islam. Everyone in the fractured and fractious West—Christians, Jews, other religious believers, atheist humanists— ought to be able to agree that this is a concept worth defending, even if they disagree about its particulars.

What we are fighting today is not precisely a "war on terror." Terror is a tactic, not an opponent. To wage a "war on terror" is like waging a "war on bombs"; it focuses on a tool of the enemy rather than the enemy itself. A refusal to identify the enemy is extremely dangerous: It leaves those who refuse vulnerable to being blindsided—as proven by the White

House access granted by both Bill Clinton and George W. Bush to now-jailed jihadists such as Abdurrahman Alamoudi and Sami al-Arian.

A forthright acknowledgment that we are facing a renewed jihad would go a long way to preventing that sort of diplomatic and intelligence embarrassment. This is not really as far-fetched as it may seem. Jihad terrorists have declared war on the United States and other non-Muslim nations—all the U.S. and Western European countries need to do is identify the enemy as they have identified themselves.

Defeating the jihad internationally

After the September 11 terrorist attacks, President Bush warned the world, "You're either with the terrorists or you're with us." But because of official Washington's persistent refusal to acknowledge exactly who the terrorists are and why they are fighting, that bold line in the sand has been obscured time and again. And few, if any, are even asking the right questions.

During her Senate confirmation hearings, Secretary of State Condoleezza Rice was grilled about Iraq, weapons of mass destruction, and how long our troops will be in that strife-ridden country. But no one bothered to ask her a more important question: When and how will American foreign policy be adjusted to defeat the goals, not just the tactics, of our jihad opponents?

Three years after September 11, this has still not been done. It should have been the first order of business. Other nations take this as axiomatic—including our enemies. Article 3 of the Iranian constitution stipulates that Iran must base its foreign policy on "Islamic criteria, fraternal commitment to all Muslims, and unsparing support to the freedom fighters of the world."

I recommend that the United States do the same: state its goals and interests regarding the global jihad. This would involve a serious re-evaluation of American posture around the globe.

A few modest proposals to this end: In the first place, it is scandalous that so many years after President Bush announced that "you're either with the terrorists or with us," the United States still counts as friends and allies—or at least recipients of its largesse—so many states where jihadist activity is widespread.

- ❀ *Tie foreign aid to the treatment of non-Muslims.* A State Department that really had America's interests at heart would immediately stop all forms of American aid to Kosovo, Algeria, Somalia, Sudan, Egypt, Jordan, the Palestinians, Pakistan, Indonesia, and even Iraq and Afghanistan, and any other state, until each demonstrably ends all support—material, educational, and religious—for jihad warfare, and grants full equality of rights to any non-Muslim citizens.
- ❀ *Reconfigure our global alliances on the same basis.* Pakistan, Saudi Arabia, and the other exporters of jihad should be put on notice. Continued friendly relations with the United States absolutely depend on an immediate and comprehensive renunciation of the jihad, including a reformation of schools that teach it. It cannot be enough for a state to denounce or renounce terror; each must stop Islamic jihad as a means of undermining the integrity of other states. At the same time, the United States should try to cultivate closer ties with states that have been victims of jihad violence—most notably, Russia. So far, Russia's resistance to the global jihad has been even more inconsistent and shortsighted than our own. However, if the U.S. were to acknowledge that we are up against a worldwide jihad and seek closer ties on that basis, this might start to change.
- ❀ *Call on Muslim states to renounce sharia's expansionist imperative.* To be a friend of the United States, each state

must renounce any intention to try to realize the Islamic goals enunciated by Pakistani Islamic leader Syed Abul Ala Maududi, who declared that when Muslims are ruled by non-Muslims, "the believers would be under an obligation to do their utmost to dislodge them from political power and to make them live in subservience to the Islamic way of life."[11]

His comments were in full accord with Islamic theology and history, as well as with the Qur'an as it has been read and understood by Muslims for centuries. This is the goal of the jihadists today; it should be the fundamental defining point of U.S. alliances with Muslim states.

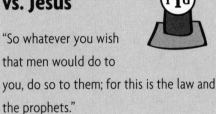

Muhammad vs. Jesus

"So whatever you wish that men would do to you, do so to them; for this is the law and the prophets."

Jesus (Matthew 7:12)

"None of you will have faith till he likes for his (Muslim) brother what he likes for himself."[12]

The Muslim version of the Golden Rule extends only to fellow Muslims, not to unbelievers.

Initiate a full-scale Manhattan Project to find new energy sources—so that the needed reconfiguration of our alliances can be more than just words. President Bush took a first tentative step toward this in April 2005, when he called for the construction of new nuclear power plants and oil refineries to decrease American dependence on foreign (i.e., Saudi) energy supplies.[13] But this was to propose only a stopgap when a total overhaul is needed; much more needs to be done. The "Manhattan Project" is a deliberate choice of analogy. During World War II, the United States invested millions and set the brightest scientific minds in the world on the atomic bomb project. Is a similar effort being made today to end our dependence on Saudi oil?

A Book You're Not Supposed to Read

Infiltration: How Muslim Spies and Subversives Have Penetrated Washington by Paul Sperry; Nashville, TN: Nelson Current, 2005. Sperry details just how bad things have gotten in America: Muslims with clear ties to jihad terrorists have entrenched themselves deeply in our political system and military establishment. This book underscores the urgency of mounting a full and effective resistance to the Islamic jihad—before it's too late.

In a larger sense, does anyone in the State Department have the will to advocate these and other measures? Or is it only regimes like the bloody mullahocracy in Tehran that are allowed to speak openly about their principles and goals, and take all the necessary measures for their own defense?

Secretary Rice needs to ask and answer these questions. The State Department's bureaucracy has been playing realpolitik for so long that it reflexively thinks it can work with the Islamic jihadists—as if dropping care packages into Indonesia will somehow blunt the force of the Maududi dictum that "non-Muslims have absolutely no right to seize the reins of power."

The State Department needs to come to grips with the fact that it is facing a totalitarian, supremacist, and expansionist ideology—and plan accordingly. Not only has it not been done, but it is so far off the table that it never even occurred to Democratic senator Barbara Boxer to use it as another partisan stick with which to batter Dr. Rice's competence and veracity at her confirmation hearing.

Now it is up to Secretary Rice herself to demonstrate whether she has the vision to do what is needed.

Defeating the jihad domestically

The first thing we need in order to defeat the jihad at home is an informed citizenry:

Read the Qur'an.

In 1141, Peter the Venerable, the abbot of Cluny, had the Qur'an translated into Latin. After that, every preacher of the Crusades was required to have read it.[14] If Europeans were going to go to the Middle East to fight Muslims, it was clear to virtually everyone that they needed to have a working knowledge of their opponents' mindset. Yet in the United States, the idea that knowing something about Islam and the Qur'an might help clarify some issues regarding the War on Terror meets with ridicule, indifference, or charges of "racism." Mahmood Mamdani, Herbert Lehman Professor of Government in the department of anthropology and school of international affairs at Columbia University, recently heaped contempt on the idea that the Qur'an had anything to tell us about modern terrorism:

> I was in New York City on 9/11. In the weeks that followed, newspapers reported that the Koran had become one of the biggest-selling books in American bookshops. Astonishingly, Americans seemed to think that reading the Koran might give them a clue to the motivation of those who carried out the suicide attacks on the World Trade Center. Recently, I have wondered whether the people of Falluja have taken to reading the Bible to understand the motivation for American bombings. I doubt it.[15]

It was astonishing indeed—that Mandani and his publishers evidently thought this is a cogent argument. Was it really astonishing that Americans would read the Qur'an to discover the motivation of men who cited the Qur'an repeatedly in their communiqués to explain their actions? It was more astonishing that Mahmood Mamdani would think that Fallujans reading the Bible was an appropriate *reductio ad absurdum* to dispose of this idea, despite the demonstrable fact that for all the dark suspicions of the PC crowd about Bush's Christianity, modern American foreign policy has never proceeded according to Biblical or Christian precepts, either explicitly or implicitly—except perhaps in the military's zeal to avoid civilian casualties as much as possible (a principle that has been contravened more than once). The contrast with Osama bin Laden's Qur'an-filled messages should be immediately obvious—except to all who don't wish to see it, or who wish to obscure it.

Report honestly about jihadist activity in the U.S. and the West.

An informed citizenry doesn't just read the Qur'an and other Islamic sources. It also demands responsible reporting from the media and honesty from law enforcement officials about jihadist attacks in the United States. We saw in chapter sixteen how common it is for such attacks to be explained away. This obfuscation no doubt stems from an official fear of stirring up vigilantes who will victimize Muslims in America. But this insults the intelligence and decency of the American public. Official unwillingness to draw obvious conclusions hinders our ability to make informed decisions about how to conduct the War on Terror. It has to stop.

Reclassify Muslim organizations.

Any Muslim group in America that does not explicitly renounce, in word and in deed, any intention now or in the future to replace the Constitution of the United States with Islamic sharia should be classified as a political rather than a religious organization, and should be subject to all the responsibilities and standards to which political organizations must adhere.

Take pride in Western culture.

It's time for all the schools that dropped "Crusaders" as their team name to readopt it. The corrosive effects of multiculturalism have bred a suicidal hatred of the West among our own children. It's time to roll this back through a concerted effort to extirpate the multiculturalist ethos from school textbooks and the culture at large. Western civilization has given the world notions of human rights that are universally accepted (except in the Islamic world), technological advancement beyond the wildest dreams of people of previous ages, and a great deal more. Yet our own leaders and teachers tell us we must stand before the world in a posture of shame.

It's time to say "enough," and teach our children to take pride in their own heritage. To know that they have a culture and a history of which they can and should be grateful; that they are not the children and grandchildren of oppressors and villains; and that their homes and families are worth defending against those who want to take them away, and are willing to kill to do so.

Call it a Crusade.

ACKNOWLEDGMENTS

Hearty thanks first of all to the Jihad Watch staff: Hugh Fitzgerald, Rebecca Bynum, and all the others who were patient and kind enough to discuss much of the material here with me, review it at various stages, and contribute many helpful suggestions for its improvement. Hugh Fitzgerald's brilliance and erudition are a godsend and a tremendous boon, not only to this book but also to the entire Jihad Watch effort—and the resistance to the global jihad in general. There are many others I would like to name, but am unable to do so for fear of putting them in various kinds of danger: these courageous ones, laboring on the front lines of the anti-jihad resistance, are the true heroes of this age.

As has been true many times in the past, I owe a great debt of gratitude to Jeff Rubin, whose conceptual skill and vision are unparalleled. I am particularly grateful as well to the Regnery editors Harry Crocker and Stephen Thompson, whose deft and insightful touch is responsible for sharpening much of what is successful in these pages. As ever, what is good here is theirs, and the errors are only mine.

NOTES

Introduction:

Islam and the Crusades

1. Bill Clinton, "Remarks as delivered by President William Jefferson Clinton, Georgetown University, November 7, 2001." Georgetown University Office of Protocol and Events, www.georgetown.edu.

2. "World Islamic Front Statement," Jihad Against Jews and Crusaders, February 23, 1998. http://www.fas.org/irp/world/para/docs/980223-fatwa.htm.

3. Middle East Media Research Institute (MEMRI), "Ramadan Sermon From Iraq," MEMRI Special Dispatch No. 438, November 8, 2002. www.memri.org.

4. "Al Qaeda-linked group takes credit for Saudi attack," CNN, December 7, 2004.

5. Karen Armstrong, *Islam: A Short History* (New York: Modern Library, 2000), 179–180.

Chapter 1:

Muhammad: Prophet of War

1. A. Guillaume, *The Life of Muhammad: A Translation of Ibn Ishaq's Sirat Rasul Allah*, Oxford University Press, 1955, 287–288.

2. Cf. *'Umdat al-Salik* o9.10; al-Mawardi, *al-Akham as-Sultaniyyah*, 4.2.

3. Ibn Ishaq, 289.

4. Ibid., 300.

5. Muhammed Ibn Ismaiel Al-Bukhari, *Sahih al-Bukhari: The Translation of the Meanings*, translated by Muhammad M. Khan, Darussalam, 1997, vol. 4, book 58, no. 3185.

6. Ibn Ishaq, 308.

7. Ibid., 304.

8. Bukhari, vol. 4, book 58, no. 3185.

9. Ibn Ishaq, 306.

10. Ibid., 308.

11. Ibid., 363.

12. Ibid., 367.

13. *Sahih Muslim*, translated by Abdul Hamid Siddiqi, Kitab Bhavan, revised edition 2000, vol. 3, book 17, no. 4436.

14. Bukhari, vol. 4, book 56, no. 3032.

15. Bukhari, vol. 5, book 64, no. 4037.

16. Ibn Ishaq, 369.

17. Ibid., 382.

18. Ibid., 386.

19. Ibid., 387.

20. Sayyid Qutb, *Social Justice in Islam*, translated by John B. Hardie and Hamid Algar, revised edition, Islamic Publications International, 2000, 19.

21. Deroy Murdock, "'The Great Satan' on Devastated Muslim Streets," National Review Online, January 6, 2005.

22. Ibn Ishaq, 509.

Chapter 2:

The Qur'an: Book of War

1. "I have a question about offensive Jihad," Islam Q & A Online with Mufti Ebrahim Desai, Question 12128 from Canada, http://www.islam.tc/ask-imam/view.php?q=12128.

2. Sidik Aucbur, "The true meaning of Jihad," www.khilafah.com, May 11, 2003.

3. Ibn Arabi, in Suyuti, *Itqan* iii, 69. Cf. John Wansbrough, *Quranic Studies*, Prometheus, 2003, 184.

4. "Surat at-Tawba: Repentance," *Tafsir al-Jalalayn*, anonymous translation, reprinted at http://ourworld.compuserve.com/homepages/ABewley/tawba1.html.

5. Ibn Kathir, vol. 4, 377.

6. "Surat at-Tawba: Repentance," *Tafsir Ibn Juzayy*, anonymous translation, reprinted at http://ourworld.compuserve.com/homepages/ABewley/tawba1.html.

7. Ibn Kathir, vol. 8, 668.

8. "Question #34770: There is no compulsion to accept Islam," *Learn Hajj Jurisprudence*, Islam Q & A, http://63.175.194.25/index.php?ln=eng&ds=qa&lv=browse&QR=34770&dgn=4.

9. Middle East Media Research Institute (MEMRI), "PA TV Broadcasts call for Killing Jews and Americans," MEMRI Special Dispatch No. 138, October 13, 2000. www.memri.org.

10. Osama bin Laden, "Declaration of War against the Americans Occupying the Land of the Two Holy Places," 1996. http://www.mideastweb.org/osamabinladen1.htm.

11. Middle East Media Research Institute (MEMRI), "Bin Laden's Sermon for the Feast of the Sacrifice," MEMRI Special Dispatch No. 476, March 5, 2003.

Chapter 3:

Islam: Religion of War

1. Bukhari, vol. 1, book 2, no. 26; cf. vol. 2, book 25, no. 1519 and many others.

2. Bukhari, vol. 4, book 56, no. 2892.

3. *Muslim*, book 20, no. 4642.

4. Abu-Dawud Sulaiman bin Al-Aash'ath Al-Azdi as-Sijistani, *Sunan abu-Dawud*, Ahmad Hasan, translator, Kitab Bhavan, 1990, book 14, no. 2497.

5. *Muslim*, book 20, no. 4645.

6. Bukhari, vol. 4, book 56, no. 2785.

7. *Muslim*, book 19, no. 4294.

8. "Full text: bin Laden's 'letter to America,'" *Observer*, November 24, 2002.

9. Bukhari, vol. 1, book 2, no. 25. The transliterated Arabic of the Muslim confession of faith has been omitted from this translation for ease of reading. The same statement is repeated in Bukhari, vol. 1, book 8,

no. 392; vol. 4, book 56, no. 2946; vol. 9, book 88, no. 6924; and vol. 9, book 96, nos. 7284–7285, as well as in other hadith collections.

10. Ibn Abi Zayd al-Qayrawani, *La Risala* (*Epitre sur les elements du dogme et de la loi de l'Islam selon le rite malikite.*) Translated from Arabic by Leon Bercher. 5th ed. Algiers, 1960, 165. Cited in Andrew G. Bostom, "Khaled Abou El Fadl: Reformer or Revisionist?," http://www.secularislam.org/articles/bostom.htm.

11. Ibn Taymiyya, "Jihad," in Rudolph Peters, *Jihad in Classical and Modern Islam*, Markus Wiener Publishers, 1996, 49. Cited in Andrew G. Bostom, "Khaled Abou El Fadl: Reformer or Revisionist?," http://www.secularislam.org/articles/bostom.htm.

12. From the *Hidayah*, vol. I, 140, quoted in Thomas P. Hughes, *A Dictionary of Islam* (W.H. Allen, 1895), "Jihad," 243–248. Cited in Andrew G. Bostom, "Khaled Abou El Fadl: Reformer or Revisionist?," http://www.secularislam.org/articles/bostom.htm.

13. Abu'l Hasan al-Mawardi, *al-Ahkam as-Sultaniyyah (The Laws of Islamic Governance),* Ta-Ha Publishers, 1996, 60.

14. Ahmed ibn Naqib al-Misri, *Reliance of the Traveller ('Umdat al-Salik): A Classic Manual of Islamic Sacred Law,* translated by Nuh Ha Mim Keller. Amana Publications, 1999, xx.

15. Ibid., o9.0.

16. Ibid., o9.8.

17. Ibid., o9.6.

18. Quoted in Jonathan Riley-Smith, *The Oxford Illustrated History of the Crusades* (Oxford University Press, 1995), 250–251.

19. Qutb, *Milestones*, 63.

20. Shariah Council of State Defense Council (Majlis al-Shura) of CRI, "Jihad and Its Solution Today," *Jihad Today*, Kavkaz Center, November 26, 2003. http://kavkazcenter.com/eng/content/2003/11/26/2028.shtml.

21. See, for example, "Fears as young Muslims 'opt out,'" *BBCNews*, March 7, 2004.

22. "Interview Sahim Alwan," *Frontline*, October 16, 2003. http://www.pbs.org/wgbh/pages/frontline/shows/sleeper/interviews/alwan.html.

23. Peter Ford, "Listening for Islam's silent majority," *Christian Science Monitor*, November 5, 2001.

24. Debbie Schlussel, "Bush's scary CAIR friends," WorldNetDaily.com, October 16, 2001.

25. Jagan Kaul, "Kashmir: Kashmiri Pundit View-point," *Kashmir Telegraph*, May 2002.

26. Daniel Pipes, "The Danger Within: Militant Islam in America," *Commentary,* November 2001.

Chapter 4:

Islam: Religion of Intolerance

1. Emrah Ulker, "UN Uses Ottoman Tolerance Concept as Model," *Zaman Daily Newspaper*, December 9, 2004.

2. Abu'l Hasan al-Mawardi, *al-Ahkam as-Sultaniyyah (The Laws of Islamic Governance)* Ta-Ha Publishers, 1996, 28.

3. Ibn Kathir, vol. 4, 406.

4. Ibid., 407.

5. Ibid.

6. *'Umdat al-Salik*, o11.3, 5.

7. "The Charter of Allah: The Platform of the Islamic Resistance movement (Hamas)," translated and annotated by Raphael Israeli, The International Policy Institute for Counter-Terrorism, April 5, 1998. http://www.ict.org.il/documents/documentdet.cfm?docid=14.

8. Middle East Media Research Institute (MEMRI), "Islamist Leader in London: No Universal Jihad As Long As There is No Caliphate," MEMRI Special Dispatch No. 435, October 30, 2002.

9. Jonathan Adelman and Agota Kuperman, "Christian Exodus from the Middle East," Foundation for the Defense of Democracies, December 19, 2001. Reprinted at: http://www.defenddemocracy.org/publications/publications_show.htm?doc_id=155713.

10. Middle East Media Research Institute (MEMRI), "Friday Sermons in Saudi Mosques: Review and Analysis," MEMRI Special Report No. 10, September 26, 2002. www.memri.org. This sermon is undated, but it recently appeared on the Saudi website www.alminbar.net.

11. Abdullah Azzam, *Defence of the Muslim Lands*, Mohammed Taqi-ud-Oin AI-Hilali and Mohammed Muhsin Khan, translators. Maktaba Dar-us-Salam, 1993. Reprinted at http://www.religioscope.com/info/doc/jihad/azzam_defence_1_table.htm.

12. Stephen Schwartz, "Reductio ad Jihadam," TechCentralStation.com, February 17, 2005.

13. Quoted in Steven Runciman, *History of the Crusades* Volume I, (Oxford: Cambridge University Press, 1951), 27.

14. A. S. Tritton, *Caliphs and Their Non-Muslim Subjects: A Critical Study of the Covenant of 'Umar*, Idarah-I-Adabiyat-I Delli, 1950, 229.

15. Philip K. Hitti, *The Arabs: A Short History* (Washington, DC: Regnery, 1996), 137.

16. Steven Runciman, *The Great Church in Captivity* (Oxford: Cambridge University Press, 1968), 179.

17. Quoted in Philip Mansel, *Constantinople: City of the World's Desire 1453–1924* (New York: St. Martin's Griffin, 1998), 51.

18. Bat Ye'or, *The Decline of Eastern Christianity Under Islam* (Madison, NJ: Fairleigh Dickinson University Press, 1996), 296.

19. Michael the Syrian, quoted in Ye'or, *The Decline of Eastern Christianity Under Islam*, 78.

20. Ibid.

21. Tritton, 227.

22. Quoted in Ibn Warraq, *Why I Am Not A Muslim* (Amherst, NY: Prometheus Books, 1995), 228.

23. Quoted in Bat Ye'or, *Islam and Dhimmitude: Where Civilizations Collide* (Madison, NJ: Fairleigh Dickinson University Press, 2002), 70.

24. Ye'or, *The Decline of Eastern Christianity Under Islam*, 78.

25. Ibid., 112–13.

26. Maxime Rodinson, *Muhammad*, translated by Anne Carter (New York: Pantheon Books, 1971), 296.

27. Apostolos E. Vacolopolous, "Background and Causes of the Greek Revolution," *Neo-Hellenika*, vol. 2, 1975, 54–55; cited in Andrew G. Bostom, "The Islamization of Europe," FrontPageMagazine.com, December 31, 2004.

28. Paul Johnson, *A History of the Jews* (New York: Harper & Row, 1987), 175.

29. This is an old Arabic signal of danger.

30. Bukhari, vol. 6, book 65, no. 4971.

31. Gregory X, "Papal Protection of the Jews," in *The Portable Medieval Reader* (New York: Viking Press, 1949), 170–71.

32. "Egypt: Police Arrest 22 Christians in New Crackdown," Barnabas Fund, October 24, 2003. www.barnabasfund.org.

33. "Egyptian officials revoke church license to build *after* demolition of church," U.S. Copts Association, December 2, 2003.

34. "Christian Captured At Border," Compass Direct, December 4, 2003. www.compassdirect.org.

35. "Christian Couple Escapes," Compass Direct, May 17, 2004.

36. "Police arrests Christian for 'blasphemy', lets attackers go," *Daily Times*, November 29, 2003.

37. "Dajkot Church attacked. PCP Report," *Pakistan Christian Post*, December 11, 2003.

38. "Pakistan blasphemy suspect dies, beaten by cop," Reuters, May 29, 2004.

39. Quoted in Robert Hussein, *Apostate Son* (Najiba Publishing Company, 1998), 161.

40. V. S. Naipaul, *Among the Believers: An Islamic Journey* (New York: Vintage Books, 1982), 65.

41. Ibid., 141–42.

42. Ibid., 119.

Chapter 5:

Islam Oppresses Women

1. Lisa Anderson, "Islamic woman sparks controversy by leading prayers," *Chicago Tribune*, March 18, 2005.

2. "Woman leads Muslim prayer service in New York City despite criticism in the Middle East," Associated Press, March 19, 2005.

3. Muslim Women's League, "Gender Equality in Islam," September 1995, http://www.mwlusa.org/pub_gender.html.

4. Nawal El-Saadawi, quoted in Muhammad Ali Al-Hashimi, *The Ideal Muslimah: The True Islamic Personality of the Muslim Woman as Defined in the Qur'an and Sunnah*, International Islamic Publishing House, 1998, http://www.usc.edu/dept/MSA/humanrelations/womeninislam/idealmuslimah/.

5. Christine Armario, "U.S. Latinas seek answers in Islam," *Christian Science Monitor*, December 27, 2004.

6. Quoted in al-Hashimi, *The Ideal Muslimah*.

7. Abu Dawud, book 32, no. 4092.

8. See Christopher Dickey and Rod Nordland, "The Fire That Won't Die Out," *Newsweek*, July 22, 2002, 34–37.

9. See United Nations Children's Fund, "UNICEF: Child marriages must stop," March 7, 2001, http://www.unicef.org/newsline/01pr21.htm.

10. Bukhari, vol. 5, book 63, no. 3896; cf. Bukhari, vol. 7, book 67, no. 5158.

11. Amir Taheri, *The Spirit of Allah: Khomeini and the Islamic Revolution* (New York: Adler and Adler), 1986, 90–91.

12. Lisa Beyer, "The Women of Islam," *Time*, November 25, 2001. Reprinted at http://www.time.com/time/world/article/0,8599,185647,00.html.

13. Andrew Bushell, "Child Marriage in Afghanistan and Pakistan," *America*, March 11, 2002, 12.

14. Abu Dawud, book 11, no. 2141.

15. Ibid., book 11, no. 2142.

16. Bukhari, vol. 7, book 77, no. 5825.

17. See Amnesty International, "Media briefing: Violence against women in Pakistan," April 17, 2002, http://web.amnesty.org/ai.nsf/Index/ASA330102002?OpenDocument&of=THEMES\WOMEN.

18. *Muslim*, book 4, no. 2127.

19. Bukhari, vol. 4, book 59, no. 3237. This hadith is repeated in many other places.

20. *'Umdat al-Salik*, m11.9.

21. Ibid., m10.4.

22. Ibid., m10.3.

23. Amnesty International, "Saudi Arabia: End Secrecy End Suffering: Women," http://www.amnesty.org/ailib/intcam/saudi/briefing/4.html.

24. Bukhari, vol. 7, book 67, no. 5206.

25. *'Umdat al-Salik*, n7.7.

26. Bukhari, vol. 3, book 52, no. 2639.

27. "Ninth Pakistani school destroyed," *BBC News*, February 20, 2004.

28. Nicholas Hellen, "Muslim second wives may get a tax break," The Sunday Times, December 26, 2004.

29. Bukhari, vol. 7, book 67, no. 5119.

30. Ibid., vol. 7, book 67, nos. 5117–5118.

31. *'Umdat al-Salik,* o24.8.

32. See also Bukhari, vol. 3, book 52, no. 2661.

33. *Muslim*, vol. 3, book 17, no. 4206.

34. See Sisters in Islam, "Rape, Zina, and Incest," April 6, 2000, http://www.muslimtents.com/sistersinislam/resources/sdefini.htm.

35. See Stephen Faris, "In Nigeria, A Mother Faces Execution," www.africana.com, January 7, 2002.

36. *'Umdat al-Salik,* e4.3.

37. Quoted in Geneive Abdo, *No God But God: Egypt and the Triumph of Islam* (Cambridge: Oxford University Press, 2000), 59.

38. Frank Gardner, "Grand Sheikh condemns suicide bombings," *BBC News*, December 4, 2001, www.bbc.co.uk.

Chapter 6:

Islamic Law: Lie, Steal, and Kill

1. *Muslim*, book 32, no. 6309.

2. Bukhari, vol. 4, book 56, no. 3030; Muslim, vol. 4, book 32, no. 6303.

3. Ibn Kathir, vol. 2, 141–42.

4. Bernard Lewis, *The Assassins* (New York: Basic Books, 1967), 25. For *taqiyya* among al Qaeda members, see Charles M. Sennott, "Exposing Al Qaeda's European Network," *Boston Globe*, August 4, 2002.

5. Ibn Kathir, vol. 5, 530.

6. *'Umdat al-Salik*, o1.0, o1.1, o1.2.

7. Sultanhussein Tabandeh, *A Muslim Commentary on the Universal Declaration of Human Rights*, translated by F. J. Goulding (London: F. T. Goulding and Co., 1970), 18.

8. Ali Sina, "The Golden Rule and Islam," Faith Freedom International, April 28, 2005.

9. *'Umdat al-Salik* o9.10, cf. al-Mawardi, *al-Akham as-Sultaniyyah*, 4.2.

10. *'Umdat al-Salik*, xx.

11. "Al-Qaradawi full transcript," *BBCNews*, July 8, 2004.

Chapter 7:

How Allah Killed Science

1. *'Umdat al-Salik*, r40.1.

2. Quoted in Amir Taheri, *The Spirit of Allah: Khomeini and the Islamic Revolution* (New York: Adler and Adler, 1986), 259.

3. Bukhari, vol. 4, book 59, no. 3225.

4. Oleg Grabar, "Palaces, Citadels and Fortifications," *Architecture of the Islamic World: Its History and Social Meaning,* edited by George Michell (New York: Thames & Hudson, 1995).

5. Caesar E. Farah, *Islam*, Sixth Edition (New York: Barrons, 2000), 198.

6. Elias B. Skaff, *The Place of the Patriarchs of Antioch in Church History* (Manchester, NH: Sophia Press, 1993), 169.

7. Bat Ye'or, *The Decline of Eastern Christianity Under Islam*, p. 233.

8. Philip Hitti, *The Arabs: A Short History* (Washington, DC: Regnery, 1996), 67.

9. Ibid., 141–42.

10. "Islam." *Encyclopædia Britannica,* 2005. Encyclopædia Britannica Premium Service, http://www.britannica.com/eb/article?tocId=69186.

11. Ibid.

12. Abu Hamid al-Ghazali, *The Incoherence of the Philosophers*, translated by Michael E. Marmura. (Provo, UT: Brigham Young University Press, 2000), 2.

13. Ibid., 8.

14. Al-Ghazali, 226. Emphasis added.

15. St. Thomas Aquinas, *Summa Contra Gentiles*, Book Two: Creation, Chapter 25, section 14. Translated by James F. Anderson. (Notre Dame, IN: University of Notre Dame Press, 1975).

16. James V. Schall, S. J., *War-Time Clarifications: Who Is Our Enemy?* 2001.

Chapter 8:

The Lure of Islamic Paradise

1. *The History of al-Tabari* (*Ta'rikh al-rusul wa'l-muluk*), vol. VIII: The Victory of Islam, translated by Michael Fishbein (New York: State University of New York Press, 1997), 26.

2. Ibn Ishaq, 300.

3. Ibid., vol. 2, book 23, no. 1365.

4. "Al-Qaradawi full transcript," *BBC News*, July 8, 2004. For Esposito's praise, see John L. Esposito, "Practice and Theory: A response to 'Islam and the Challenge of Democracy,'" *Boston Review*, April/May 2003.

5. Middle East Media Research Institute (MEMRI), "An Interview with the Mother of a Suicide Bomber," MEMRI Special Dispatch No. 391, June 19, 2002.

6. Abu Dawud, book 38, no. 4448.

7. *'Umdat al-Salik*, p17.3 (1).

8. "Two Saudis beheaded for killing Pakistani who witnessed 'shameful' incident," Associated Press, March 15, 2005.

9. Quoted in Ibn Warraq, *Why I Am Not A Muslim* (New York: Prometheus, 1995), 342–43.

10. David Brooks, "Among the Bourgeoisophobes: Why the Europeans and Arabs, each in their own way, hate America and Israel," *Weekly Standard*, April 15, 2002.

11. "'Little bomber' fascinates Israeli media," *BBC News*, March 25, 2004.

12. Tom Lasseter, "Iraqi teen tells how he joined Ansar al Islam," Knight Ridder, February 13, 2004.

13. Steven Runciman, *The Fall of Constantinople 1453* (Cambridge: Cambridge University Press, 1965), 151.

14. Bukhari, vol. 4, book 56, no. 2818.

15. Bernard Lewis, *The Assassins* (New York: Basic Books, 1967), 127.

16. Marco Polo, *The Travels*, Ronald Latham, translator (New York: Penguin, 1958), 70–71.

17. Paul Sperry, "Airline denied Atta paradise wedding suit," WorldNetDaily.com, September 11, 2002.

Chapter 9:

Islam—Spread by the Sword? You Bet.

1. *Muslim*, book 19, no. 4382.

2. Bukhari, vol. 4, book 56, no. 2941.

3. Ibid., no. 2924.

4. *The History of al-Tabari*, Volume XII: The Battle of al-Qadisiyyah and the Conquest of Syria and Palestine, translated by Yohanan Friedmann (New York: State University of New York Press, 1992), 167. Cited in Andrew Bostom, "The Legacy of Jihad in Palestine," FrontPage Magazine.com, December 7, 2004. http://www.frontpagemag.com/Articles/ReadArticle.asp?ID=16235.

5. Steven Runciman, *A History of the Crusades*, Volume I (Cambridge: Cambridge University Press, 1951), 3.

6. Quoted in Bat Ye'or, *The Decline of Eastern Christianity Under Islam*, 271–72.

7. Ibid., 275.

8. Ibid., 276–77.

9. Ya'qub Abu Yusuf, in Ye'or, *The Decline of Eastern Christianity Under Islam*, 274.

10. Bukhari, vol. 4, book 56, no. 2818.

11. Quoted in V. S. Naipaul, *Among the Believers: An Islamic Journey* (New York: Vintage Books, 1982), 103.

12. Pierre Lance, "Jacques Chirac, avez-vous des racines?" *Les 4 Vérités*, January 17, 2004.

13. Quoted in Paul Fregosi, *Jihad in the West: Muslim Conquests from the 7th to the 21st Centuries* (New York: Prometheus Books, 1998), 99.

14. Sita Ram Goel, *The Story of Islamic Imperialism in India* (Voice of India, revised edition, 1994), 70–71.

15. Ibid., 44.

16. Bukhari, vol. 1, book 2, no. 25. The transliterated Arabic of the Muslim confession of faith has been omitted from this translation for ease of reading. The same statement is repeated in Bukhari, vol. 1, book 8, no. 392; vol. 4, book 56, no. 2946; vol. 9, book 88, no. 6924; and vol. 9, book 96, nos. 7284–7285, as well as in other hadith collections.

17. Sayyid Qutb, "The Right to Judge," http://www.islamworld.net/justice.html.

18. Sayyid Abul A'la Maududi [here, Mawdudi], *Towards Understanding the Qur'an*, Zafar Ishaq Ansari, translator (The Islamic Foundation, revised edition, Vol. 3, 1999), 202.

Chapter 10:

Why the Crusades Were Called

1. Amin Maalouf, *The Crusades Through Arab Eyes* (New York: Schocken Books, 1984), xvi.

2. John Esposito, *Islam: The Straight Path*, third edition (Oxford: Oxford University Press, 1998), 58.

3. Bukhari, vol. 4, book 56, no. 2941.

4. Esposito, 58.

5. Quoted in Bat Y'eor, *The Decline of Eastern Christianity Under Islam* (Madison, NJ: Fairleigh Dickinson University Press, 1996), 44.

6. Bukhari, vol. 1, book 2, no. 36.

7. Moshe Gil, *A History of Palestine 634–1099* (Cambridge: Cambridge University Press, 1992), 473–76. To his credit, Caliph al-Muqtadir did respond to the 923 persecutions by ordering the church rebuilt.

8. Steven Runciman, *A History of the Crusades, Volume I* (Cambridge: Cambridge University Press, 1951), 30–32.

9. Carole Hillenbrand, *The Crusades: Islamic Perspectives* (Oxford: Routledge, 2000), 101.

10. Runciman, 33.

11. Gil, 376.

12. Runciman, 35–36; Hillenbrand, 16–17; Jonathan Riley-Smith, *The Crusades: A Short History* (New Haven, CT: Yale University Press, 1987), 44.

13. Bernard Lewis, *The Assassins* (New York: Basic Books, 2002), 33.

14. Runciman, 36.

15. Ibid., 49.

16. Gil, 412.

17. Pope Urban II, "Speech at Council of Clermont, 1095, according to Fulcher of Chartres," quoted in Bongars, *Gesta Dei per Francos*, 1, 382 ff., trans. in Oliver J. Thatcher, and Edgar Holmes McNeal, eds., *A Source Book for Medieval History* (New York: Scribners, 1905), 513–17. Reprinted at *Medieval Sourcebook*, http://www.fordham.edu/halsall/source/urban2-fulcher.html.

18. *'Umdat al-Salik*, o9.1.

19. Quoted in Hillenbrand, 71.

20. Ibn Taymiyya, "The Religious and Moral Doctrine of Jihad," in Rudolph Peters, *Jihad in Classical and Modern Islam: A Reader* (Princeton, NJ: Markus Wiener Publishers, 1996), 53.

21. Shariah Council of State Defense Council "Majlis al-Shura" of the Chechen Republic of Ichkeria, "Jihad And Its Solution Today," *Jihad Today*, no. 7. Reprinted at http://kavkazcenter.com/eng/content/2003/11/26/2028.shtml, November 26, 2003.

22. Middle East Media Research Institute (MEMRI), "Jihad Against the U.S.: Al-Azhar's Conflicting Fatwas," MEMRI Special Dispatch No. 480, March 16, 2003. www.memri.org.

23. Middle East Media Research Institute (MEMRI), "Islamist Leader in London: No Universal Jihad As Long As There Is No Caliphate," MEMRI Special Dispatch No. 435, October 30, 2002. www.memri.org.

24. Tawfiq Tabib, "Interview with Sheikh al-Mujahideen Abu Abdel Aziz," *Al-Sirat Al-Mustaqeem* (The Straight Path), August 1994. Reprinted at http://www.seprin.com/laden/barbaros.html.

25. Stephen Graham, "Muslim Militants From Europe Drawn to Iraq," Associated Press, November 3, 2003.

26. James Harvey Robinson, ed., *Readings in European History: Vol. I* (Boston, MA: Ginn and Co., 1904), 312–16. Reprinted at *Medieval Sourcebook*, http://www.fordham.edu/halsall/source/urban2a.html.

27. Ibid.

28. Ibid.

29. Thomas Madden, *The New Concise History of the Crusades* (Lanham, MD: Rowman & Littlefield, 2005), 19–20.

30. Ibid., 12.

31. Quoted in August C. Krey, *The First Crusade: The Accounts of Eyewitnesses and Participants*, (Princeton, NJ: 1921), 280–81. Reprinted at Medieval Sourcebook, http://www.fordham.edu/halsall/source/fulcher-cde.html.

32. Jonathan Riley-Smith, *The Oxford Illustrated History of the Crusades* (Oxford: Oxford University Press, 1995), 116.

33. Quoted in Maalouf, *The Crusades Through Arab Eyes*, p. 263.

Chapter 11:

The Crusades: Myth and Reality

1. Quoted in August C. Krey, *The First Crusade: The Accounts of Eyewitnesses and Participants* (Princeton, NJ: 1921), 280–81. Reprinted at Medieval Sourcebook, http://www.fordham.edu/halsall/source/fulcher-cde.html.

2. R. G. D. Laffan, ed. and trans., *Select Documents of European History 800–1492*, volume I, Henry Holt, 1929. See also "The Crusaders Capture Jerusalem, 1099," EyeWitness to History, www.eyewitnesstohistory.com (2000).

3. Archbishop Daimbert, Duke Godfrey, and Count Raymond, "Letter to Pope Paschal II, September, 1099," in Colman J. Barry, ed., *Readings In Church History* (Christian Classics, 1985), 328.

4. Moshe Gil, *A History of Palestine 634–1099* (Cambridge: Cambridge University Press, 1992), 827.

5. Francesco Gabrieli, ed. and trans., *Arab Historians of the Crusades* (Berkeley, CA: University of California Press, 1957), 11.

6. Bill Clinton, "Remarks as delivered by President William Jefferson Clinton, Georgetown University, November 7, 2001." Georgetown University Office of Protocol and Events, www.georgetown.edu.

7. Amin Maalouf, *The Crusades Through Arab Eyes* (New York: Schocken Books, 1984), xvi.

8. Warren Carroll, *The Building of Christendom* (Front Royal, VA: Christendom College Press, 1987), 545.

9. For the Crusaders reneging, see Gil, 827. For their allowing some to leave, see Thomas F. Madden, *The New Concise History of the Crusades* (Lanham, MD: Rowman & Littlefield, 2005), 34.

10. Quoted in Hillenbrand, *The Crusades: Islamic Perspectives* (Oxford: Routledge, 2000), 64–65.

11. Quoted in Madden, 181–82.

12. Steven Runciman, *The Fall of Constantinople 1453* (Cambridge: Cambridge University Press, 1965), 145.

13. Maalouf, 179.

14. Madden, 74.

15. Quoted in ibid., 76.

16. Ibid., 78.

17. Ibid., 54.

18. Jonathan Riley-Smith, *The Oxford Illustrated History of the Crusades* (Oxford: Oxford University Press, 1997), 116.

19. Hilaire Belloc, *The Crusades: The World's Debate* (Rockford, IL: Tan, 1992), 248–50.

20. Alan Cooperman, "For Victims, Strong Words Were Not Enough," *Washington Post*, April 3, 2005.

21. Pope John Paul II, "Homily of the Holy Father: 'Day of Pardon,'" March 12, 2000. http://www.vatican.va/holy_father/john_paul_ii/homilies/2000/documents/hf_jp-ii_hom_20000312_pardon_en.html.

Chapter 12:

**What the Crusades Accomplished—
And What They Didn't**

1. Steven Runciman, *A History of the Crusades*, Volume III (Cambridge: Cambridge University Press, 1951), 398–402.

2. Bernard Lewis, *The Assassins* (New York: Basic Books, 1967), 5. For the Crusades as rape, see Amin Maalouf, *The Crusades Through Arab Eyes* (New York: Schocken, 1989), 266.

3. Godfrey Goodwin, *The Janissaries* (London: Saqi Books, 1997), 34.

4. Mufti Ebrahim Desai, Ask the Imam Question 1394, "The west is often criticised by Muslims for many reasons, such as allowing women go to work," October 25, 2000. http://islam.tc/ask-imam/view.php?q=1394.

5. Paul Fregosi, *Jihad* (New York: Prometheus Books, 1998), 225.

6. Beatrice Forbes Manz, *The Rise and Rule of Tamerlane* (Cambridge: Cambridge University Press, 1989), 17.

Chapter 13:

What If the Crusades Had Never Happened?

1. Amin Maalouf, *The Crusades Through Arab Eyes* (New York: Schocken, 1989), 266.

2. Napier Malcolm, *Five Years in a Persian Town* (New York: E. P. Dutton, 1905), 45–50. Cited in Andrew G. Bostom, "The Islamization of Europe," FrontPageMagazine.com, December 31, 2004.

3. From Sistani's website, www.sistani.org.

4. *'Umdat al-Salik*, o11.5(6).

5. "Fundamentalists vow to kill female students without head cover," *AsiaNews*, October 22, 2004.

6. "Iraqi Columnist: 'It Is Difficult to Recall a Period in Which Christian Arabs Were in Greater Danger Than Today,'" Middle East Media Research Institute, Special Dispatch No. 789, September 24, 2004.

7. E. A. Wallis Budge, trans., *The Monks of Kublai Khan, Emperor of China*, (The Religious Tract Society, 1928). Reprinted at http://www.aina.org/books/mokk/mokk.htm#c72.

Chapter 14:

Islam and Christianity: Equivalent Traditions?

1. Alan Riding, "The Crusades as a Lesson in Harmony?" *New York Times*, April 24, 2005.

2. Charlotte Edwardes, "Historians say film 'distorts' Crusades," *London Sunday Telegraph*, January 18, 2004.

3. Hani Ramadan, "La charia incomprise," *Le Monde*, September 10, 2002. For a typical blasphemy killing in Pakistan, see "Man Accused of Blasphemy Shot Dead," Reuters, April 20, 2005.

4. *Sahih Bukhari*, vol. 1, book 4, no. 233.

5. "Lawyer Convicted of Helping Terrorists," Associated Press, February 10, 2005.

6. David A. Yeagley, "What's Up With White Women?" FrontPageMagazine.com, May 18, 2001.

Chapter 15:

The Jihad Continues

1. Quoted in Carole Hillenbrand, *The Crusades: Islamic Perspectives* (Oxford: Routledge, 2000), 165.

2. Middle East Media Research Institute, "Al-Qa'ida Internet Magazine Sawt Al-Jihad Calls to Intensify Fighting During Ramadan—the Month of Jihad," Special Dispatch No. 804, October 22, 2004. www.memri.org.

3. Middle East Media Research Institute, "Egyptian Cleric: Ramadan the month of Jihad," Special Dispatch No. 308, December 5, 2001. www.memri.org.

4. "Full text: bin Laden's 'letter to America,'" *Guardian*, November 24, 2002.

5. Hizb ut-Tahrir, "The Khilafah was destroyed in Turkey 79 years ago; so let the Righteous Khilafah be declared again in Turkey," www.islamic-state.org, February 22, 2003.

6. Neil MacFarquhar, "Rising Tide of Islamic Militants See Iraq as Ultimate Battlefield," *New York Times*, August 13, 2003.

7. Brynjar Lia, *The Society of the Muslim Brothers in Egypt* (Ithaca, NY: Ithaca Press, 1998), 28.

8. Syed Abul Ala Maududi, "Jihad in Islam," Address at the Town Hall, Lahore, April 13, 1939. Reprinted at http://host06.ipowerweb.com/~ymofmdc/books/jihadinislam/.

9. Craig Pyes, Josh Meyer, and William C. Rempel, "Officials Reveal Bin Laden Plan," *Los Angeles Times,* May 18, 2002.

10. Daniel Simpson, "British Moslem radicals urge Islamic fightback," Reuters, March 6, 1999.

11. Steve Zwick, "The Thinker," in "The Many Faces of Islam," *Time Europe*, December 16, 2002.

12. Lisa Gardiner, "American Muslim leader urges faithful to spread Islam's message," *San Ramon Valley Herald*, July 4, 1998.

13. Art Moore, "Should Muslim Quran be USA's top authority?" WorldNetDaily.com, May 1, 2003.

14. John Perazzo, "Hamas and Hizzoner," FrontPageMagazine.com, March 5, 2003.

15. See the *Dallas News* blog, December 17, 2004.

16. Quoted in Amir Taheri, *Holy Terror: Inside the World of Islamic Terrorism* (New York: Adler & Adler, 1987), 241–43.

17. Quoted in Amir Taheri, *The Spirit of Allah: Khomeini and the Islamic Revolution* (New York: Adler and Adler, 1986), 20, 45.

18. Daniel Pipes, "Advancing U.S. National Interests Through Effective Counterterrorism," Testimony presented to Secretary's Open Forum, Department of State, January 30, 2002. www.danielpipes.org.

19. "O'Reilly Factor Flash," August 5, 2004, http://www.billoreilly.com/pg/jsp/general/genericpage.jsp?pageID=368.

20. William Glaberson, "Defense in Terror Trial Paints a Rosier Picture of 'Jihad,'" *New York Times*, February 25, 2005.

21. Bukhari, vol. 1, book 2, no. 25. The transliterated Arabic of the Muslim confession of faith has been omitted from this translation for ease of reading. The same statement is repeated in Bukhari, vol. 1, book 8, no. 392; vol. 4, book 56, no. 2946; vol. 9, book 88, no. 6924; and vol. 9, book 96, nos. 7284–7285, as well as in other hadith collections.

22. Kathy Gannon, "Radical Islamic Group Growing in Asia," Associated Press, May 1, 2005.

23. Khalid A-H Ansari, "65% Pakistanis support Osama, says report," *Mid-Day*, March 27, 2004.

24. Qutb, *Milestones* (New Delhi: Islamic Book Service, 2002), 10–11.

25. Bernard Lewis, *The Assassins* (New York: Basic Books, 1967), 35.

26. Ibid., 58.

Chapter 16:

"Islamophobia" and Today's Ideological Jihad

1. Universal Declaration of Human Rights, 1948. http://www.un.org/Overview/rights.html.

2. The Cairo Declaration on Human Rights in Islam, August 5, 1990. http://www.religlaw.org/interdocs/docs/cairohrislam1990.htm.

3. Stephen Schwartz, "The 'Islamophobes' That Aren't," TechCentral Station.com, April 28, 2005.

4. "Atheist Becomes Theist: Exclusive Interview with Former Atheist Antony Flew," *Philosophia Christi*, Winter 2004.

5. "Swiss arrests over Saudi attacks," BBCNews, January 9, 2004; "Muslims in Switzerland fear 'witch-hunt,'" *Swissinfo*, April 22, 2004.

6. Stuart Jeffries, "Coming to a small screen near you," *Guardian*, January 13, 2005.

7. Victor Davis Hanson, "Cracked Icons," *National Review*, December 17, 2004.

8. Abu Dawud, book 32, no. 4092.

9. Bukhari, vol. 7, book 77, no. 5825.

10. Council on American-Islamic Relations, "CAIR Calls on Wiesenthal Center to Repudiate 'Islamophobia,'" December 11, 2004.

11. Council on American-Islamic Relations, "About CAIR," http://www.cair-net.org/asp/aboutcair.asp.

12. Pam Easton, "Terrorism Ruled Out in Oil Refinery Blast," Associated Press, March 25, 2005.

13. SITE Institute, "Qaeda al-Jihad in the United States Claims Responsibility For Texas Refinery Bombing," March 25, 2005; "Terror cover-up in Texas City?" WorldNetDaily.com, April 5, 2005.

14. "Terror cover-up in Texas City?" WorldNetDaily.com, April 5, 2005.

15. "Multiple blasts struck refinery," Associated Press, April 29, 2005.

16. Uriel Heilman, "Murder on the Brooklyn Bridge," *Middle East Quarterly*, Summer 2001.

17. Daniel Pipes, "Denying Terrorism," *New York Sun,* February 8, 2005.

18. "Gunman shoots 7, kills self at Empire State Building," CNN, February 24, 1997.

19. Pipes, "Denying Terrorism."

20. Daniel Pipes, "Terror & Denial," *New York Post*, July 9, 2002.

21. Michelle Malkin, "Lee Malvo, Muslim hatemonger," Townhall.com, December 10, 2003.

22. Andrew Tilghman, "Saudi pleads guilty to killing Jewish friend in Houston," *Houston Chronicle*, January 12, 2004.

23. Pipes, "Denying Terrorism."

Chapter 17:

Criticizing Islam May Be Hazardous to Your Health

1. E-mail to author, March 31, 2005.

2. Dana Parsons, "'24's' Latest Plot Twist Pains Some Muslims," *Los Angeles Times*, January 12, 2005.

3. Adam Wild Aba, "Fox Features 'Muslim Terrorists' in '24' Drama," IslamOnline, January 10, 2005.

4. "Muslim-rights voice indicted in jihad plot," WorldNetDaily.com, July 9, 2003.

5. Joe Kaufman, "A Night of Hamas 'Heroes,'" FrontPageMagazine.com, March 8, 2004.

6. "Religious Hate Law: A Threat to Free Speech?" Barnabas Fund, April 6, 2005. http://www.barnabasfund.org/news/itrhc/about_itrhc.htm.

7. Michael Higgins, "Summary of Reasons for Decision," Victorian Civil and Administrative Tribunal, Human Rights Division, December 17, 2004.

8. Mark Durie, "Daniel Scot's (in)credible testimony,"jihadwatch.org., February 1, 2005.

9. Patrick Goodenough, "Verdict in 'Vilifying Islam' Case Exposes Christian Fault Lines," CNSNews.com, December 20, 2004.

10. Toby Sterling, "Dutch Filmmaker Theo Van Gogh Murdered," Associated Press, November 2, 2004.

11. "Dutch Filmmaker Killed, Muslims Condemn," IslamOnline.net, November 2, 2004.

12. Sterling, "Dutch Filmmaker Theo Van Gogh Murdered."

13. Andrew Osborn, "'I shot Fortuyn for Dutch Muslims,' says accused," *Guardian,* March 28, 2003.

14. Bukhari, vol. 9, book 88, no. 6922.

15. "Thousands remember slain van Gogh," *BBCNews*, November 2, 2004.

16. Ashok K. Behuria, "It is Election Time...," *Asian Affairs*, October 2002.

17. Amy Doolittle, "Muslim peril in a new faith," *Washington Times*, September 6, 2004.

18. Bukhari, vol. 9, book 88, no. 6922.

Chapter 18:

The Crusade We Must Fight Today

1. Daniel Williams and Alan Cooperman, "Vatican Is Rethinking Relations With Islam," *Washington Post,* April 15, 2005.

2. "Europa wird am Ende des Jahrhunderts islamisch sein," *Die Welt*, July 28, 2004.

3. Steve Harrigan, "Swedes Reach Muslim Breaking Point," FOX News, November 26, 2004.

4. "100 percent immigrants at Danish school," *DR Nyheder*, September 9, 2004.

5. "Islam part of core curriculum in Danish schools," *DR Nyheder*, September 13, 2004.

6. "Bin Laden backer on his way to Oslo," *Aftenposten*, August 9, 2004.

7. "Qazi Hussain Ahmed refused to comment on capital punishment on blasphemy and homosexuality during visit to Norway," *Pakistan Christian Post*, September 9, 2004.

8. "Secret arrests as Dutch terror threat 'worse than thought,'" *Expatica*, September 14, 2004.

9. "Row as Muslim prisoners take on governors," *Expatica*, September 9, 2004; Giles Tremlett, "Spanish jail wing 'run by inmates,'" *Guardian*, September 10, 2004.

10. Bat Ye'or, "How Europe Became Eurabia," FrontPageMagazine.com, July 27, 2004.

11. Sayyid Abul A'la Maududi [here, Mawdudi], *Towards Understanding the Qur'an*, Zafar Ishaq Ansari, trans., The Islamic Foundation, revised edition, 1999. Vol. 3, 202.

12. Bukhari, vol. 1, book 2, no. 13.

13. Warren Vieth and Edwin Chen, "Bush touts technology to help solve energy troubles," *Los Angeles Times*, April 28, 2005.

14. Régine Pernoud, *Those Terrible Middle Ages! Debunking the Myths*, Anne Englund Nash, trans., (Fort Collins, CO: Ignatius Press, 2000), 135.

15. Mahmood Mamdani, "Inventing political violence," *Global Agenda*, 2005.

INDEX

A

al-Aamer, Aamer bin Abdallah, 183

Abbas, Ibn, 58

Abdullah, Jabir bin, 74

The Abolition of Man (Lewis), 84

Abraham, 33, 138

abrogation (*naskh*), 24, 27

Abu Ghraib prison scandals, 13, 141

Adams, John Quincy, 83

'Adi, Yahya ibn, 91

adultery, 75, 76, 174

Aeneid (Virgil), 84

Afghanistan, xiv, 113, 186; child marriage in, 70; jihad in, 128; Taliban government in, 63, 66; women in, 66, 70; Zoroastrians in, 164

Aftenposten, 222

ahadith. *See* Hadith

Ahmad, Omar, 190

Ahmed, Leila, 66

Ahmed, Qazi Hussain, 222–23

Aisha, 66–67, 69, 70, 74, 203

al-Akwa, Salama bin, 74

Alamoudi, Abdurrahman, 225

Al-Anfal ("The Spoils of War" or "Booty"), 9

Alayed, Mohammed Ali, 207

Al-Azhar University, Cairo, Egypt, 40, 86, 91, 127

Albania, 154

al-Basrah, Iraq, 108

Alexandria, Egypt, 107, 109

Alexius I Comnenus, 125, 130, 133, 134, 152

Ali, Abdullah Yusuf, 31

Ali, Hussein Qambar, 61

Al-Jabr aw-al Muqabilah (Khwarizmi), 93

Allah: dhimmitude and, 49, 62; jihad and, 22, 34–35, 37–40; lying and, 80; as merciful, 20, 22; Muhammad as man of war and, 4–10, 14–16; murder and, 82; music and, 88; Paradise and, 101, 103, 104; Qur'an and, 20, 33; rape and, 74; science and, 95–96; theft and, 81; women and, 69, 70, 71, 76. *See also* Islam; Muhammad

Al-Muhajiroun, 189

al Qaeda, xiv, 44, 54, 104, 183

Alwan, Sahim, 44

Amnesty International, 71

'Amr, Suhayl bin, 16

Analects (Confucius), 84

Annan, Kofi, 195–96

Ansar al-Islam, 187

Antioch, 54

Antioch, Asia Minor, 107, 108, 123, 133–34, 138–39, 149, 160

apostasy, 59–60, 62

Aquinas, Saint Thomas, 96

Arabia: child marriage in, 69; Islamic conquest in, 108; pagans of, 10

Arab League, 224

Arabs: Muslims vs., 43, 47; in Persia, 62
Arghun, Mongol ruler, 149–51, 160
al-Arian, Sami, 225
Aristotle, 87, 90, 91, 94, 97
Armenia, 110, 113
Armstrong, Karen, xv
art, Islamic, 87–89
al-Ashraf, K'ab bin, 11–12
As-Salat (prayers), 37
Assassins, 105–6
Assem, Shaker, 189
Assyrian International News Agency, 160
Assyrians, 166–69
Assyrian School of Nisibis, 91
Ataturk, Kemal, 185, 185–87
al-Athir, Ibn, 136–37
Atta, Muhammad, 106
Attar, Farid, ud-Din, 88
Attaullah, 61
Aucbur, Sidik, 23
Augustine, Saint, 116
Australia, criticizing Islam in, 209, 211–13
Averroes, 90, 94, 95
Avicenna, 90, 94, 95
Awad, Boulos Farid Rezek-Allah, 60
Awad, Nihad, 211
Ayat al-Sayf (Verse of the Sword). *See* Verse of the Sword (Ayat al-Sayf)
al-Ayubi, 184
Azerbaijan, 167
al-'Azimi, 138
Aziza, Majid, 166
Azzam, Abdullah, 54

B

Badr, Battle of, 7–10, 99, 184
Baghdad, Iraq, xiv, 56
Bakhtishu, Jabrail ibn, 91
Bakr, Abu, 68
Bakri, Omar, 189
Balderic, 136
Balian of Ibelin, 142

al-Balik, Abd, 167
Balkenende, Jan Peter, 214
Bangladesh, 70
al-Banna, Hasan, 188
Banu Hawazin, 5
Baptist General Association of Virginia, 218
Bara'ah, Sura, 25
Battle of Badr, 7–10, 99, 184
Battle of Hunayn, 23
Battle of Mut'ah, 23
Battle of Tabuk, 23
Battle of Trench (627), 15, 99
Baybars, 138
Baz, Rashid, 206
de Beert, Gaston, 136
believers: distinction between unbelievers and, 13, 16; religion and, 3–4. *See also* unbelievers
Belloc, Hilaire, 144
Bernard of Clairvaux, 143–44
Bhagavad Gita, 84
Bible, 37; Crusades and, 28; desecration of, 61; New Testament, 27–28, 84; Old Testament, 28–29, 84; Qur'an vs., 19, 26–32, 58, 85, 94, 101, 143, 154, 168; violence in, 19, 26–32
bin Laden, Osama, 53, 141, 175, 176, 199; Crusades and, xiv; fanaticism of, 47; goals of, 189; Islam and, 36, 201; jihad and, 184, 205, 222, 223; Qur'an and, 31, 230; September 11 and, 6, 86
Blair, Tony, 212
blasphemy, 60–61, 174, 215, 217
Bohemond VI, 138–39
Bolshevism, 173
Bosnia-Herzegovina, 128, 186, 197
Boxer, Barbara, 227
Brethren Church of Assiout, 60
Britain, 116, 209; criticizing Islam in, 212; Islamophobia in, 200; Muslims in, 73; religious vilification laws in, 213
Buddha, Buddhists: 3, 4, 49

Budge, Sir E. A. Wallis, 160
Bulgaria, 154
Buraid, Sulaiman b., 35
Buscarel of Gisolf, 151
Bush, George W., 176, 225, 226, 227, 229
Byzantine Empire: Crusades and, 123–25, 130, 133, 148; death of, 97; Islamic conquest of, 107–9, 113
Byzantines, 41

C

Caesarea, 110
CAIR. *See* Council on American-Islamic Relations
Cairo, Egypt, 40
Cairo Declaration on Human Rights in Islam (1990), 196
Calcutta, India, 3
caliphate: abolition of, 36, 185, 185–87; in Britain, 189; democracy and, 183; jihad and, 185–90; restoration of, 36, 183, 187–89; Sunni Islam and, 36; in United States, 189–90
Caner, Ergun Mehmet, 76
capital punishment, 84, 215
Cappadocia, 110
Catch the Fire Ministries, 212
Catholic Church: Crusades and, xiii, 133; just-war theory of, 22; West and, 179
Chechnya, 42, 127, 128, 186
Chicago, Illinois, 3
Chirac, Jacques, 112
Chosroes, King of Persia, 108
Christianity: adultery and, 75; defense of, 4; forced conversion and, 57–58; Islamic tolerance and, 51; Islam vs., 4, 12, 26–32, 35, 47, 58, 75, 85, 94, 101, 107, 111, 116–17, 122, 141, 143, 154, 168, 171–79, 192, 199, 217, 227; Judaism and, 179; moral equivalence theory and, 116–17, 171–79; science and, 87; spread of, 107, 116–17; West and, 178–79. *See also* Christians

Christians: Coptic, 162; evangelical, 174–75; Islam and, 47–48; jihad and, 41; moral equivalence theory and, 26–32; Muslim persecution of, 123–25; Ottoman, 54; Qur'an and, 19, 20. *See also* Christianity; dhimmitude
Christian Science Monitor, 65
Churchill, Winston, 92
Church of Calvary, 123
Church of the Holy Sepulcher, 124, 129, 149
Church of the Jews, 138
Church of the Resurrection, 122, 123, 124
Cilicia, 110, 123
circumcision, female, 76–77
Clinton, Bill, xiii–xiv, 137, 141, 225
Cohen, Job, 214–15
Columbus, Christopher, 97
Communism, 15, 173
The Conference of the Birds (Attar), 88
"Confronting Islamophobia: Education for Tolerance and Understanding" (United Nations), 48
Confucius, 84
Constantine, 155
Constantinople: Crusades and, 148, 157; fall of, 97, 157; Islamic conquest of, 97, 107, 111, 139–40, 160; Turkish invasion of, 54
Coptic Christians, 162
Council of Clermont (1095), 125–26, 130, 143
Council of Florence, 156
Council on American-Islamic Relations (CAIR), 172, 189–90, 204–5, 209–11, 219
Crete, 111, 123
Croatia, 154
Crusades: accomplishments of, 147–57, 159–61; Assyrians and, 166–69; beginning of, 113; Catholic Church and, xiii, 133; as chance for gain, 129–30;

Crusades (continued):
  European colonialism and, 133–36;
  failure of, 157, 159; Fifth, 148; First,
  xiii, xvi, 130, 142, 147; forced conversion and, 121, 130–32; Fourth,
  148; Hollywood and, 171–74; Islam
  and, 224; Islamic conquest of Europe
  and, 159–61; Jerusalem, Israel and,
  xiii, 121, 122–25, 133–40, 144–45;
  Jews and, 133, 142–44; jihad and, 10,
  141; John Paul II and, 133, 145; Mongols and, 149–51, 155–57; Muslim
  agreements and, 151–54; Nestorians
  and, 167–69; PC myths about,
  122–32, 133–45, 159–61; purpose of,
  121–32; religious imperialism and,
  121, 125–29; Second, 143, 147; Seventh, 149; Sixth, 148–49; Third,
  147–48; as unprovoked, 121, 122–25;
  Urban II and, 113, 125–29, 133, 142,
  143, 160; West and, xiii; Zoroastrians
  and, 161–66
The Crusades: The World's Debate
  (Belloc), 144
The Crusades Through Arab Eyes
  (Maalouf), 121, 140
Cyprus, 55, 63, 111, 123, 155
Cyril, Saint, 116
Cyrus, 110

D

Daily Times (Pakistan), 60
Daimbert, Archbishop, 136, 137
Dajkot, Pakistan, 61
Dallas, Texas, 191
Damascus, Syria, 3, 108
Dar al-Islam, 186
Dar al-Kufr, 186
al-Darazi, Muhammad ibn Isma'il, 124
Dark Ages, 87
Dashti, 'Ali, 218
al-Daulah, Iftikar, 137
al-Dawla, Saif, 123, 127
Dawood, N. J., 31

Day of Discrimination, 9
Dearborn, Michigan, 190–92
death penalty, 84, 215
"Declaration of War against the Ameri-
  cans Occupying the Land of the Two
  Holy Places" (1996), 31
*The Decline and Fall of the Roman
  Empire* (Gibbon), 63
*The Decline of Eastern Christianity
  Under Islam: From Jihad to Dhimmi-
  tude* (Ye'or), 60
deconstructionism, 3
Defence of the Muslim Lands (Azzam),
  54
democracy, 14–15, 165, 183
Derbyshire, John, 209
Derwish, Kamal, 44
Desai, Ebrahim, 22, 153
Dhimmah (promise of protection), 50
*The Dhimmi: Jews and Christians
  Under Islam* (Ye'or), 60
dhimmitude: Allah and, 49, 62; Chris-
  tians and, 49–56, 166; conversion
  and, 55, 56; dress regulations and,
  51, 163, 166; effects of, 162; Islamic
  law (Sharia) and, 47, 49, 51, 53, 59;
  Islamic tolerance and, 49–56; Jews
  and, 49, 51–53; jihad and, 161; *jizya*
  (poll tax) and, 51, 53, 54, 54–56,
  163–64; *kharaj* (land tax) and, 55–56;
  modern, 59–62; Muhammad and, 49;
  PC myths about, 53–54, 57–63;
  Qur'an and, 50, 55; response to,
  56–57; restoration of, 53; spread of
  Islam and, 117
Die Welt, 222
Dimashqi, Isma'il bin 'Amr bin Kathir
  al. *See* Ibn Kathir
ed-Din, Imad, 142
ed-Din, Nur, 138
divorce, 69, 71–72
domestic violence, 65, 66, 69–70,
  212–13
Durie, Mark, 212–13

E

Edward I, 150–51
Egypt: Crusades and, 148; female circumcision in, 76; Islamic conquest in, 107, 110, 111; jihad in, 23; modern dhimmitude in, 59–60
Egyptian Sharia Association, 184
Eid al-Adha (Feast of Sacrifice), 31
Emicho of Leiningen, 143
Emir ul-Momineen (Commander of the Faithful), 189
Esposito, John, 102, 121
Eugenius IV, 156
Eurabia (Ye'or), 223
Europe: Christianity in, 116; Crusades and colonialism of, 133–36; Dark Ages in, 87; intellectual tradition of, 93–94; Islamic conquest in, 111–13, 154; Islamic conquest of, 147, 159–61; Islamization of, 221–23; Jews in, 142–43; Jews in Christian, 47, 57–59; jihad in, 128, 155, 221–23; Renaissance in, 96–97
European Union, 224

F

Fadayan-e Islam, 215
Fadl, Khaled Abou El, 173
Falls Church, Virginia, 217–18
Falwell, Jerry, 165, 174
al-Farabi, 95
Farhat, Muhammad, 102
fatawa (Islamic rulings), 27
Fatwa Council (Palestinian Authority), 30
Federal Bureau of Investigation (FBI), 205, 206
Firdowsi, Hakim Abu al-Qasim Mansur, 87
Fire of Jahannum (Hell), 23
First Crusade. *See* Crusades
Fitnah (disbelief and polytheism), 27
Fitzgerald, Michael, 221, 223
Five Pillars of Islam, 20

Flew, Antony, 199
Foda, Faraj, 215
Fortuyn, Pim, 216
The Fourth Crusade and the Sack of Constantinople (Philips), 173
FOX TV, 209–11
Franciscans, 131
Franks, xiii, 138, 140, 144
Frederick Barbarossa, 147
Frederick II, 148–49, 152
Fregosi, Paul, 115
Fulcher of Chartres, 130, 134–35

G

Gabriel, 5
Galen, 91
Germany, 128, 143
al-Ghambdi, Marzouq Salem, 53
al-Ghazali, Sufi Abu Hamid, 94–95, 96
Ghazwan, 'Utbah ibn, 108
Gibbon, Edward, 63, 161
Giuliani, Rudolph, 206
Godfrey of Bouillon, 130, 136, 137, 138, 160, 224
Goel, Sita Ram, 113–14
Gold, Dore, 156
Goodwin, Godfrey, 153
Grabar, Oleg, 90
Great Britain, 53
Greece, 56–57, 154
Gregory Palamas, 41
Gregory VIII, 147
Gregory X, 57–59

H

Hadayet, Hesham Mohamed Ali, 206
Hadith, 15; female circumcision and, 76; jihad and, 11, 43; Muhammad and, 33. *See also* Muhammad; Qur'an
hadith qudsi (holy hadith), 33
Hagia Sophia, 139–40
al-Hakim, Abu 'Ali al-Mansur, 123–24
Halabiya, Ahmad Abu, 30
Hamas, 51, 53, 102, 141, 192, 211

Hamza, 14
Hanafi Islam, 38, 39–40
Hanbali Islam, 38, 42
Hanson, Victor Davis, 200–201
Hatred's Kingdom (Gold), 156
Hawazin tribe, 108
Haykel, Bernard, 192
Hell (Fire of Jahannum), 23
Heraclius, 108
Higgins, Michael, 212, 214
Hindus, 49, 161
Hippocrates, 91
Hisham, Abu Jal bin, 7
Hisham, 'Amr ibn, 8
Hitler, Adolf, 200
Hitti, Philip, 54
Hizb ub-Tahrir (Islamic Liberation
    Party), 23, 185, 187, 189, 192, 193
Hollywood, Crusades and, 171–74
homophobia, 200
homosexuality, 103–5
Honorius IV, 150
Hooper, Ibrahim, 190
*How the Catholic Church Built Western
    Civilization* (Woods), 179
al-Humam, 'Umayr bin, 100, 101
Humani Corporis Fabrica (On the Fab-
    ric of the Human Body) (Vesalius), 93
Hunayn, Battle of, 23
Hungary, 143, 156–57
Hussein, Saddam, xiv, 141, 166, 224
Huwayissa, 12
hypocrites, 20

I

IAP. *See* Islamic Association for
    Palestine
Ibn Jubayr, 131–32
Ibn Abbas, 58
Ibn Ishaq, 11
Ibn Juzayy, 25
Ibn Kathir, 25–26, 49–50, 80, 81
Ibn Khaldun, 54
Ibn Sunayna, 12

Ibn Taghribirdi, 137
Ibn Taymiyya, 39, 127
Ibn Warraq, 11
Ichkeria, 42
idolaters, 20, 25
ijmaa (Consensus) of Sahaba (compan-
    ions of Muhammad), 23
Incoherence of the Incoherence (Aver-
    roes), 95
Incoherence of the Philosophers (Ghaz-
    ali), 94–95
India, 113–14, 161, 167
Indonesia, 15, 31
infidels. *See* unbelievers
*Infiltration: How Muslim Spies and
    Subversives Have Penetrated Wash-
    ington* (Sperry), 228
Institute of Islamic Studies, Jakarta, 201
Inviolable Place of Worship, 22
Inyadullah, Maulana, 104
Iran, 13; Islamic conquest in, 107;
    Islamic law (Sharia) in, 36; jihad in,
    23
Iraq, xiv, 6, 186; Christian persecution
    in, 166; democracy in, 165; invasion
    of, 13; Islamic conquest in, 108; jihad
    in, 23, 128; U.S. presence in, 13
Iraq War (2003), 128
Ireland, 116
Ishaq, Huneyn ibn, 91
Islam: blasphemy and, 60–61, 174, 215,
    217; Christianity vs., 4, 12, 26–32, 35,
    47, 58, 75, 85, 94, 101, 107, 111,
    116–17, 122, 141, 143, 154, 168,
    171–79, 192, 199, 217, 227; core prin-
    ciples of, 4; Crusades and, 224; cul-
    tural development and, 89–92;
    danger of criticizing, 209–19; defini-
    tion of, 197–99; early spread of,
    107–17; extremism in, 128; extrem-
    ists in, 47; Five Pillars of, 20; four
    principle schools of, 38; Golden Age
    of, 92–94; Hanafi, 38, 39–40; Hanbali,
    38, 42; imperialism of, 107–17; Jews

and, 47–48; jihad and, 22, 23, 33–45, 175–77; Judaism vs., 47; mainstream, 33, 38; Maliki, 38, 42; moderate, 43–45, 176–77; moral equivalence theory and, 26–32, 116–17, 171–79; moral equivalence theory of, 4; negotiated settlements and, 3, 15–17; Paradise and, 99–106; PC myths about, 34–35, 41–42, 47–48, 89–92, 108–13, 174–75, 216–17; as peaceful, 41–42, 47, 191; reform of, 201–2; rejection of, 10, 14–15, 19; as religion of war, 33–45, 47; science and, 87–97; Shafi'i, 38, 40; Shi'ite, 73–74, 80–81, 105–6, 123; Sufi, 156; Sunni, 36, 38, 42, 80–81, 83–84, 123; theology of, 5–6, 24, 38, 62, 99; tolerance and, 47–63; universal moral principles in, 84–85; Wahhabi, 156; women in, 65–77, 201–4. *See also* Allah; Islamic law (Sharia); Muhammad; Muslims
Islam and Dhimmitude: Where Civilizations Collide (Ye'or), 60
Islamic Association for Palestine (IAP), 211
Islamic Council of Victoria, 213
Islamic law (Sharia): apostasy and, 59–60; Christians and, 47; democracy and, 183; dhimmitude and, 47, 49, 51, 53, 59; divorce and, 72; forced conversion and, 57–58; hegemony of, 22, 191; homosexuality and, 103; Jews and, 47; jihad and, 11, 22, 37–41, 42, 45, 127, 185; jizya and, 26; lying and, 79–81; murder and, 82–84, 85–86; music and, 88; non-Muslims and, 47; rape and, 76; theft and, 81–82; women and, 65, 68, 71. *See also* Islam
Islamic Liberation Party (Hizb ub-Tahrir), 25, 185, 187, 189, 192, 193
Islamic Republic, 84
Islamic Resistance Movement. *See* Hamas

Islamic rulings (*fatawa*), 27
Islamikaze: Manifestations of Islamic Martyrology (Israeli), 103
Islamization: of Europe, 221–23; resistance to, 56–57
IslamOnline, 210
Islamophobia: in Britain, 200; hate speech and, 195, 204–5; jihad and, 195–208; moderate Muslims and, 195, 197; UN and, 195–97; Universal Declaration of Human Rights (1948) and, 196–97
Israel, 13, 30. *See also* Jerusalem, Israel
Israeli, Raphael, 103
itijihad, 38

J

Jackson, Jesse, 178
jahiliyya (ignorance), 62, 115, 193
Jahl, Abud, 8
Jakarta, 199, 201
Jamaat-e-Islami (Muslim Party), 115–16, 188, 222–23
Jan III Sobieski, 157
al-Jawzi, Ibn, 136
Jeddah, Saudi Arabia, xiv
Jerusalem, Israel, 3, 53, 167; Crusades and, xiii, 121, 122–25, 133, 135–40, 144–45; Islamic conquest in, 107, 108–9; Saladin and, 141–42
Jerusalem Post, 210
Jesus, Muhammad vs., 4, 12, 28, 29, 35, 58, 75, 85, 94, 101, 111, 122, 143, 154, 168, 174, 192, 199, 217, 227
Jews: in Christian Europe, 47, 57–59; Crusades and, 133, 142–44; in Europe, 142–43; Islam and, 47–48; jihad and, 41; Muhammad as man of war and, 11–12; Qur'an and, 19, 20. *See also* dhimmitude
jihad: Allah and, 22, 34–35, 37, 40; Badr, Battle of, and, 10; bin Laden, Osama and, 184, 205; caliphate and, 185–87, 187–89, 189–90; centrality of, 38;

jihad (continued):
  Crusades and, 10, 141; defeating, 223–31; as defensive, 13, 22–24, 111–13, 176; dhimmitude and, 161; early, 107–17, 111–13; Hadith and, 11, 43; Islam and, 22, 23, 33–45, 175–77; Islamic law (Sharia) and, 11, 22, 37–41, 42, 45, 127, 185; Islamophobia and, 195–208; modern, 138, 141, 183–93, 195–208; Muhammad and, 33, 34, 37, 40, 43, 184; Paradise and, 21, 34–35, 104; purpose of, 184–85; Qur'an and, 11, 19–21, 31–32, 34, 43, 142; recruitment and, 13, 42, 44; religious fundamentalism and, 171, 175–77; Sunni Islam and, 38, 42; Sunni/Shi'ite disunity and, 123; unbelievers and, 43–45; in United States, 44–45, 205–8
"Jihad and Its Solution Today" (State Defense Council), 42
Jihad in the West: Muslim Conquests from the 7th to the 21st Centuries (Fregosi), 115
Jihad Today, 42
jizya (poll tax): Crusades and, 122; dhimmitude and, 51, 53, 54, 54–56, 163–64; humiliation of, 54–56; Islamic law (Sharia) and, 26; jihad and, 54; non-Muslims and, 36, 37, 39–40, 41; Qur'an and, 20; unbelievers and, 20, 26
John I, 156
John VI Cantacuzenus, 152, 153, 154
John VIII, 156
John Paul II, 133, 145, 221
Johnson, Paul, 57
Jordan, 70
Jubayr, Ibn, 131–32
Judaism: Christianity and, 179; Islamic tolerance and, 51; Islam vs., 47; science and, 87
Julius II, 185

K

Kafirs (infidels). *See* unbelievers
Kahane, Meir, 207
Kalaf, Ubai bin, 7
Kamal, Ali Abu, 206
al-Kamil, Sultan, 148
Karmous, Nadia, 200
Kashmir, 127, 186
Kasravi, Ahmad, 215
Kathir, Ibn, 25–26, 49–50, 80, 81
Kazakhstan, 199
Keller, Nuh Ha Mim, 86
Khalaf, 'Umaiya bin, 7
Khaldun, Ibn, 54
Khan, Genghis, 156
Khan, Hulagu, 149
Khan, Kublai, 149
Khan, Sabiha, 210
kharaj (land tax), 55–56
al-Khattab, Umar ibn, 49
Khilafah. *See* caliphate
Khilafah.com, 23
Khomeini, Ayatollah, 84, 190–92, 216; child marriage and, 70; music and, 89
Khorassani, Sa'id Raja'i-, 191
al-Khwarizmi, Abu Ja'far Muhammad ibn Musa, 93
al-Kindi, Abu Ysusuf Yaqub ibn Ishaq al-Sabbah, 94
Kingdom of Heaven, 171
Kirbuka, 149–50
kitman (religious deception), 80, 81
Knights Templar, 172
Koran. *See* Qur'an
The Koran (Dawood), 31
Kosovo, 127, 154, 160
Kreikar, Mustapha, 187–88
Kuffaar (unbelievers). *See* unbelievers
Kulthum, Umm, 16–17
Kuwait, 61–62

L

Lackawanna, New York, 44
Lahab, Abu, 5, 58

Latin America, 65

Lehman, Herbert, 229

Letholdus, 135

Lewis, Bernard, 221–22

Lewis, C. S., 84–85

Libya, 63

The Life of Muhammad: A Translation of Ibn Ishaq's Sirat Rasul Allah (Guillaume), 16

literature, Islamic, 87–89

Louis IX, 149

Luke, Saint, 27

lying, 79–81

M

Maalouf, Amin, 121, 140, 159

Macedonia, 154

Madden, Thomas F., 131

Madrid, Spain, bombings (2004), 48, 223

al-Mahalli, Jalal al-Din Muhammad ibn Ahmad, 25

al-Mahdi, 167–68

Mahfouz, Naguib, 215–16

Majlis al-Shura (State Defense Council), 42

Malcolm, Napier, 162–64

Malik, Charles, 196

Maliki Islam, 38, 42

Malvo, Lee, 206–7

Mamdani, Mahmood, 229

Mandela, Nelson, 142

al-Mansur, Caliph, 55

Manuel I Comnenus, 152

Manzikert, Armenia, 113

Mar Dinkha IV, 166

marriage: child, 65, 68–69; polygamy, 65, 66, 201; temporary, 65, 73–74

Martel, Charles, 112

Marwan II, 54–55

Marx, Karl, 173

Masih, Anwar, 60–61

Maslama, Muhammad bin, 12

al-Masri, Abu Hamza, 189

Matthew of Paris, 152

Maududi, Sayyid Abul Ala, 115–16, 188–89, 227

al-Mawardi, Abu'l Hasan, 40

al-Mawsilaya, Ibn, 183

McVeigh, Timothy, 175

Mecca, Saudi Arabia, 5, 6, 53

media: moderate Islam and, 45; September 11 and, xv

Medina, Saudi Arabia, 5, 16

Mehmed II, 104

Mehmed III, 54

Mehmet II, 140

Mehmet V, 127

Methodius, Saint, 116

Metroplex Organization of Muslims, 190

Michael the Syrian, 54–55

Middle East: democracy in, 165; dhimmitude in, 55; Islamic conquest in, 109–11, 160

Milestones (Qutb), 193

Mongols: Crusades and, 149–51, 155–57; Muslim, 155–57; pagan, 149–51

The Monks of Kublai Khan Emperor of China, or The History of the Life and Travels of Rabban Sawma, Envoy and Plenipotentiary of the Mongol Khans to the Kings of Europe, and Markos Who As Mar Yahbh-Allaha III Became Patriarch of the Nestorian Church in Asia (trans. Budge), 160

Morocco, 55

Moses, 3, 4, 33

Mossadegh, 13

Mother of All Battles mosque, Baghdad, Iraq, xiv

Mu'ait, 'Uqba bin Abi, 7

Mu'awiya, 110

Muawiya II, 167

Muhammad, xvi; Badr, Battle of, and, 7–10; Crusades and, 121; dhimmitude and, 49; divorce and, 72;

Muhammad (continued):
Hadith and, 33; homosexuality and, 103; Islam and, xvi; Jesus vs., 4, 12, 28, 29, 35, 58, 75, 85, 94, 101, 111, 122, 143, 154, 168, 174, 192, 199, 217, 227; Jews and, 11–12; jihad and, 33, 34, 37, 40, 43, 184; lying and, 79; as man of war, 3, 3–17, 23; murder and, 82; music and, 88; negotiated settlements and, 15–17; Paradise and, 99; PC myths about, 15–17; as peaceful, 3, 16; polygamy and, 72–73; rape and, 74; theft and, 81–82; tolerance and, 3; women in Islam and, 68, 69, 70, 202–3. *See also* Allah; Islam
Muhammad ibn Abdallah ibn Abd al-Muttalib. *See* Muhammad
Muhammad, John, 206–7
Muhammad, Omar Bakri, 53, 127
Muhayissa, 12
mujahada, 40
mujahideen, 102
Mukheimar, Fuad, 184
Mulia, Musdah, 201–4
multiculturalism, 41, 216, 230–31
al-Munajid, Muhammad Saalih, 27
Murad I, 152–53
Murad II, 156
Murad III, 54
murder, 82–84, 85–86
Murdoch, Rupert, 210
Musa, 112
mushrikun (infidels). *See* unbelievers
music, Islamic, 87–89
"Muslim Background Believers Convention," 217–18
Muslim Brotherhood, 14, 41, 115, 188
A Muslim Commentary on the Universal Declaration of Human Rights (Tabandeh), 84
Muslims: Arabs vs., 43, 47; in Britain, 73; Christian relations with, xiii; in Latin America, 65; moderate, 195, 197; Mongols and, 149–51; Muhammad as man of war and, 4–17; Quraysh tribe and, 4–8, 12–14; in United States, xv. *See also* Islam
Muslim Women's League, 65
Mut'a (marriage). *See* marriage
Mut'ah, Battle of, 23
al-Mutanabbi, 87
al-Mutawakkil, Caliph, 54, 168
muttawa, 68

N

Naipaul, V. S., 62
Nakhla, 5–6
Naseer, 60
National Review, 209
Nawash, Kamal, 192
an-Nawawi, 55
Negus, King of Abyssinia, 108
neo-colonialism, 13
Nesimi, Sufi, 87
Nestorians, 160, 167–69
Nestorius, 167
Netherlands, 214
The New Concise History of the Crusades (Madden), 131
New Testament, 27–28, 84
New World, 96–97
New York, 44, 45, 65
New York Post, 205, 210
New York Times, 171
Nicephorus Phocas, 123
Nicholas IV, 150
Nidal, Umm, 102
Nigeria, 31, 76
Nikiou, 109–10
non-combatants, killing of, 6, 85–86, 114
non-Muslims: conversion of, 55; Islamic Golden Age and, 87; Islamic law (Sharia) and, 47; jizya and, 36, 37, 39–40, 41; Muslim persecution of, 123–25; second-class status for, 47; three choices for, 33, 35–37, 54, 108. *See also* dhimmitude

North Africa: dhimmitude in, 55; Islamic conquest in, 107, 109–11, 112, 160; jihad in, 23
Norway, 187
Nosair, El Sayyid, 207
Notaras, Lukas, 104–5
Numbers, 29
Nuwas, Abu, 87, 103

O

Old Testament, 28–29, 84
Omar, Mullah, 189
O'Reilly Factor, 192
Ottoman Empire: Christians in, 54; Crusades and, 153; Islamic tolerance and, 48, 51

P

Pakistan, 113, 193; blasphemy in, 174; jihad in, 32; modern dhimmitude in, 60–61; women in, 73, 76
Pakistan Christian Post, 61
Pakistan Institute of Medical Sciences, 70
Palestine, 30, 127, 186
Palestinian Authority, 30, 53
Paradise: Allah and, 101, 103, 104; Assassins and, 105–6; homosexuality and, 103–5; Islam and, 99–106; jihad and, 21, 34–35, 104–6; lying and, 79; Muhammad and, 99; promise of, 99–106; Qur'an and, 99–103, 105; suicide bombers and, 102
Paschal II, 136
Patrick, Saint, 116
Paul, Saint, 108, 113
peace: Islam and, 41–42, 47, 191; Qur'an and, 21, 27
People of the Book, 20, 49. *See also* Christians; Jews
Perfumed Garden (Nuwas), 103
Péroncel-Hugoz, Jean-Pierre, 207
Persia: Arabs in, 62; Islamic conquest in, 107, 162

Peter I, 155
Peter the Venerable, 229
Pew Research Center, 193
Philip, 148
Philip IV, 150, 151
Philippines, 186
Philips, Jonathan, 173
Pickthall, Mohammed Marmaduke, 31
Pinet, Jasmine, 65
Pipes, Daniel, 192, 206, 210
Plato, 91
pluralism, 48, 121
Poland, 156, 157
Polo, Marco, 105–6
polygamy, 65, 66, 72–73, 201
Pontifical Council for the Inter-Religious Dialogue, 221
Probus of Antioch, 90
Prophet of Islam. *See* Muhammad
prostitution, 65, 71

Q

Qaddafi, Muammar, 63
al-Qalanisi, Ibn, 138
al-Qaradawi, Yusuf, 86, 102
al-Qayrawani, Ibn Abi Zayd, 38–39
Qilaba, Abu, 174
Qur'an: abrogation (*naskh*) and, 24–26, 27; Allah and, 20, 33; Bible vs., 19, 26–32, 58, 85, 94, 101, 143, 154, 168; bin Laden, Osama and, 31, 230; as book of war, 19–32; canceling of verses of, 19, 24–26; child marriage and, 68–69; dhimmitude and, 50, 55; divorce and, 71; female circumcision and, 76; jihad and, 11, 19–21, 22–24, 31–32, 34, 37, 38, 43, 142, 229–30; jizya and, 20; lying and, 80; Muhammad as man of war and, 5, 6, 9–10; murder and, 82–83; Paradise and, 99–103, 104–6; PC myths about, 21–24, 26–32; as peaceful, 19, 21, 27; recruitment and, 44; science and, 95–96; suicide and, 102;

Qur'an (continued):
temporary wives and, 74; terrorism and, 30; theft and, 81; tolerance and, 21, 24–26; unbelievers and, 19, 23; Verse of the Sword in, 25, 27, 31; violence in, 26–32; women and, 65–69, 73, 76, 212–13. *See also* Allah; Hadith; Islam; Muhammad
Quraysh tribe, 5–8, 11, 12–14, 15–17
Qutb, Sayyid, 14, 41, 115, 193

R

Rabi'a, Shaiba bin, 7
Rabi'a, 'Utba bin, 7
racism, 47, 200
The Raft of Mohammed (Péroncel-Hugoz), 207
Rahman, Omar Abdel, 45, 176
Rajab, 6
Ramadan, Hani, 174
rape: adultery and, 76; Islamic law (Sharia) and, 76; Muslim understanding of, 74–76
al-Rashid, Harun, 93, 168
Raymond, Count of Toulouse, 136, 137
ar-Razi, Abu Bakr, 94
Razmara, Haji-Ali, 215
recruitment: jihad and, 13, 42, 44; Qur'an and, 44
The Reformation of Morals ('Adi), 91
Reliance of the Traveller, 40–41, 86
religious fundamentalism, 171, 174–75
Revell, Oliver, 211
Reynald of Chatillon, 141–42
Rhazes, 94
Rice, Condoleezza, 225, 227
Richard the Lionhearted, 147–48, 160, 224
Riley-Smith, Jonathan, 172
Robertson, Pat, 174
Romans, 23, 41
Romanus IV Diogenes, 125
Rome, Italy, 3
Rudolph, Eric, 175

Rumi, Jalaluddin, 87
Runciman, Steven, 54, 139
Rushd, Abul-Waleed Muhammad Ibn. *See* Averroes
Rushdie, Salman, 216
Russell, Bertrand, 173
Russians, in Chechnya, 42

S

el-Saadawi, Nawal, 65, 70
Sacred Mosque, 20
Sa'deddin, Hoca, 54
Saladin: Crusades and, 136–37, 140–42, 144, 148, 173, 193; jihad and, 184
Salemah, Yussef, 53
Salfi, Younas, 61
al-Samaraai, Bakr Abed Al-Razzaq, xiv
Saracens, 106, 135
Satan, 20
Saudi Arabia, xiv; Islamic law (Sharia) in, 36, 59; jihad in, 31–32, 44, 128; Wahhabi Islam in, 156; women in, 65, 68, 71
Sauma, Rabban, 150–51, 160
Schwartz, Stephen, 53, 197, 199
science: Allah and, 95–96; Christianity and, 87; Islam and, 87–97; Judaism and, 87; Qur'an and, 95–96
Scot, Daniel, 212, 214
Scott, Sir Ridley, 171, 172, 175
Seljuk Turks, 113, 124–25
Sellouk, Ariel, 207
September 11, xv, 44, 56–57, 85, 106, 184; bin Laden, Osama and, 6; Islam and, 11; jihad and, 11; responsibility for, xv
Serbia, 154
sexism, 200
Sha'ban, 138
Shafi'i Islam, 38, 40
Shi'ite Islam: Assassins and, 105–6; religious deception and, 80–81; Sunni Islam and, 123; temporary wives and, 73–74

A Short History of the Crusades (Riley-Smith), 172
Sicily, 111, 112
Siddiqui, Haroon, 201
Simon Wiesenthal Center, 204
Sistani, Ayatollah Sayyid Ali Husayni, 165
socialism, 15
Solomon's Temple, 109
Sophronius, 109, 121–22
South Africa, 22
Spain, 48; Islamic conquest in, 112, 160; *reconquista* in, 113
Sperry, Paul, 228
Stalinism, 200
Star Tribune (Minneapolis), 190
State Defense Council (Majlis al-Shura), 42
State Department, U.S., 226, 227
Stewart, Lynne, 176
Submission, 215
Sufi Islam, 156
Sufyan, Abu, 13
suicide bombers, Paradise and, 102
Sunni Islam: caliphate and, 36; jihad and, 38, 42; murder and, 83–84; religious deception and, 80–81; Shi'ite Islam and, 123
Surat Al-Masad, 58
Suyuti, Jalal al-Din 'Abd al-Rahman ibn Abi Bakr, 25
Sweden, 222
Switzerland, 200
Syria, 7, 167–68; Islamic conquest in, 107, 110–11

T

Tabandeh, Sultanhussein, 84, 85, 196
Tabuk, Battle of, 23
Tafsir al-Jalalayn, 25
Taghribirdi, Ibn, 137
Taliban, 63, 66, 189
Tamerlane, 156, 166, 168
Tancred, 136

Tantawi, Muhammad Sayyed, 76–77
taqiyya (religious deception), 80
Tarik, 112
Tavernier, Jean-Baptiste, 55
Taymiyya, Taqi al-Din Ahmad Ibn, 39, 127
Tefft, Bruce, 204
Ten Commandments, 4, 7
terrorism. *See* jihad
Thailand, 186
Thaqif tribe, 108
theft, 81–82
Theodosius, 53
The Thousand and One Nights (Rumi), 87
Tibet, 167
Tocqueville, Alexis de, 25
tolerance: Islam and, xv, 47–63; Muhammad and, 3; Qur'an and, 21, 24–26
Torah, 51
Toronto Star, 201
Treaty of Hudaybiyya, 15–17, 81–82
Trench, Battle of (627), 15, 99
Tripoli, 63
Tritton, A. S., 53
"The True Meaning of Jihad," 23
tsunami (2004), 15, 153
Turks, 41, 152, 154, 157; Constantinople and, 54; Seljuk, 113, 124–25
23 Years: A Study of the Prophetic Career of Mohammad (Dashti), 218
24, 209–11

U

Uhud, 12–14
Ulama (Muslim scholars), 54
Umar, 50, 110–11
'Umar, Lieutenant, 14
Umdat al-Salik, 40–41, 86
umma (community), 26
unbelievers, xiv; distinction between believers and, 13, 16; Islamic theology and, 62; jihad and, 40, 43–45;

unbelievers (continued):
jizya and, 20, 26; Qur'an and, 19, 23, 24–26. *See also* dhimmitude
United Nations (UN), 191; Islamic tolerance and, 48; Islamophobia and, 195–97
United States: caliphate in, 189–90; defeat of jihad and, 223–31; energy sources of, 227–28; foreign aid of, 226; global alliances of, 226; Islam and, 36; jihad and, 44–45, 205–8; Muslims in, xv; neo-colonialism of, 13
Universal Declaration of Human Rights (1948), 191, 196–97
Urban II, Crusades and, 113, 125–26, 128–29, 130, 133, 142, 143, 160
'Utba, Hind bint, 14
Uthmani, Tafsir, 23
Uwaq, Atsiz bin, 125

V

Vacalopoulos, Apostolos E., 56
van Gogh, Theo, 209, 214–15, 216–17
Verse of the Sword (Ayat al-Sayf), 25, 27, 31
Vesalius, Andreas, 93
Victorian Civil and Administrative Tribunal, 212
Virgil, 84
Voices Behind the Veil: The World of Islam Through the Eyes of Women (ed. Caner), 76

W

Wadud, Amina, 65
Wahaj, Siraj, 44
Waheed, Imran, 192
Wahhabi Islam, 156
Wallachia, 156
War on Terror, 176, 184, 224, 229
Washington Post, 145
Washington Times, 218
Wesley, John, 188

West: Catholic Church and, 179; Christianity and, 178–79; Crusades and, xiii; defense of, 4; Islam and, 121; pride in, 171, 177–78; recovering pride in, 230–31
Williams, John. *See* Muhammad, John
women: Allah and, 69, 70, 71, 76; child marriage and, 65, 68–69; divorce and, 71–72; domestic violence and, 65, 66, 69–70, 212–13; dress regulations and, 68; education of, 73; female circumcision and, 76–77; in Islam, 201; Islamic law (Sharia) and, 65, 68, 71; Islamic oppression of, 65–77; Muhammad and, 69, 70; PC myths about Islam and, 65–68; polygamy and, 65, 67; prostitution and, 65, 71; Qur'an and, 65–69, 76, 212–13; rape and, 74–76; in Saudi Arabia, 65, 68, 71; spiritual equality of, 65–66; temporary wives and, 73–74
Woods, Thomas E., Jr., 179
World Islamic Front for Jihad Against Jews and Crusaders, xiv
World Trade Center bombing (1993), 45, 176
World War I, 127, 186
World War II, 227

Y

Yeagley, David, 177–78, 179
Yemen, 55
Ye'or, Bat, 55, 60, 223

Z

zakat, 20, 37
Zaman, 48
Zaraqawi, 175, 176, 199
Zoroaster (Zarathustra), 162
Zoroastrians, 161–66; in Afghanistan, 164; dhimmitude and, 162–66; jihad and, 41
Zur'a Abi 'Ali 'Isa ibn, 91